Dan,

This book was drawn and written by a friend of ours. We hope you enjoy it. Happy #29!

love, Shelley David + Rachael

Special Thanks to
David Mazzucchelli

FUZZ & PLUCK BY TED STEARN
EDITED BY KIM THOMPSON
DESIGN BY TED STEARN
GARY GROTH & KIM THOMPSON, PUBLISHERS

FUZZ & PLUCK WAS ORIGINALLY SERIALIZED
IN THE COMICS ANTHOLOGY "ZERO ZERO"

FANTAGRAPHICS BOOKS
7563 LAKE CITY WAY
SEATTLE WA 98115

ISBN: 1-56097-331-5
FIRST PRINTING: JULY 1999
PRINTED IN CANADA

TED STEARN

FANTAGRAPHICS BOOKS

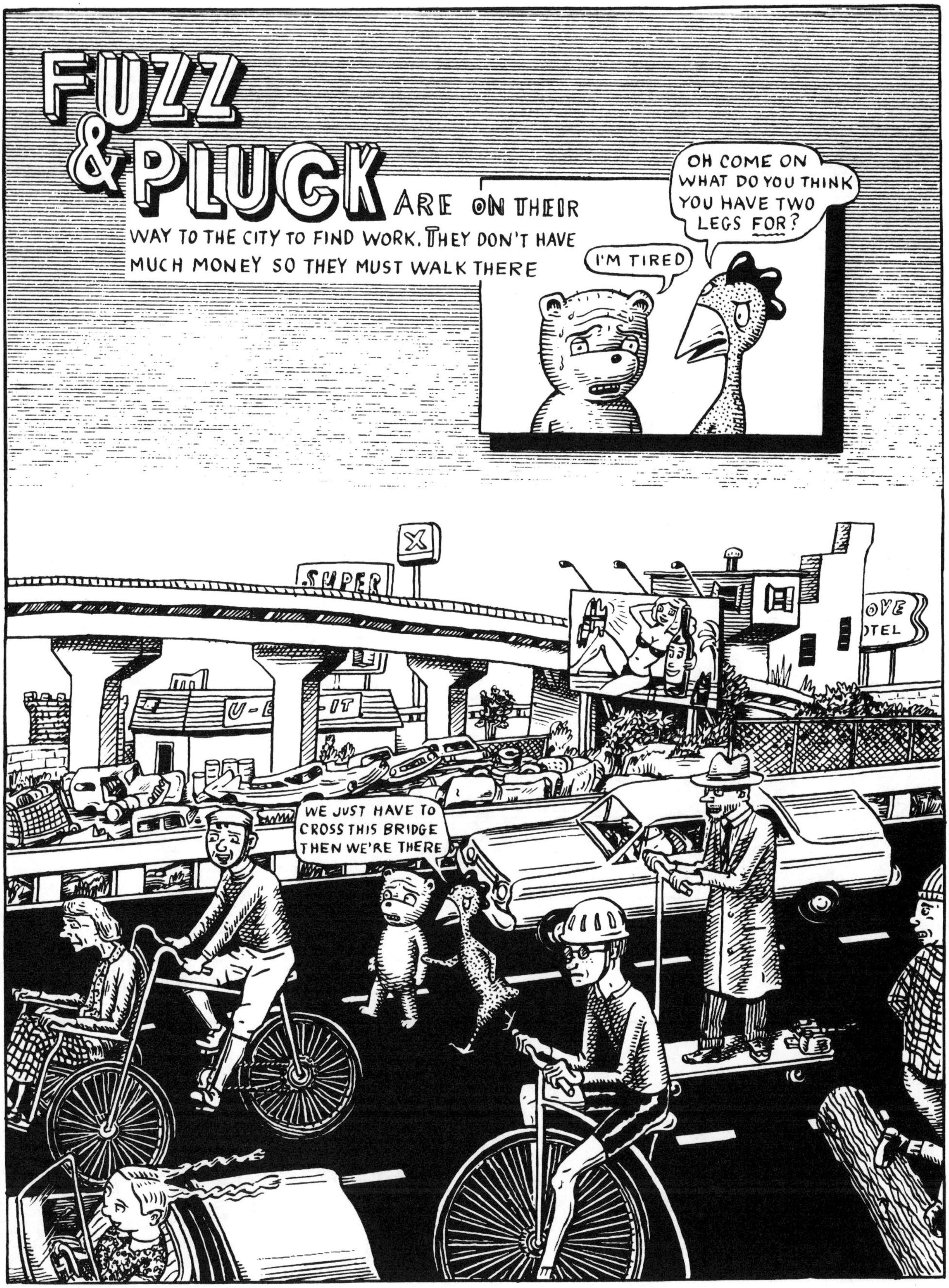
FUZZ & PLUCK
ARE ON THEIR WAY TO THE CITY TO FIND WORK. THEY DON'T HAVE MUCH MONEY SO THEY MUST WALK THERE
I'M TIRED
OH COME ON WHAT DO YOU THINK YOU HAVE TWO LEGS FOR?
SUPER
WE JUST HAVE TO CROSS THIS BRIDGE THEN WE'RE THERE

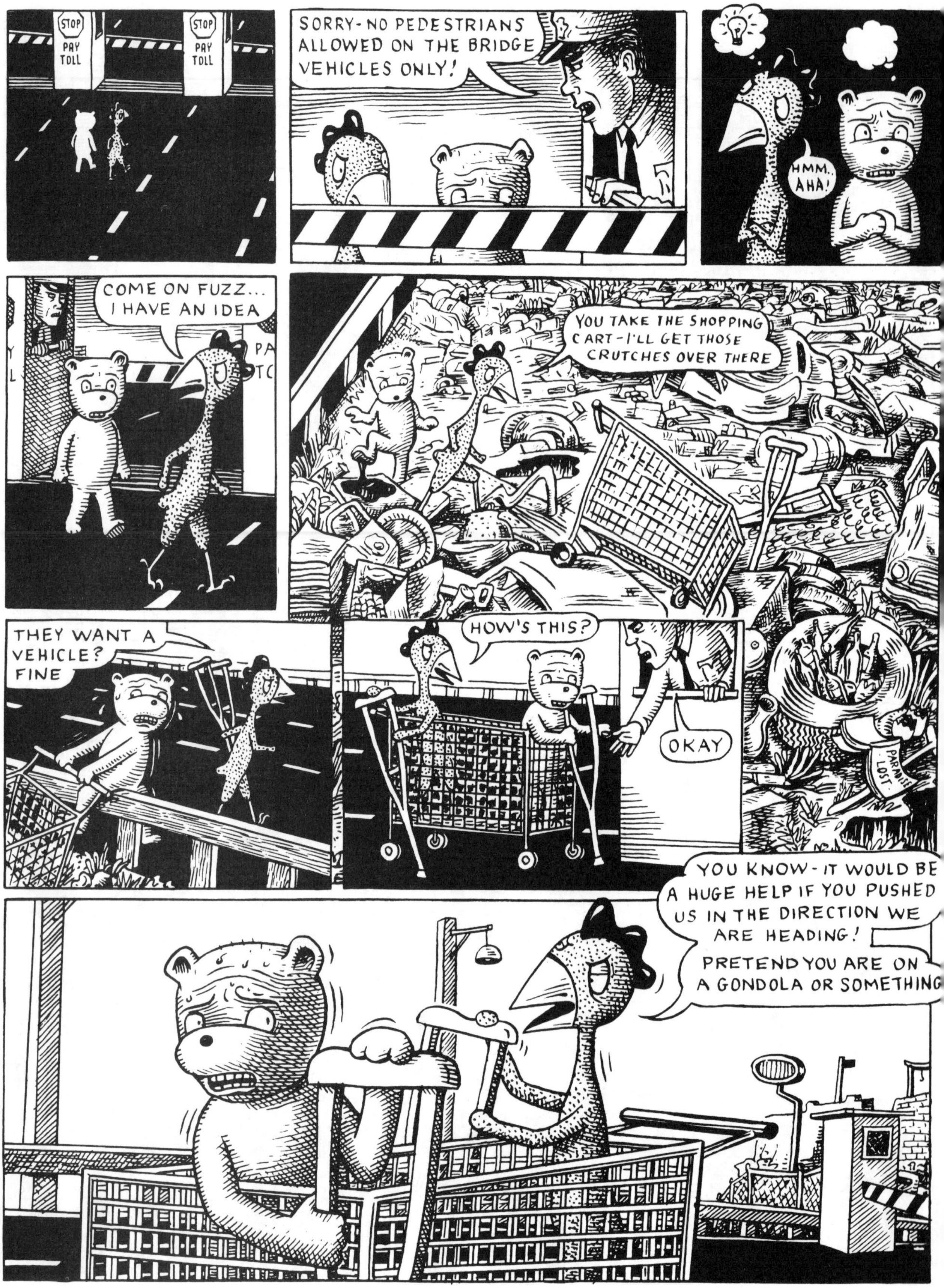
STOP PAY TOLL
STOP PAY TOLL
SORRY-NO PEDESTRIANS ALLOWED ON THE BRIDGE VEHICLES ONLY!
HMM.. AHA!
COME ON FUZZ... I HAVE AN IDEA
YOU TAKE THE SHOPPING CART-I'LL GET THOSE CRUTCHES OVER THERE
PARADISE LOST
THEY WANT A VEHICLE? FINE
HOW'S THIS?
OKAY
YOU KNOW-IT WOULD BE A HUGE HELP IF YOU PUSHED US IN THE DIRECTION WE ARE HEADING!
PRETEND YOU ARE ON A GONDOLA OR SOMETHING

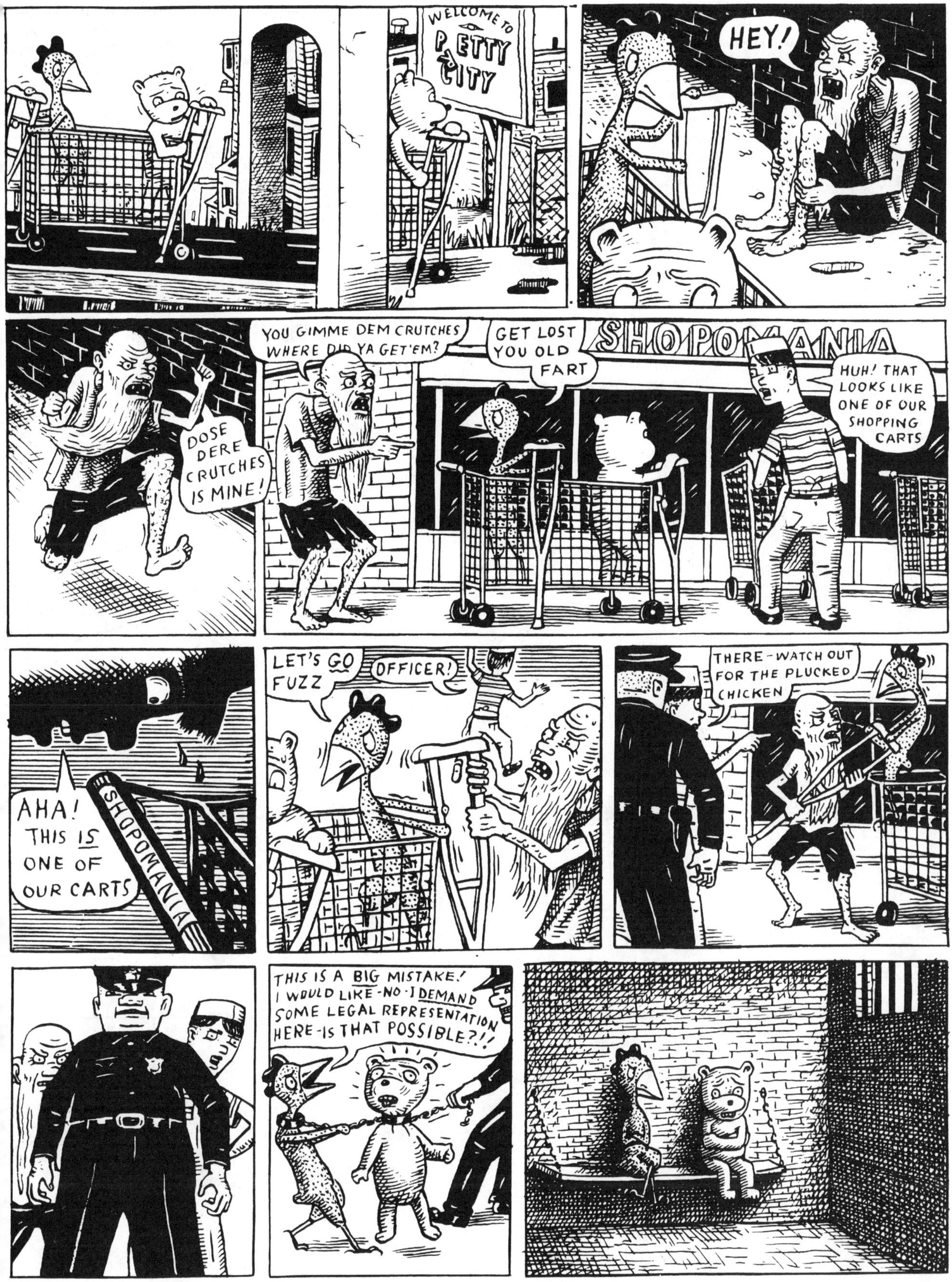
WELCOME TO
PETTY CITY
HEY!
YOU GIMME DEM CRUTCHES
DOSE DERE CRUTCHES IS MINE!
WHERE DID YA GET'EM?
GET LOST YOU OLD FART
SHOPOMANIA
HUH! THAT LOOKS LIKE ONE OF OUR SHOPPING CARTS
AHA! THIS IS ONE OF OUR CARTS
SHOPOMANIA
LET'S GO FUZZ
OFFICER!
THERE-WATCH OUT FOR THE PLUCKED CHICKEN
THIS IS A BIG MISTAKE! I WOULD LIKE-NO-I DEMAND SOME LEGAL REPRESENTATION HERE-IS THAT POSSIBLE?!!

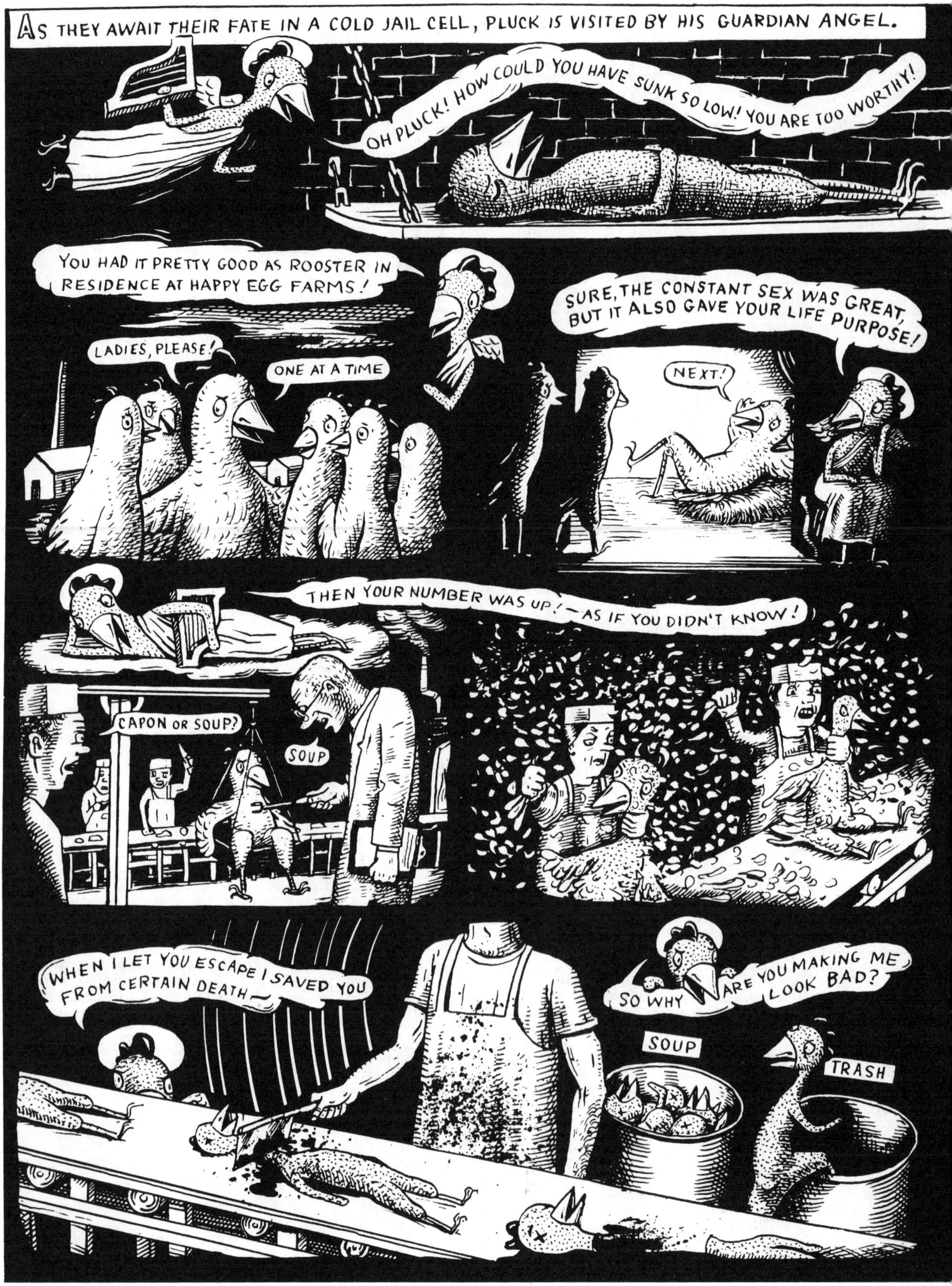
AS THEY AWAIT THEIR FATE IN A COLD JAIL CELL, PLUCK IS VISITED BY HIS GUARDIAN ANGEL.
OH PLUCK! HOW COULD YOU HAVE SUNK SO LOW! YOU ARE TOO WORTHY!
YOU HAD IT PRETTY GOOD AS ROOSTER IN RESIDENCE AT HAPPY EGG FARMS!
LADIES, PLEASE!
ONE AT A TIME
SURE, THE CONSTANT SEX WAS GREAT, BUT IT ALSO GAVE YOUR LIFE PURPOSE!
NEXT!
THEN YOUR NUMBER WAS UP! — AS IF YOU DIDN'T KNOW!
CAPON OR SOUP?
SOUP
WHEN I LET YOU ESCAPE I SAVED YOU FROM CERTAIN DEATH —
SO WHY ARE YOU MAKING ME LOOK BAD?
SOUP
TRASH

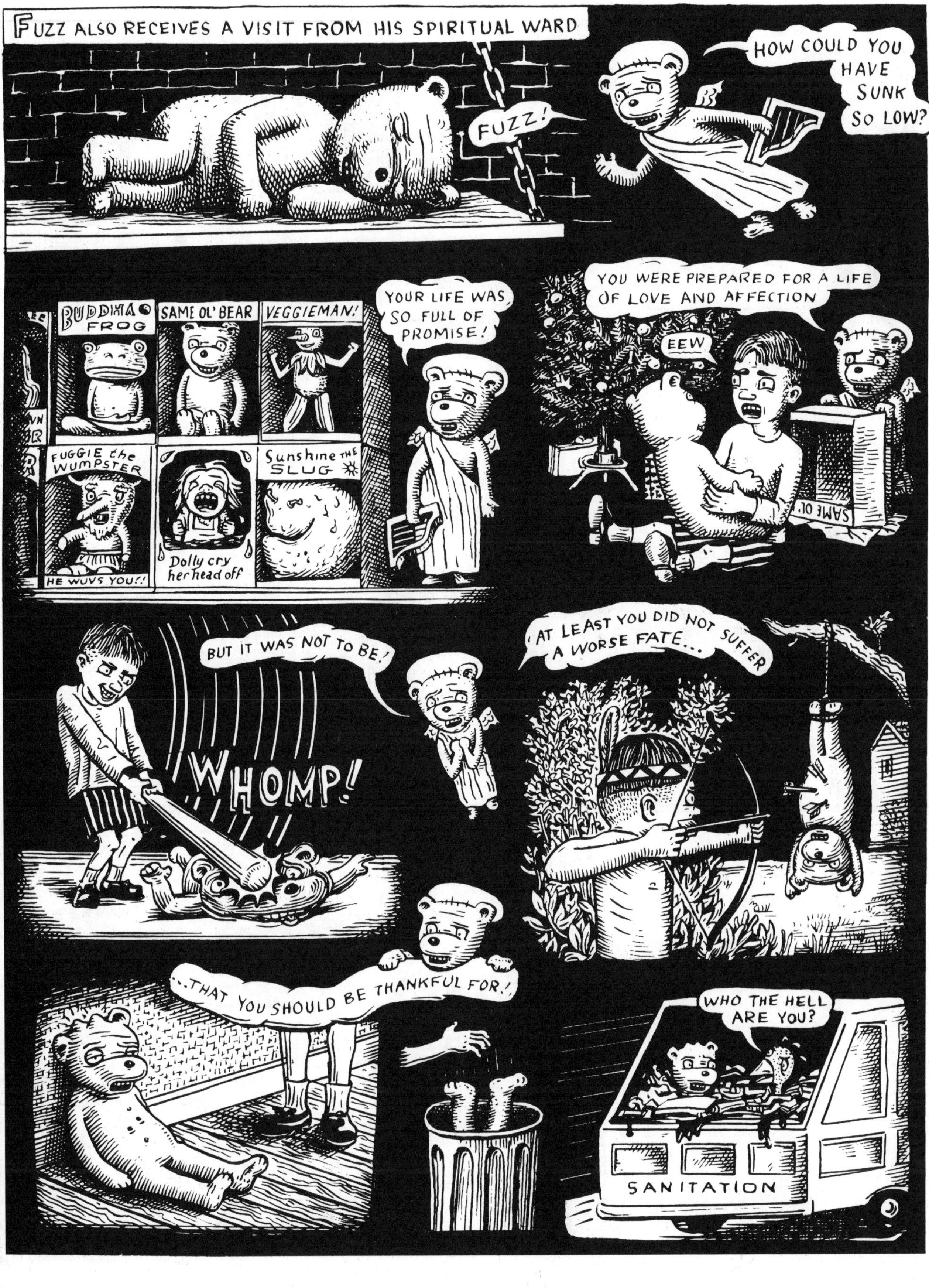
FUZZ ALSO RECEIVES A VISIT FROM HIS SPIRITUAL WARD
FUZZ!
HOW COULD YOU HAVE SUNK SO LOW?
BUDDHA FROG
SAME OL' BEAR
VEGGIEMAN!
FUGGIE the WUMPSTER
HE WUVS YOU!!
Dolly cry her head off
Sunshine THE SLUG
YOUR LIFE WAS SO FULL OF PROMISE!
YOU WERE PREPARED FOR A LIFE OF LOVE AND AFFECTION
EEW
SAME OL'
BUT IT WAS NOT TO BE!
WHOMP!
AT LEAST YOU DID NOT SUFFER A WORSE FATE...
...THAT YOU SHOULD BE THANKFUL FOR!
WHO THE HELL ARE YOU?
SANITATION

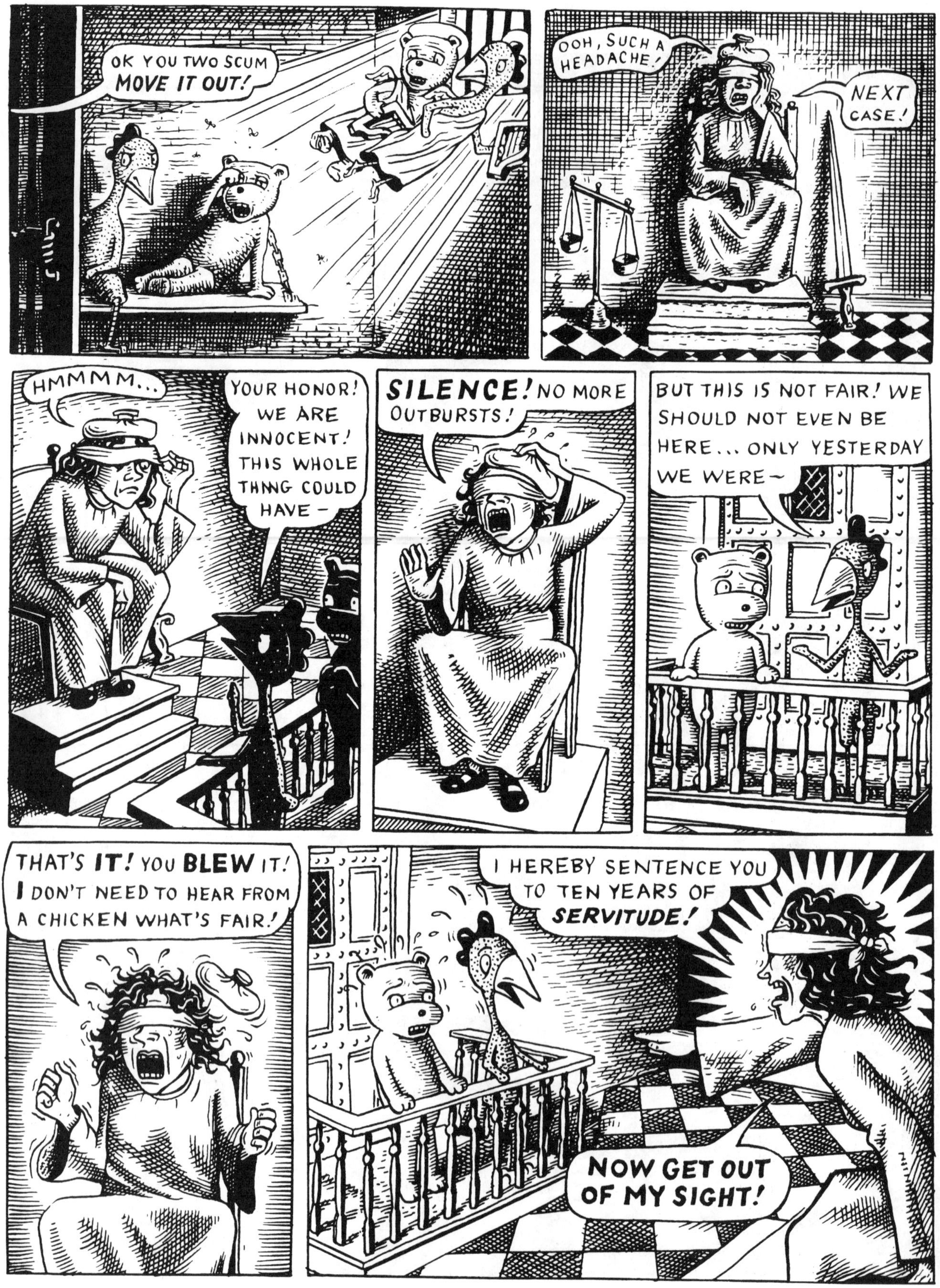
OK YOU TWO SCUM **MOVE IT OUT!**
OOH, SUCH A HEADACHE!
NEXT CASE!
HMMMM...
YOUR HONOR! WE ARE INNOCENT! THIS WHOLE THING COULD HAVE –
SILENCE! NO MORE OUTBURSTS!
BUT THIS IS NOT FAIR! WE SHOULD NOT EVEN BE HERE... ONLY YESTERDAY WE WERE –
THAT'S **IT!** YOU **BLEW** IT! I DON'T NEED TO HEAR FROM A CHICKEN WHAT'S FAIR!
I HEREBY SENTENCE YOU TO TEN YEARS OF **SERVITUDE!**
NOW GET OUT OF MY SIGHT!

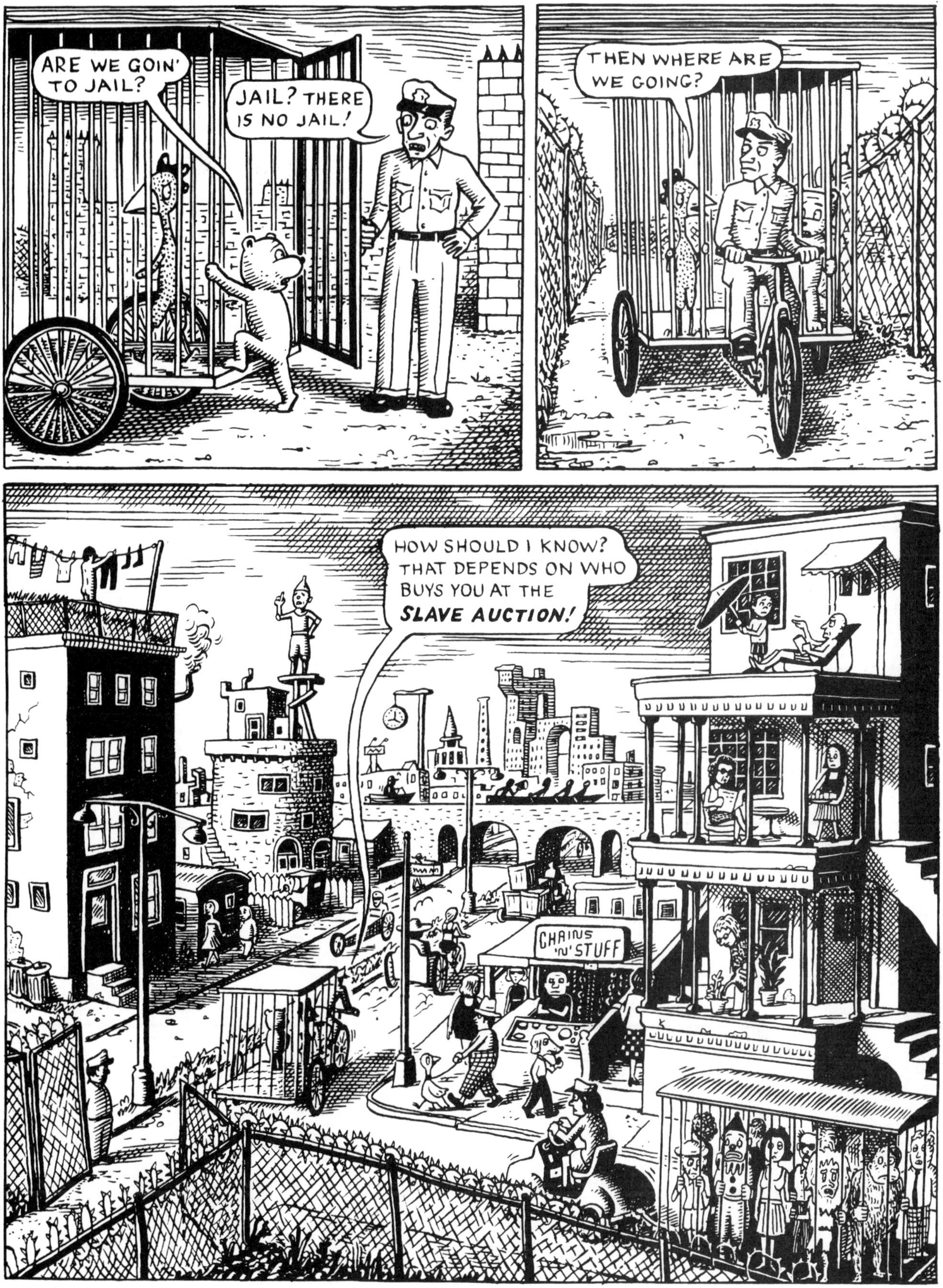
ARE WE GOIN' TO JAIL?
JAIL? THERE IS NO JAIL!
THEN WHERE ARE WE GOING?
HOW SHOULD I KNOW? THAT DEPENDS ON WHO BUYS YOU AT THE **SLAVE AUCTION!**
CHAINS 'N' STUFF

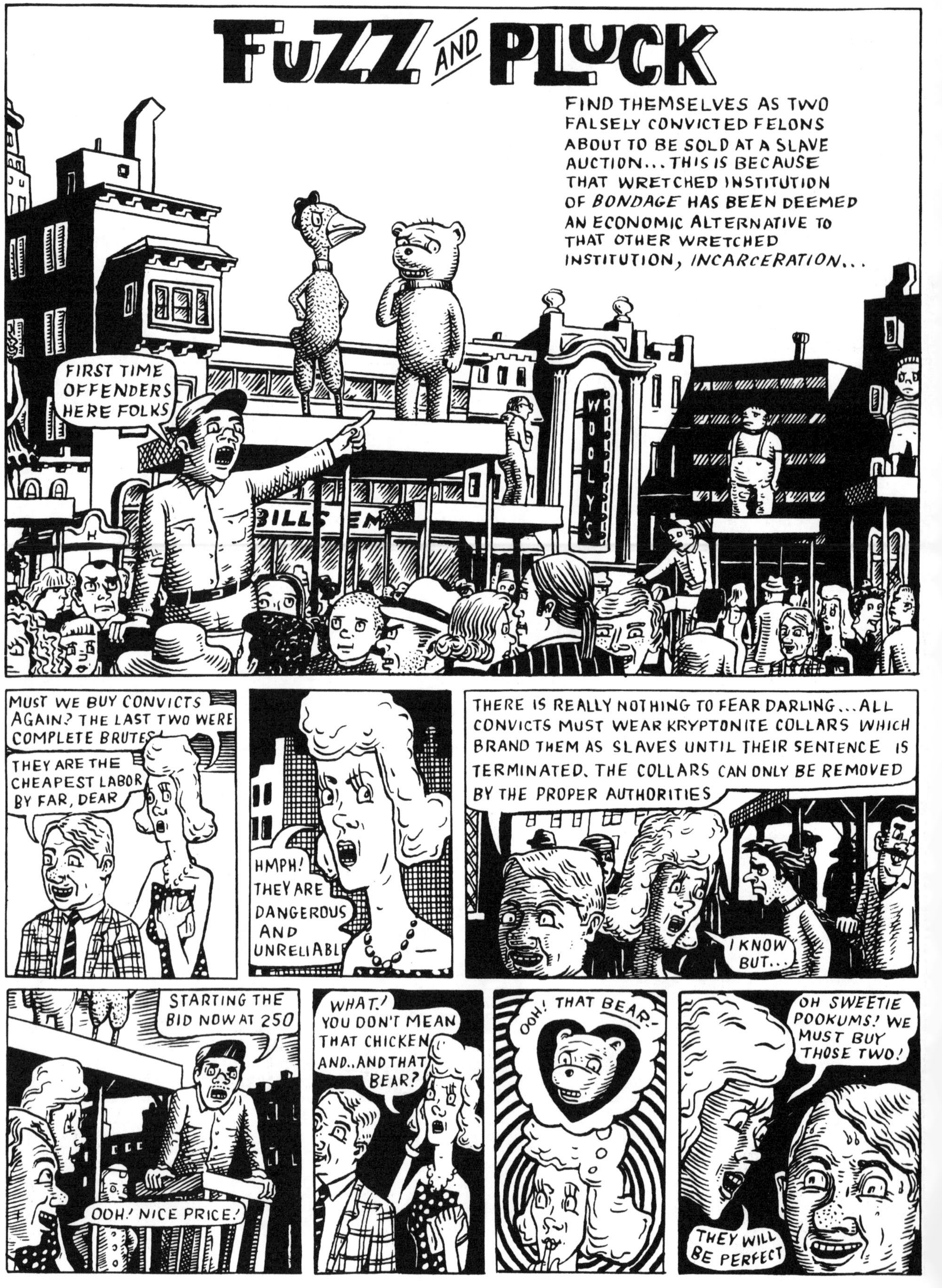
FUZZ AND PLUCK
FIND THEMSELVES AS TWO FALSELY CONVICTED FELONS ABOUT TO BE SOLD AT A SLAVE AUCTION... THIS IS BECAUSE THAT WRETCHED INSTITUTION OF *BONDAGE* HAS BEEN DEEMED AN ECONOMIC ALTERNATIVE TO THAT OTHER WRETCHED INSTITUTION, *INCARCERATION*...
FIRST TIME OFFENDERS HERE FOLKS
BILLS
WOOLY'S
MUST WE BUY CONVICTS AGAIN? THE LAST TWO WERE COMPLETE BRUTES!
THEY ARE THE CHEAPEST LABOR BY FAR, DEAR
HMPH! THEY ARE DANGEROUS AND UNRELIABLE
THERE IS REALLY NOTHING TO FEAR DARLING... ALL CONVICTS MUST WEAR KRYPTONITE COLLARS WHICH BRAND THEM AS SLAVES UNTIL THEIR SENTENCE IS TERMINATED. THE COLLARS CAN ONLY BE REMOVED BY THE PROPER AUTHORITIES
I KNOW BUT...
STARTING THE BID NOW AT 250
OOH! NICE PRICE!
WHAT! YOU DON'T MEAN THAT CHICKEN AND.. AND THAT BEAR?
OOH! THAT BEAR-
OH SWEETIE POOKUMS! WE MUST BUY THOSE TWO!
THEY WILL BE PERFECT

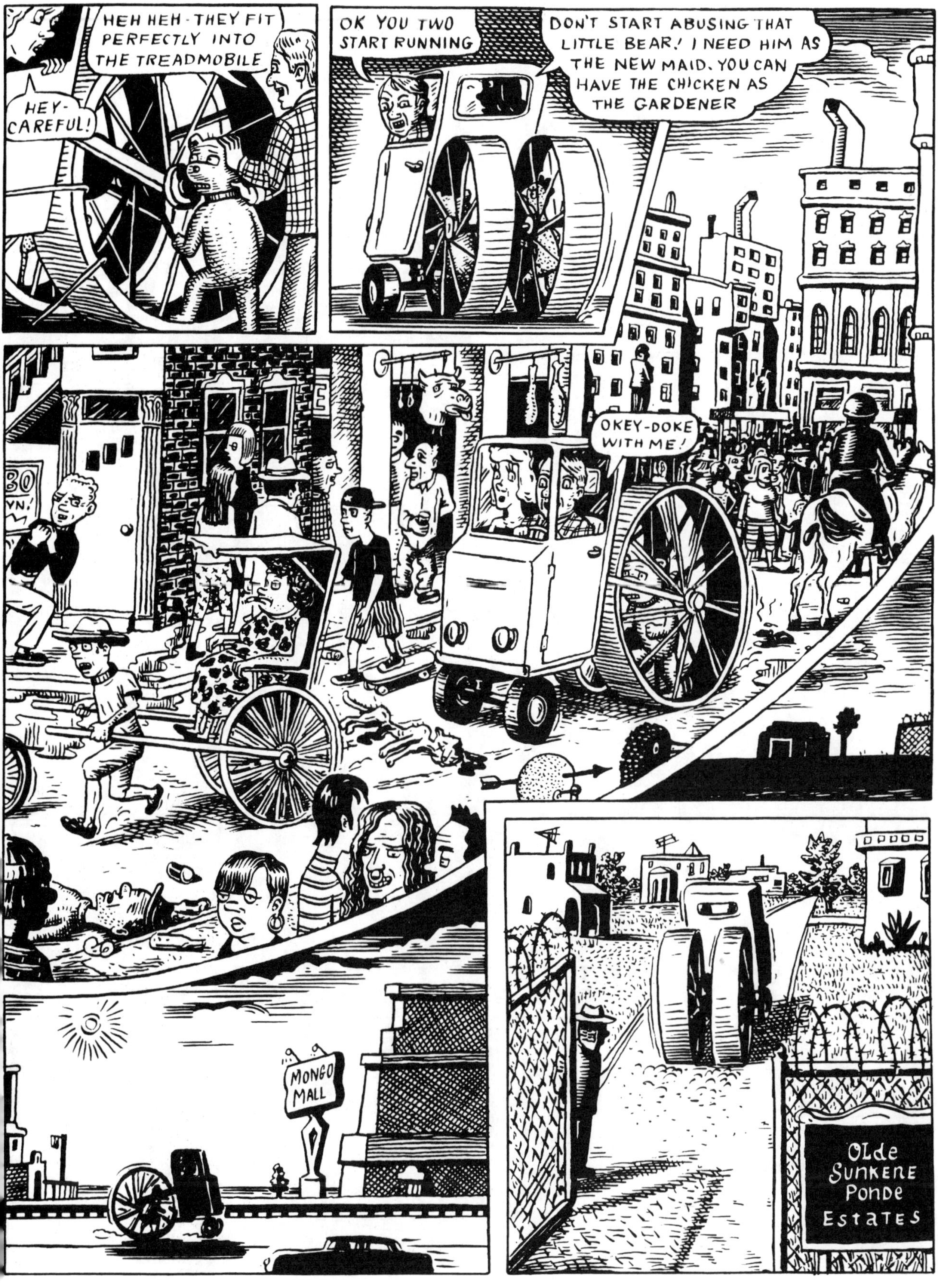
HEH HEH - THEY FIT PERFECTLY INTO THE TREADMOBILE
HEY-CAREFUL!
OK YOU TWO START RUNNING
DON'T START ABUSING THAT LITTLE BEAR! I NEED HIM AS THE NEW MAID. YOU CAN HAVE THE CHICKEN AS THE GARDENER
OKEY-DOKE WITH ME!
MONGO MALL
Olde Sunkene Ponde Estates

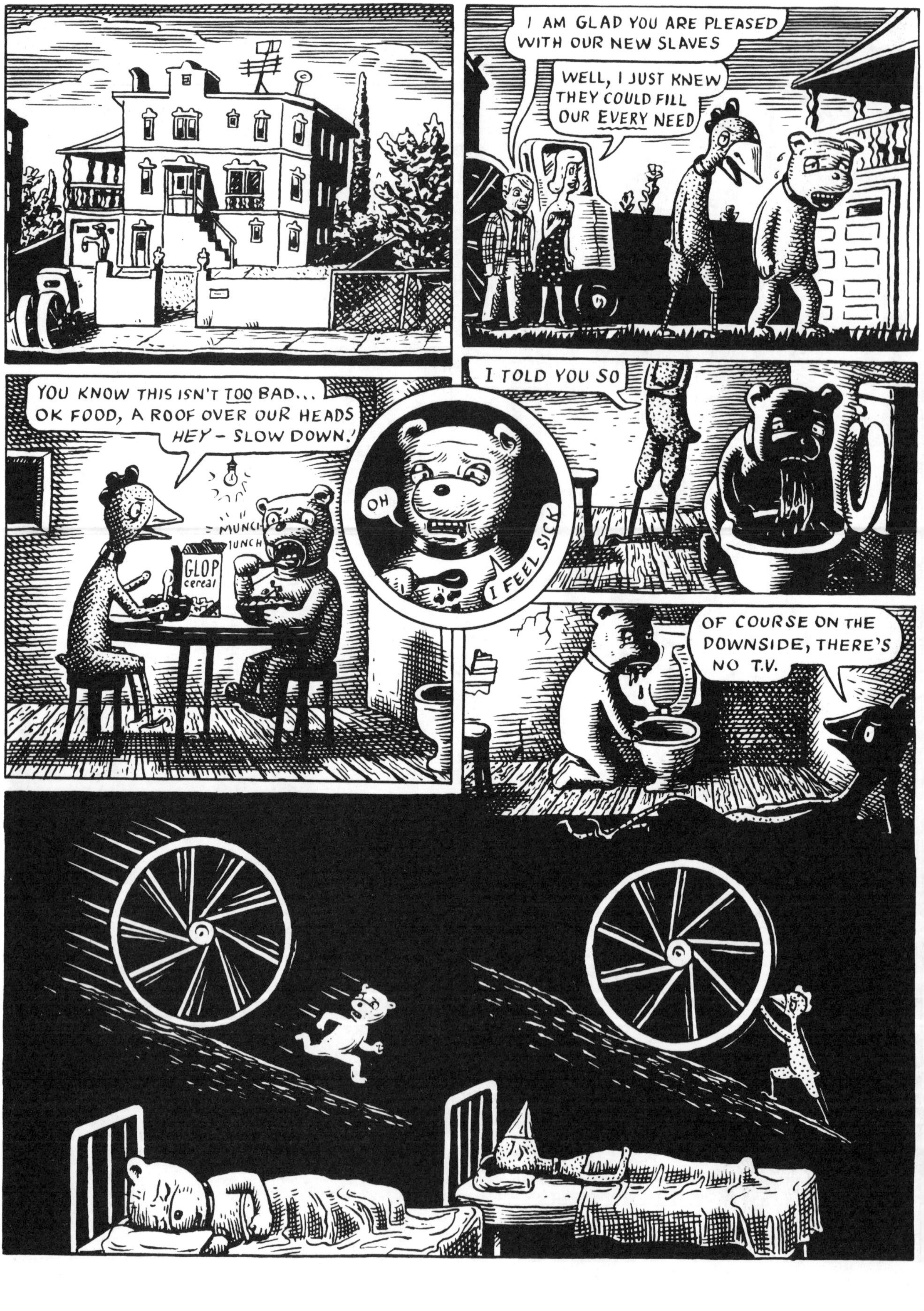

I AM GLAD YOU ARE PLEASED WITH OUR NEW SLAVES
WELL, I JUST KNEW THEY COULD FILL OUR EVERY NEED
YOU KNOW THIS ISN'T TOO BAD... OK FOOD, A ROOF OVER OUR HEADS HEY - SLOW DOWN!
MUNCH MUNCH
GLOP cereal
OH
I FEEL SICK
I TOLD YOU SO
OF COURSE ON THE DOWNSIDE, THERE'S NO T.V.

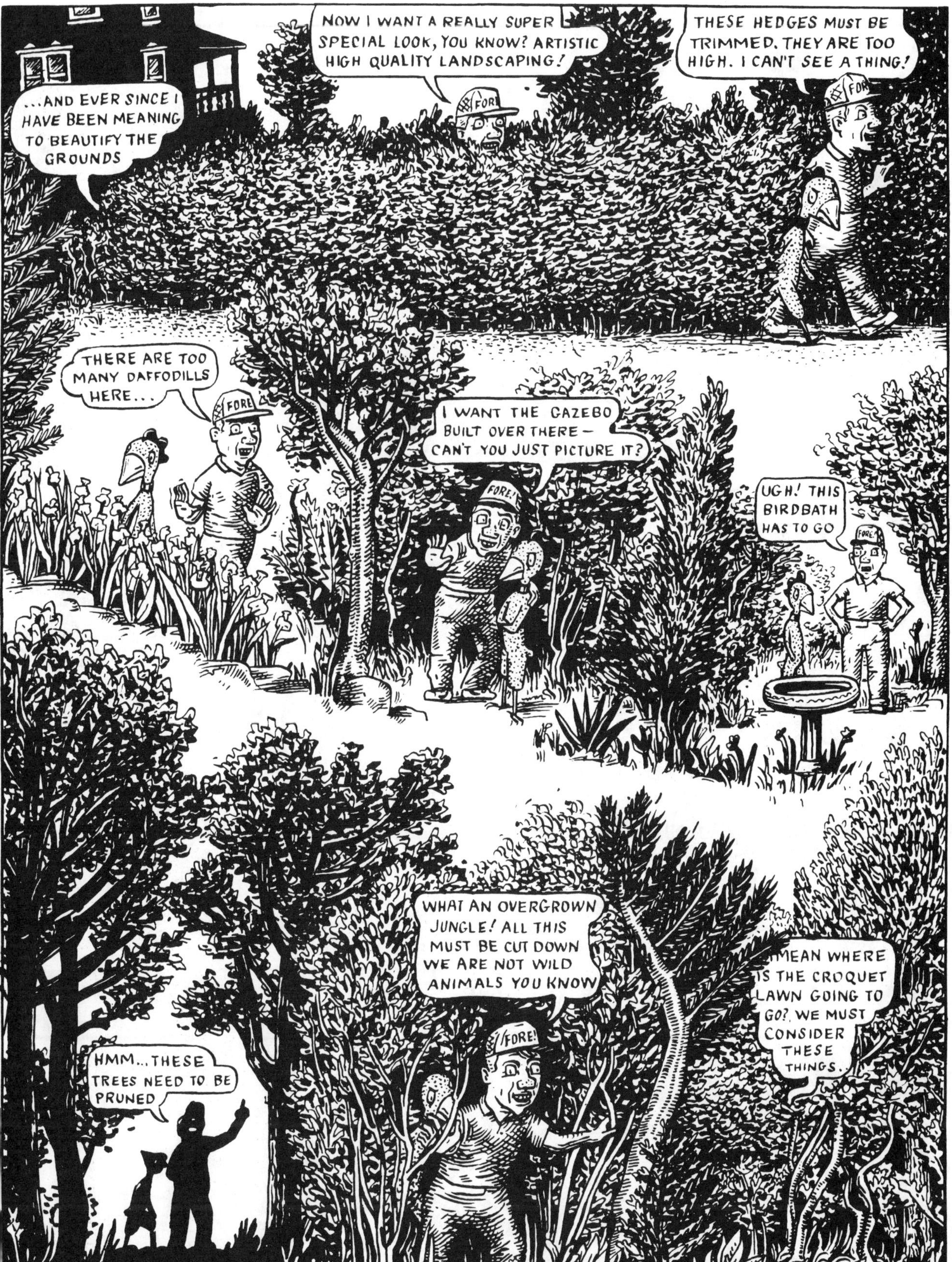
...AND EVER SINCE I HAVE BEEN MEANING TO BEAUTIFY THE GROUNDS
NOW I WANT A REALLY SUPER SPECIAL LOOK, YOU KNOW? ARTISTIC HIGH QUALITY LANDSCAPING!
FORE
THESE HEDGES MUST BE TRIMMED. THEY ARE TOO HIGH. I CAN'T SEE A THING!
FORE
THERE ARE TOO MANY DAFFODILLS HERE...
FORE
I WANT THE GAZEBO BUILT OVER THERE— CAN'T YOU JUST PICTURE IT?
FORE!
UGH! THIS BIRDBATH HAS TO GO
FORE!
WHAT AN OVERGROWN JUNGLE! ALL THIS MUST BE CUT DOWN WE ARE NOT WILD ANIMALS YOU KNOW
FORE!
I MEAN WHERE IS THE CROQUET LAWN GOING TO GO? WE MUST CONSIDER THESE THINGS.
HMM... THESE TREES NEED TO BE PRUNED

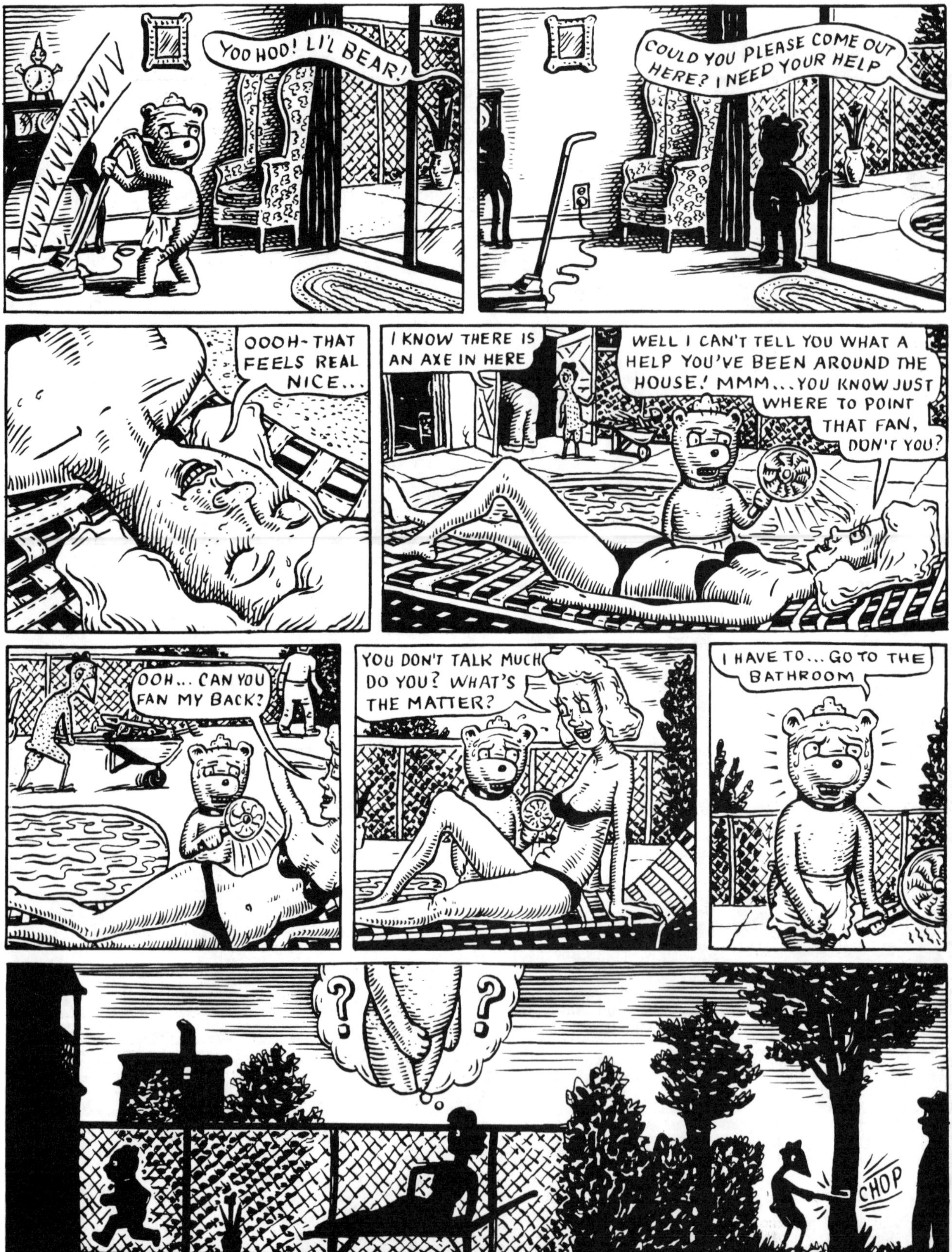

YOO HOO! LI'L BEAR!
COULD YOU PLEASE COME OUT HERE? I NEED YOUR HELP
OOOH- THAT FEELS REAL NICE...
I KNOW THERE IS AN AXE IN HERE
WELL I CAN'T TELL YOU WHAT A HELP YOU'VE BEEN AROUND THE HOUSE! MMM... YOU KNOW JUST WHERE TO POINT THAT FAN, DON'T YOU?
OOH... CAN YOU FAN MY BACK?
YOU DON'T TALK MUCH DO YOU? WHAT'S THE MATTER?
I HAVE TO... GO TO THE BATHROOM
? ?
CHOP

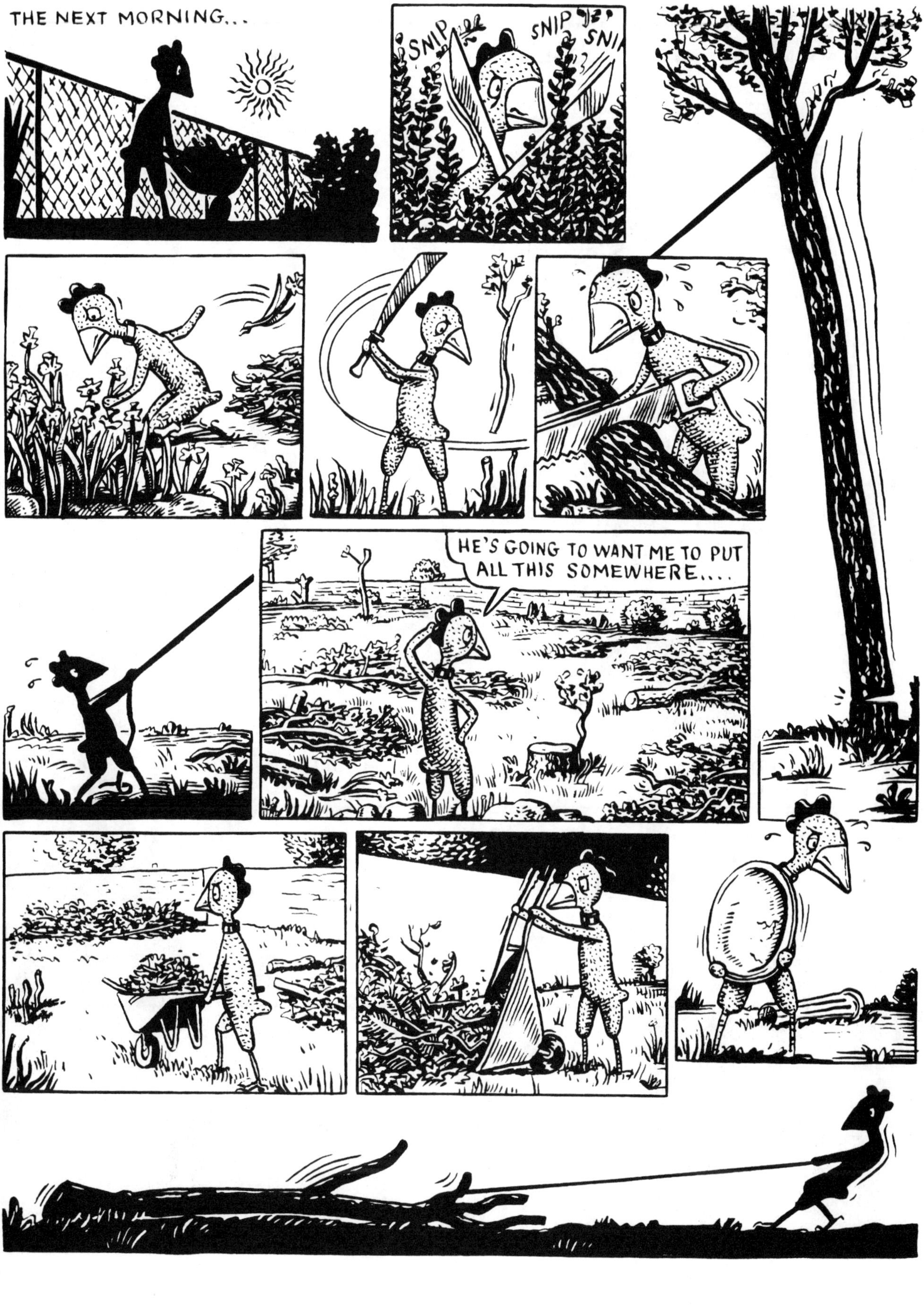
THE NEXT MORNING...
SNIP
SNIP
SNI
HE'S GOING TO WANT ME TO PUT ALL THIS SOMEWHERE....

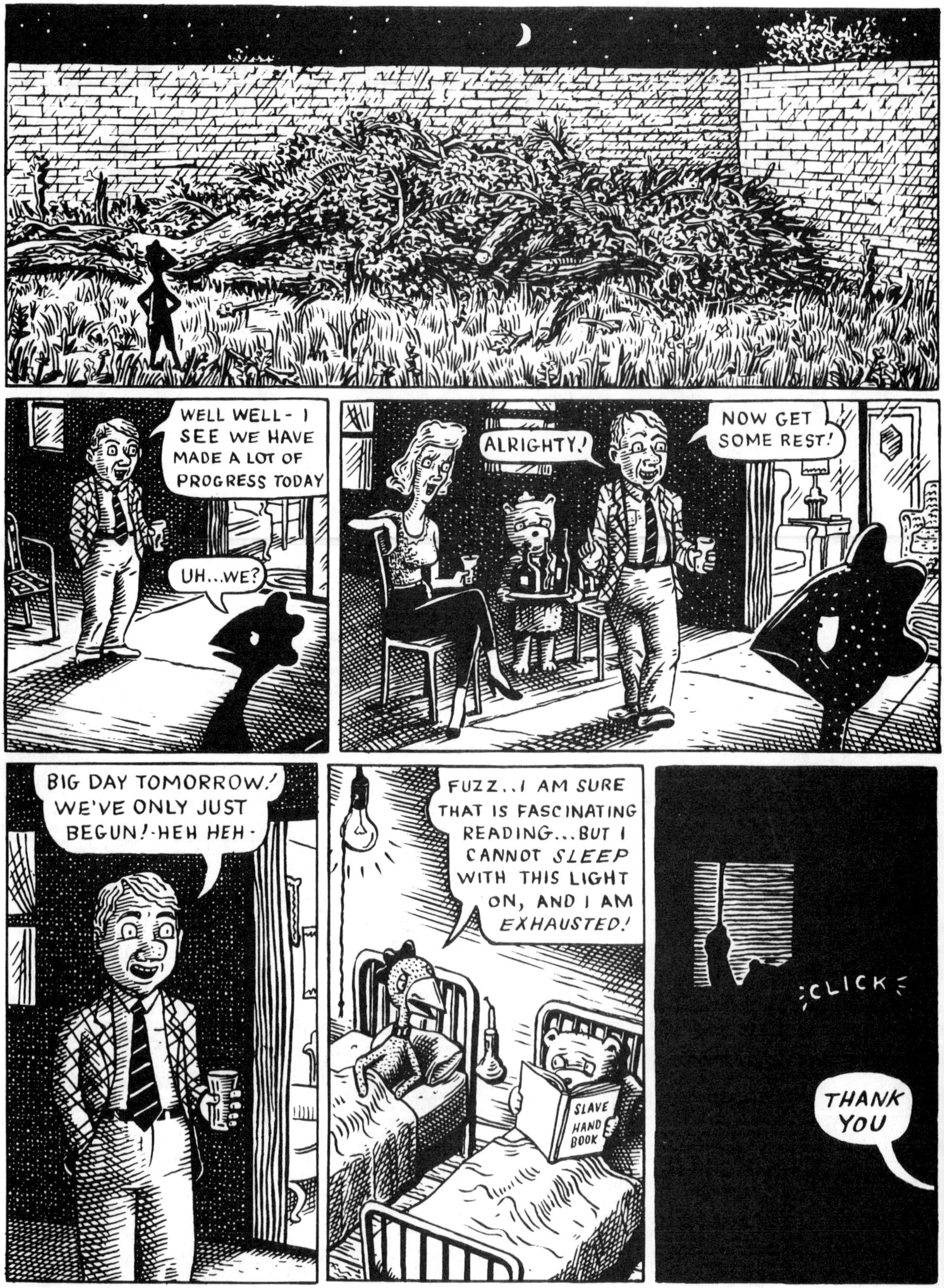
WELL WELL- I SEE WE HAVE MADE A LOT OF PROGRESS TODAY
UH...WE?
ALRIGHTY!
NOW GET SOME REST!
BIG DAY TOMORROW! WE'VE ONLY JUST BEGUN! -HEH HEH-
FUZZ..I AM SURE THAT IS FASCINATING READING...BUT I CANNOT SLEEP WITH THIS LIGHT ON, AND I AM EXHAUSTED!
SLAVE HAND BOOK
CLICK
THANK YOU

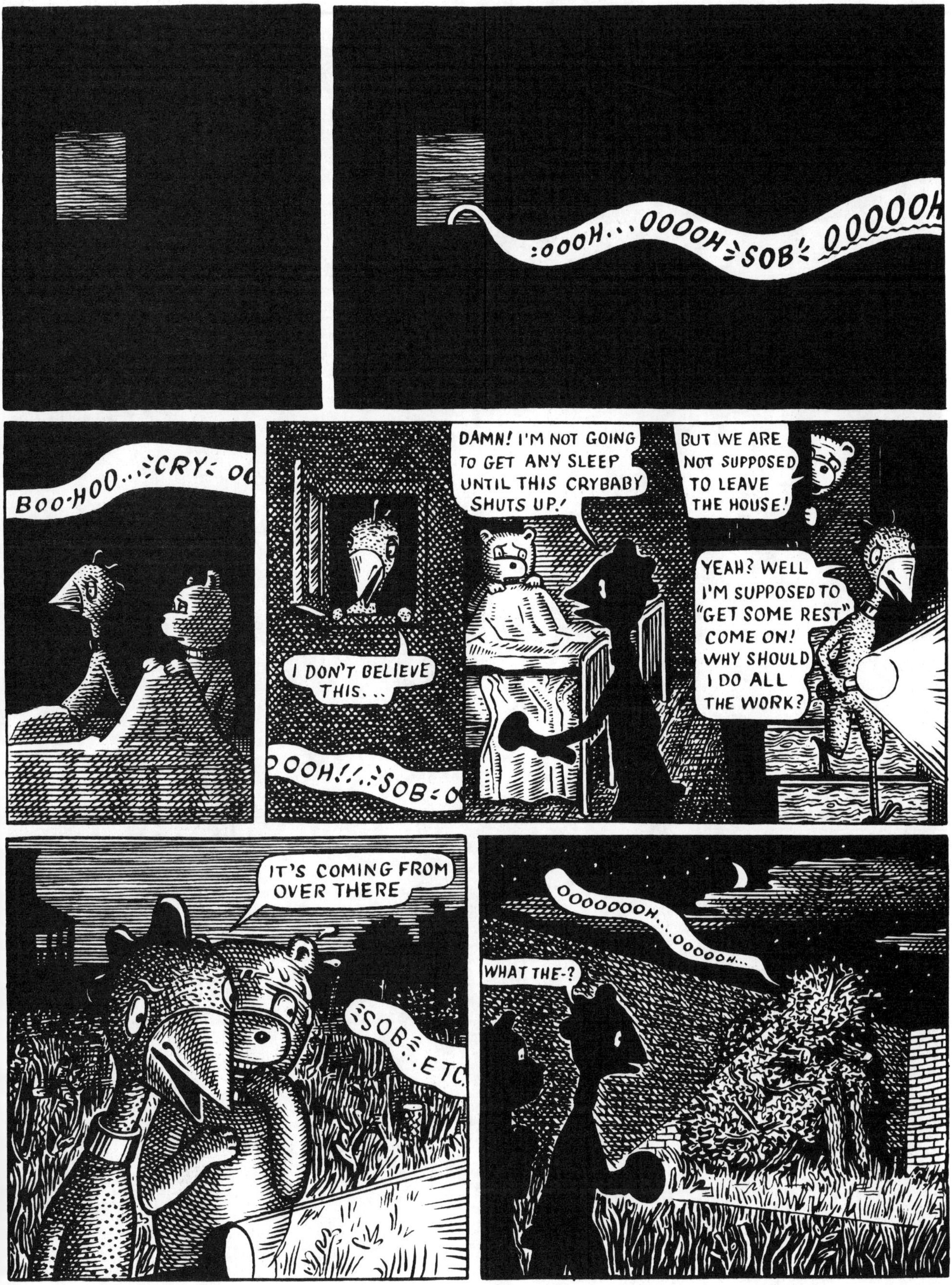
:OOOH...OOOOH:SOB: OOOOOH
BOO-HOO...:CRY: OO
I DON'T BELIEVE THIS...
OOOH!!:SOB: O
DAMN! I'M NOT GOING TO GET ANY SLEEP UNTIL THIS CRYBABY SHUTS UP!
BUT WE ARE NOT SUPPOSED TO LEAVE THE HOUSE!
YEAH? WELL I'M SUPPOSED TO "GET SOME REST" COME ON! WHY SHOULD I DO ALL THE WORK?
IT'S COMING FROM OVER THERE
:SOB:...ETC.
OOOOOOOH....OOOOOH...
WHAT THE-?

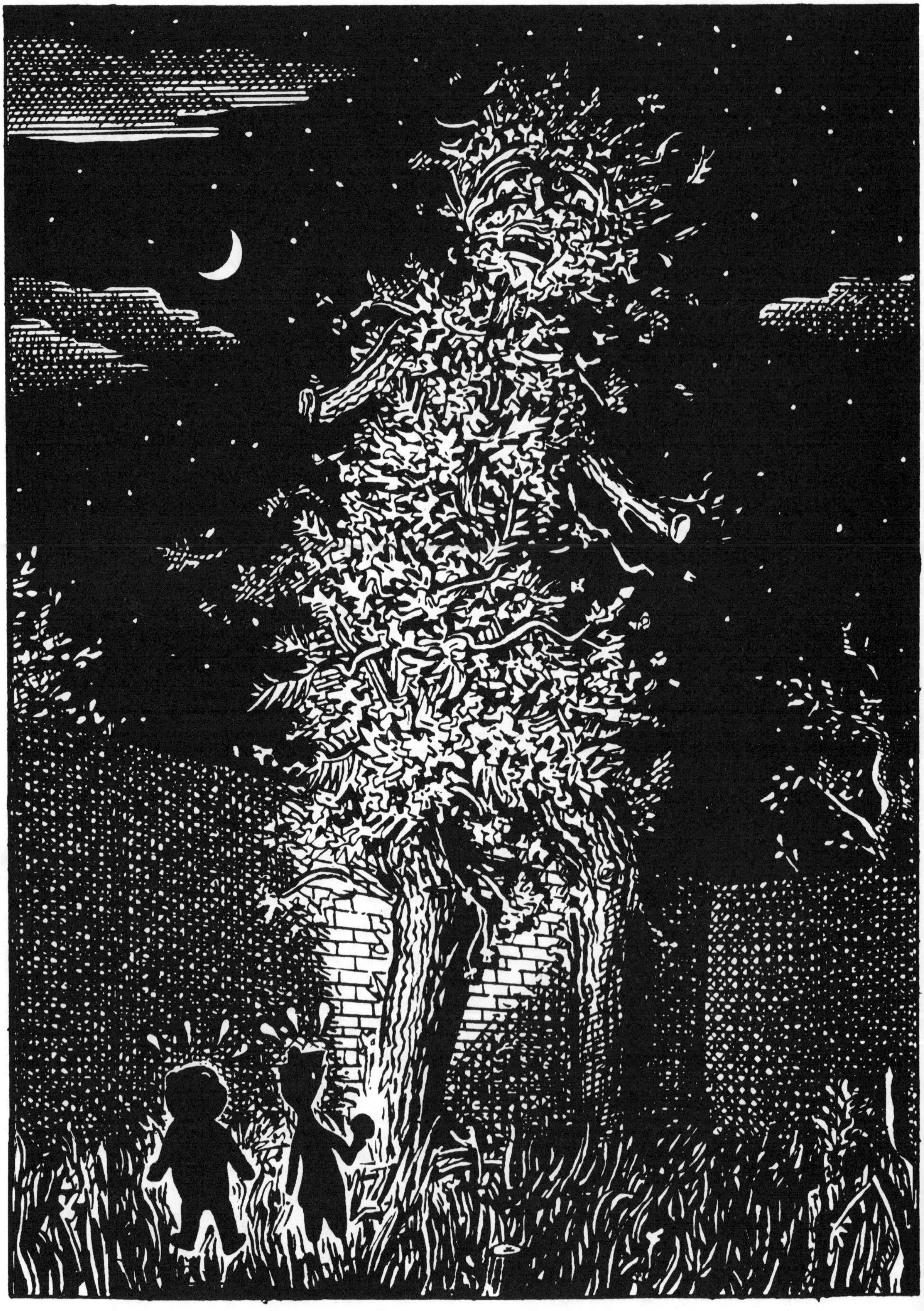

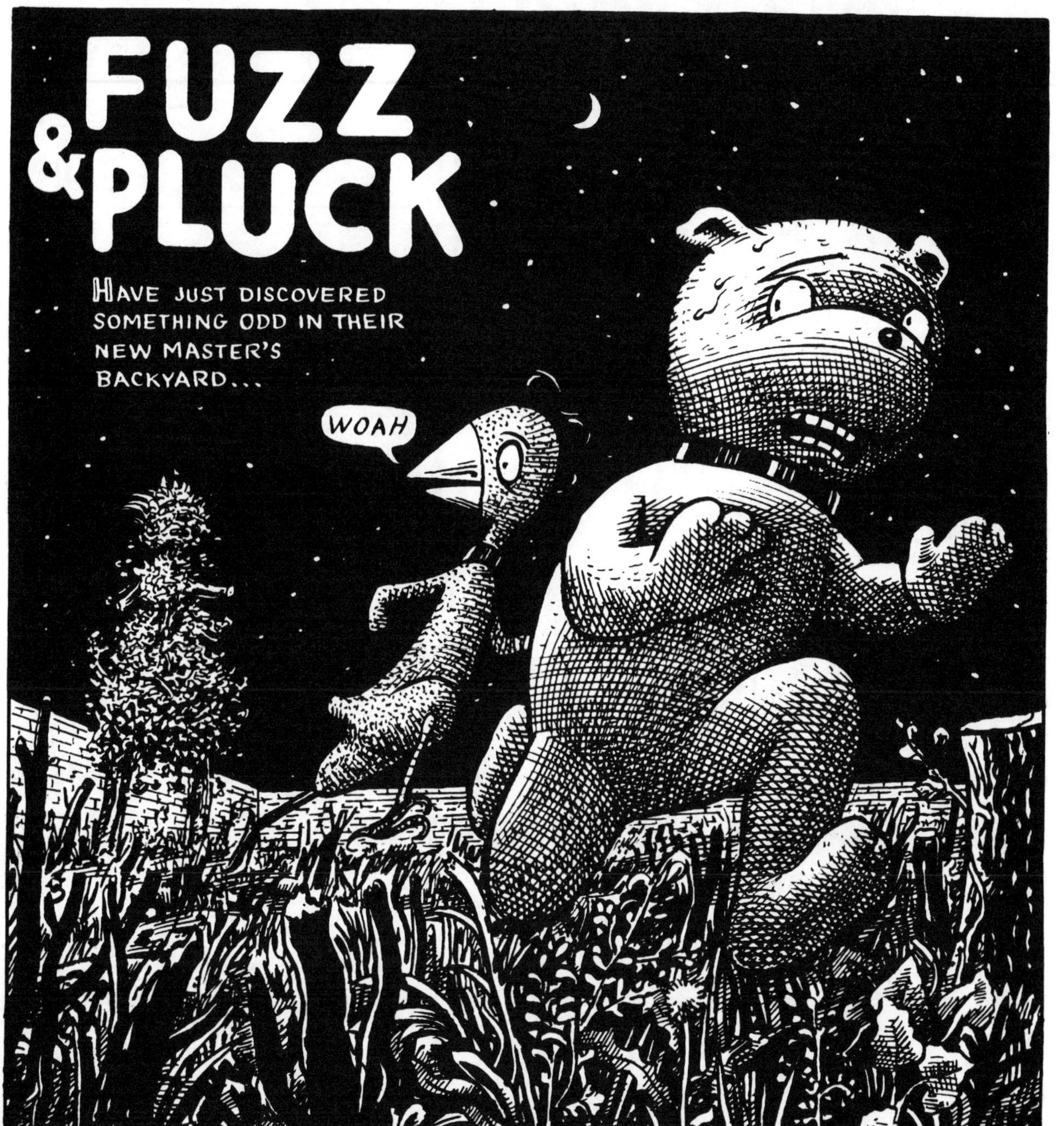
FUZZ & PLUCK
HAVE JUST DISCOVERED SOMETHING ODD IN THEIR NEW MASTER'S BACKYARD...
WOAH

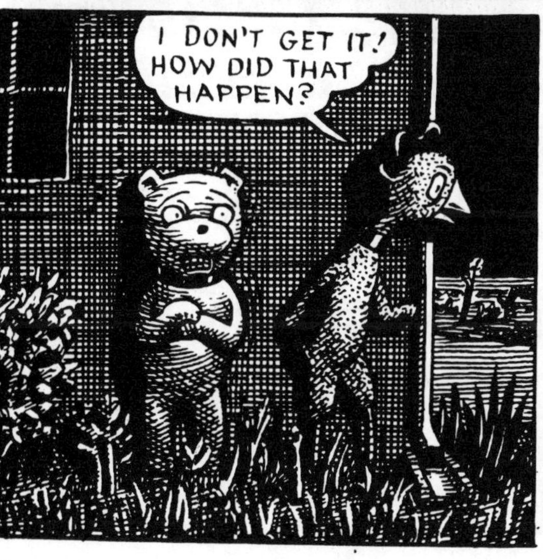
I DON'T GET IT! HOW DID THAT HAPPEN?

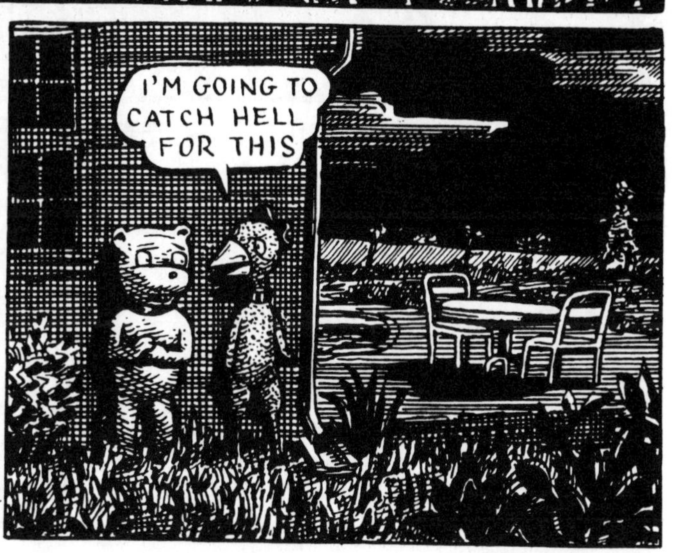
I'M GOING TO CATCH HELL FOR THIS

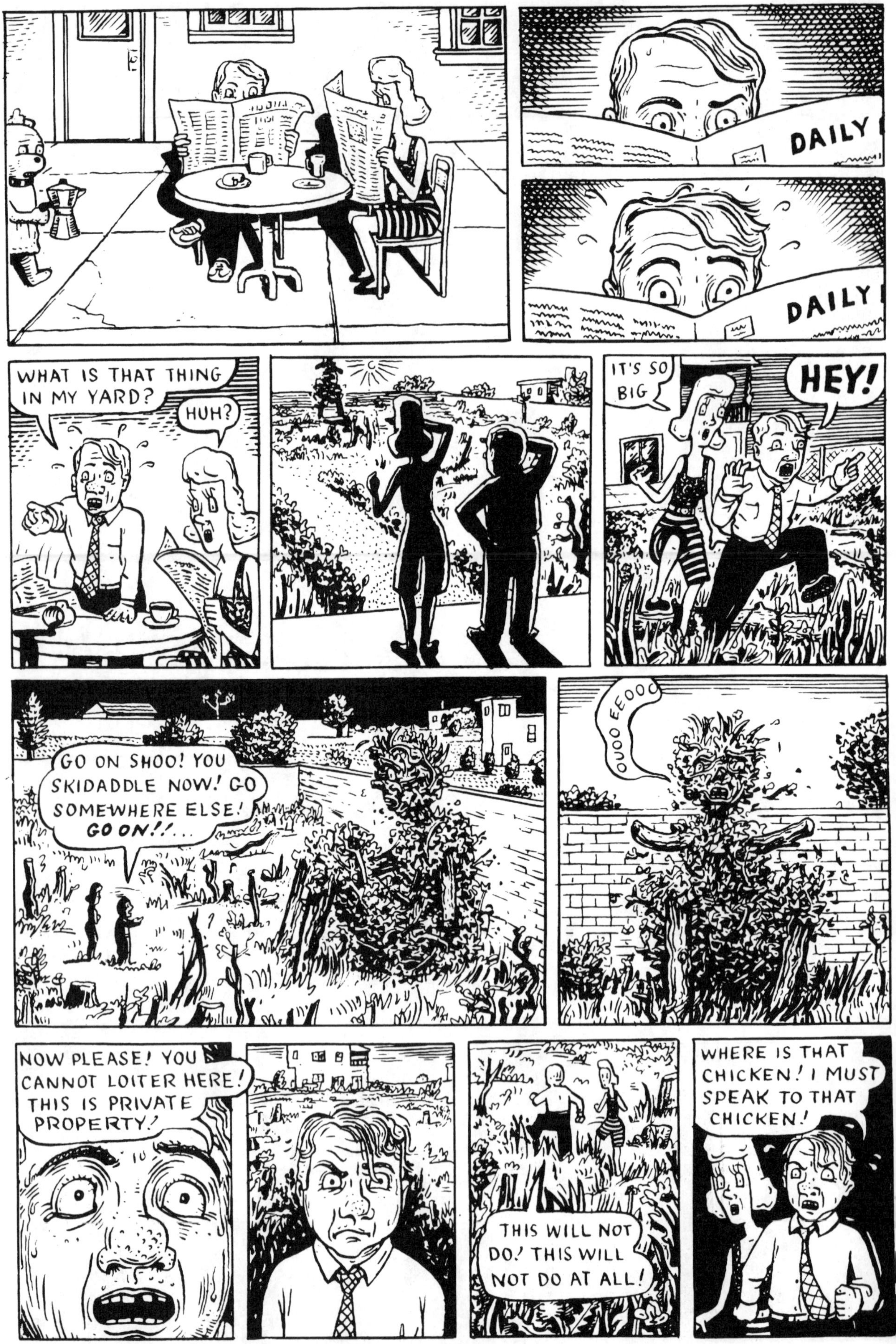
DAILY
DAILY
WHAT IS THAT THING IN MY YARD?
HUH?
IT'S SO BIG
HEY!
GO ON SHOO! YOU SKIDADDLE NOW! GO SOMEWHERE ELSE! GO ON!!...
OUOO EEOOO
NOW PLEASE! YOU CANNOT LOITER HERE! THIS IS PRIVATE PROPERTY!
THIS WILL NOT DO! THIS WILL NOT DO AT ALL!
WHERE IS THAT CHICKEN! I MUST SPEAK TO THAT CHICKEN!

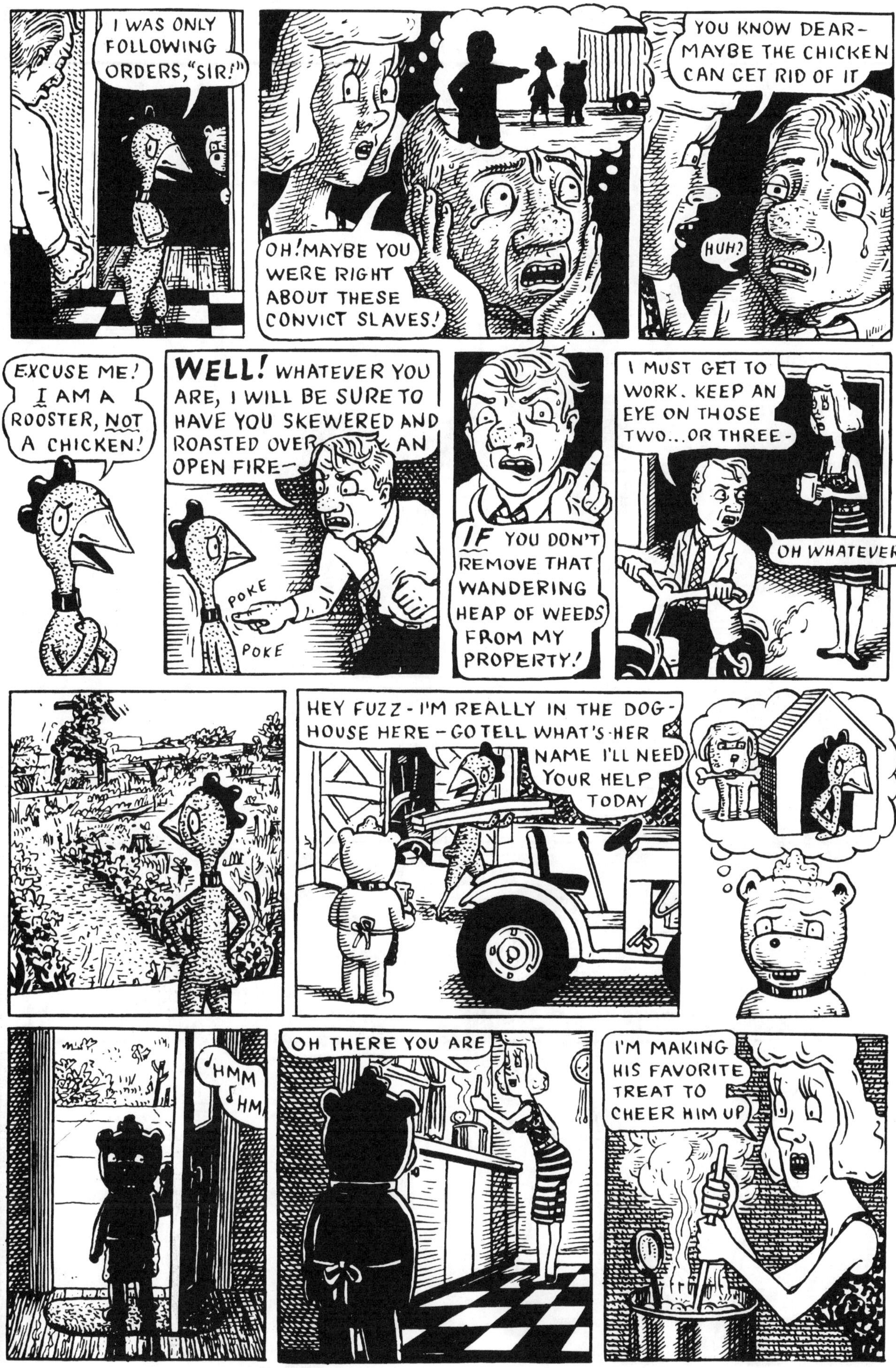
I WAS ONLY FOLLOWING ORDERS, "SIR!"
OH! MAYBE YOU WERE RIGHT ABOUT THESE CONVICT SLAVES!
YOU KNOW DEAR- MAYBE THE CHICKEN CAN GET RID OF IT
HUH?
EXCUSE ME! I AM A ROOSTER, NOT A CHICKEN!
WELL! WHATEVER YOU ARE, I WILL BE SURE TO HAVE YOU SKEWERED AND ROASTED OVER AN OPEN FIRE-
POKE
POKE
IF YOU DON'T REMOVE THAT WANDERING HEAP OF WEEDS FROM MY PROPERTY!
I MUST GET TO WORK. KEEP AN EYE ON THOSE TWO...OR THREE-
OH WHATEVER!
HEY FUZZ - I'M REALLY IN THE DOG-HOUSE HERE - GO TELL WHAT'S-HER NAME I'LL NEED YOUR HELP TODAY
HMM HMM
OH THERE YOU ARE
I'M MAKING HIS FAVORITE TREAT TO CHEER HIM UP

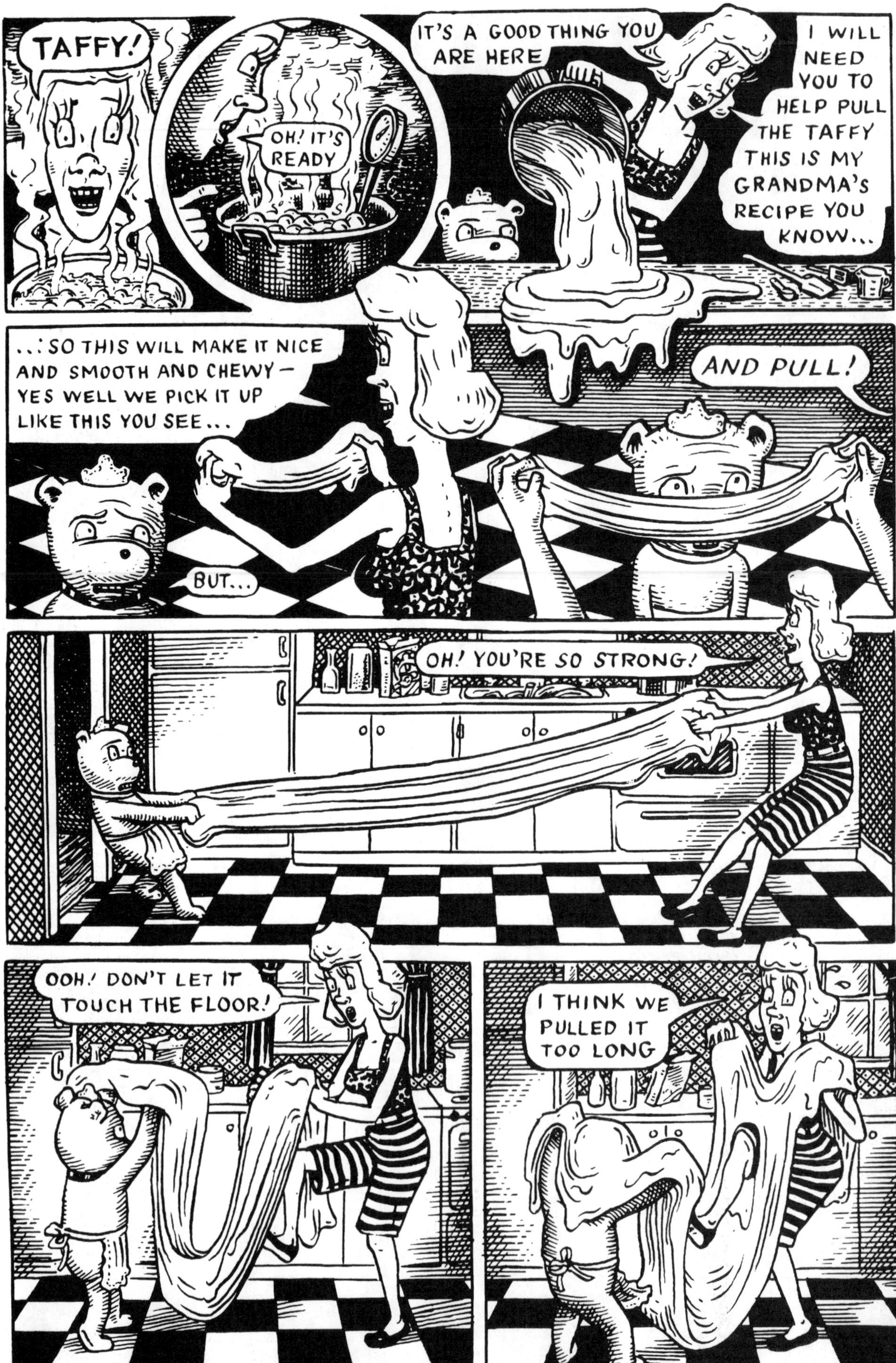
TAFFY!
OH! IT'S READY
IT'S A GOOD THING YOU ARE HERE
I WILL NEED YOU TO HELP PULL THE TAFFY THIS IS MY GRANDMA'S RECIPE YOU KNOW...
...: SO THIS WILL MAKE IT NICE AND SMOOTH AND CHEWY— YES WELL WE PICK IT UP LIKE THIS YOU SEE...
AND PULL!
BUT...
OH! YOU'RE SO STRONG!
OOH! DON'T LET IT TOUCH THE FLOOR!
I THINK WE PULLED IT TOO LONG

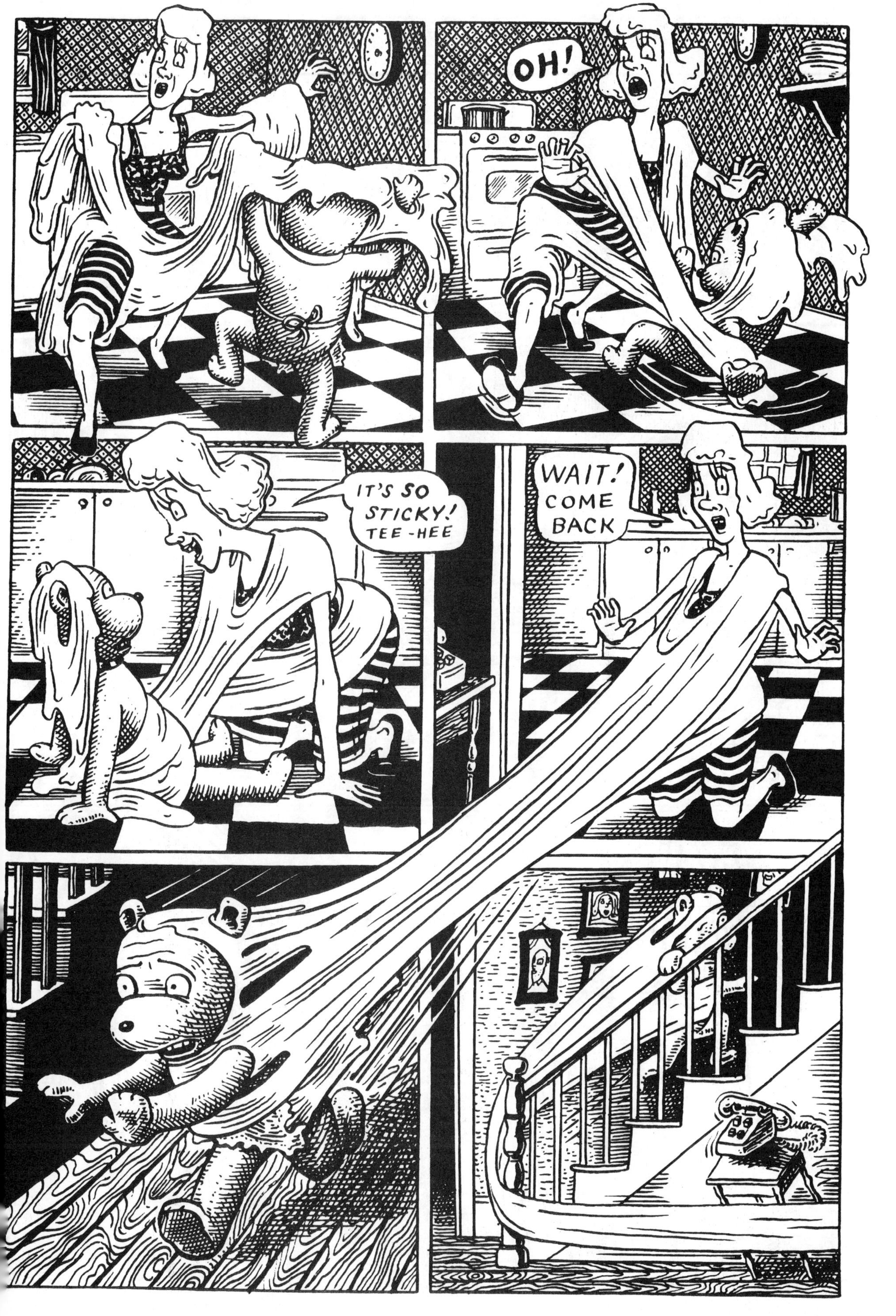
OH!
IT'S SO STICKY! TEE-HEE
WAIT! COME BACK

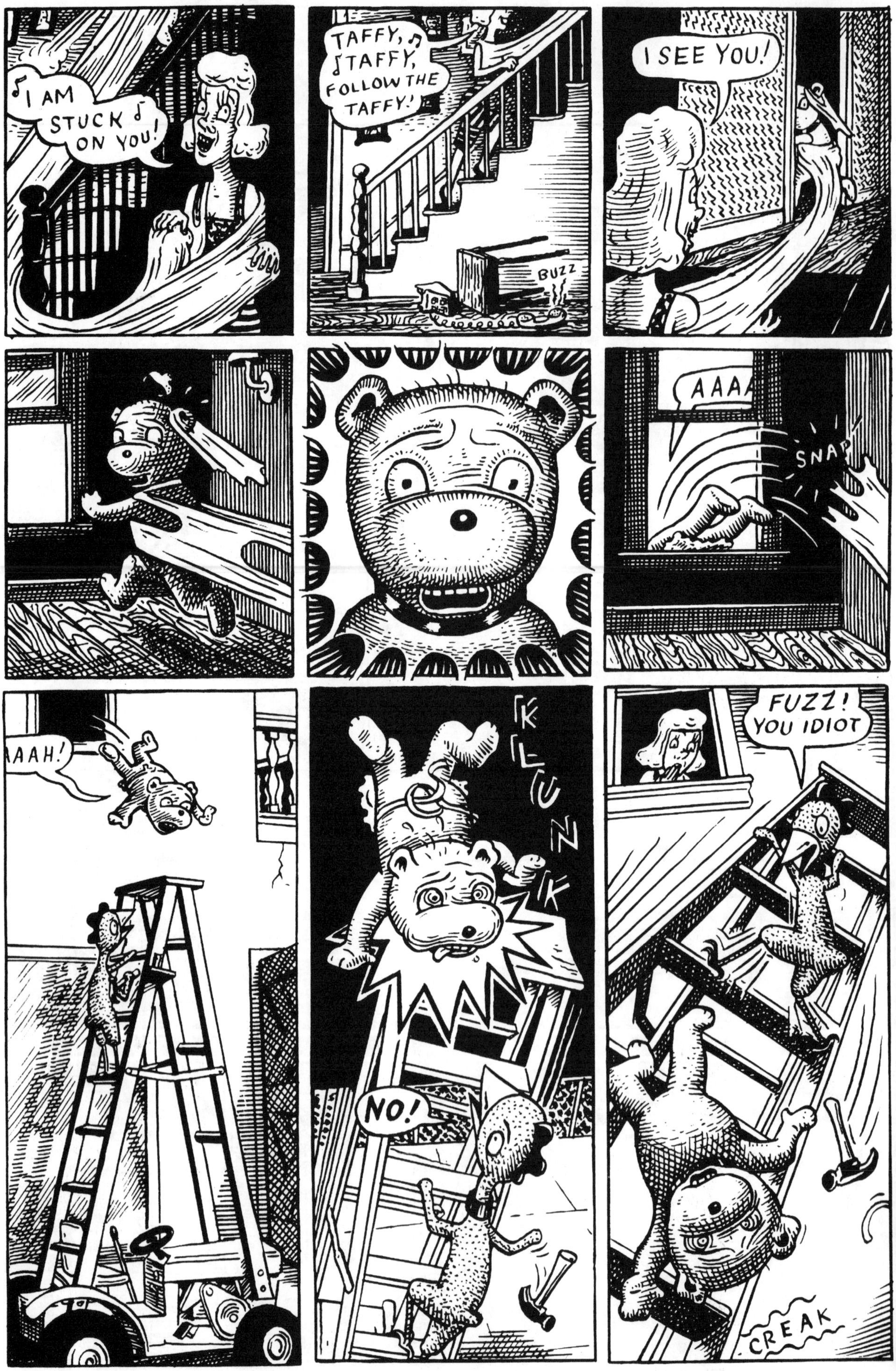
I AM STUCK ON YOU!
TAFFY, TAFFY, FOLLOW THE TAFFY!
BUZZ
I SEE YOU!
AAAA
SNAP
AAAH!
KLUNK
NO!
FUZZ! YOU IDIOT
CREAK

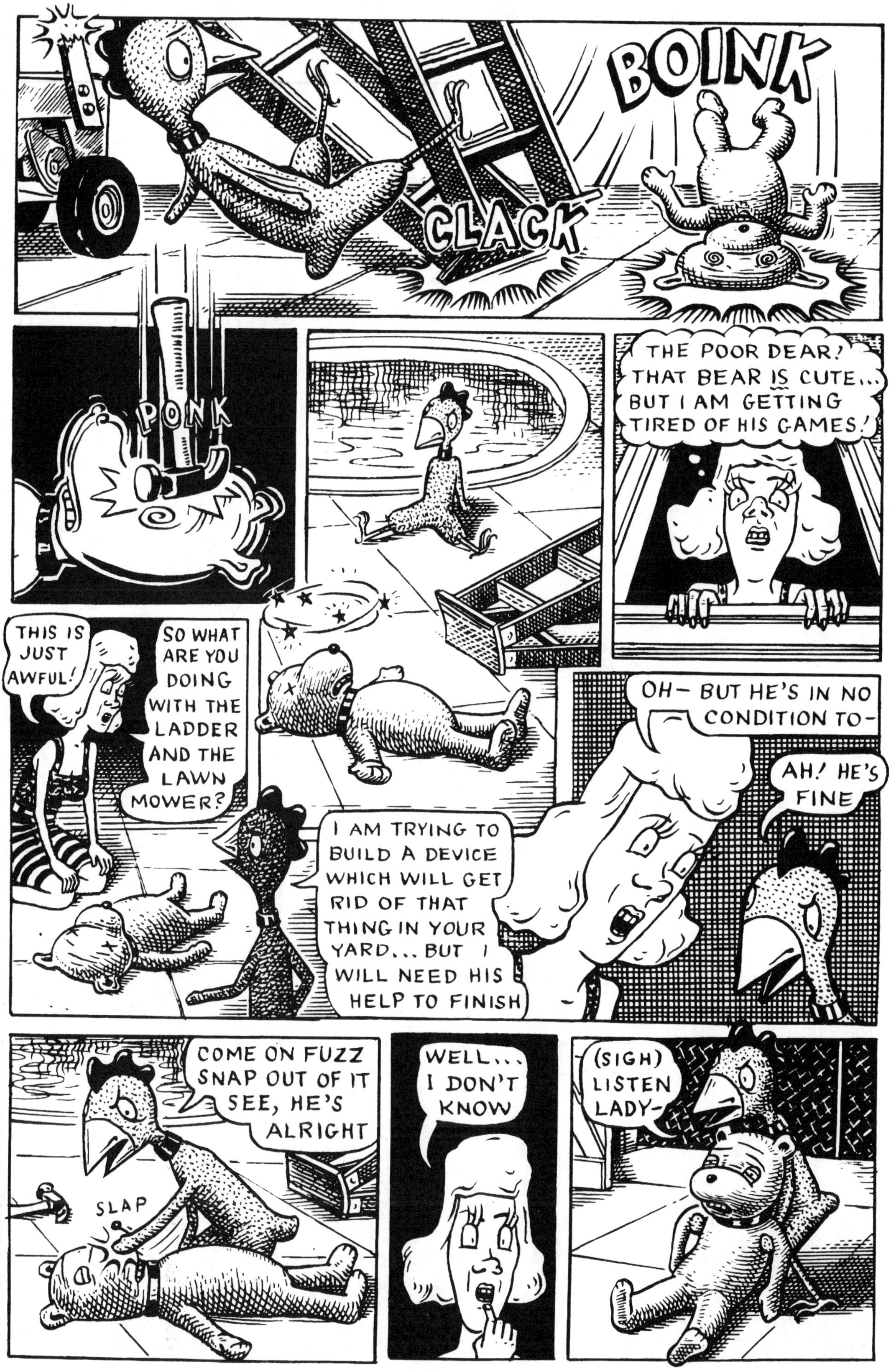
BOINK
CLACK
PONK
THE POOR DEAR! THAT BEAR IS CUTE... BUT I AM GETTING TIRED OF HIS GAMES!
THIS IS JUST AWFUL!
SO WHAT ARE YOU DOING WITH THE LADDER AND THE LAWN MOWER?
I AM TRYING TO BUILD A DEVICE WHICH WILL GET RID OF THAT THING IN YOUR YARD... BUT I WILL NEED HIS HELP TO FINISH
OH— BUT HE'S IN NO CONDITION TO—
AH! HE'S FINE
COME ON FUZZ SNAP OUT OF IT SEE, HE'S ALRIGHT
SLAP
WELL... I DON'T KNOW
(SIGH) LISTEN LADY—

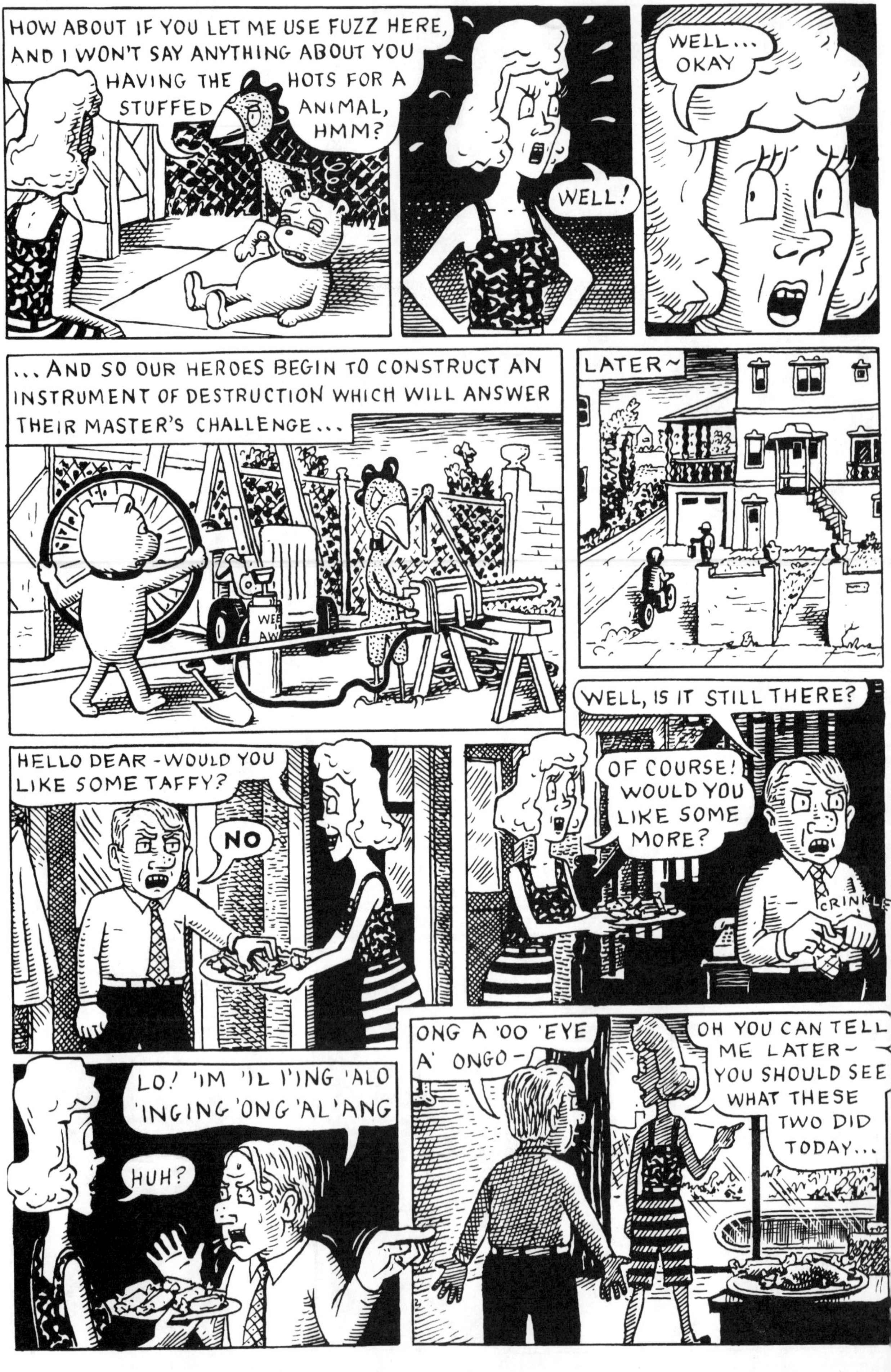
HOW ABOUT IF YOU LET ME USE FUZZ HERE, AND I WON'T SAY ANYTHING ABOUT YOU HAVING THE HOTS FOR A STUFFED ANIMAL, HMM?
WELL!
WELL... OKAY
...AND SO OUR HEROES BEGIN TO CONSTRUCT AN INSTRUMENT OF DESTRUCTION WHICH WILL ANSWER THEIR MASTER'S CHALLENGE...
LATER~
HELLO DEAR - WOULD YOU LIKE SOME TAFFY?
NO
WELL, IS IT STILL THERE?
OF COURSE! WOULD YOU LIKE SOME MORE?
CRINKLE
LO! 'IM 'IL I'ING 'ALO 'INGING 'ONG 'AL 'ANG
HUH?
ONG A 'OO 'EYE A' ONGO -
OH YOU CAN TELL ME LATER - YOU SHOULD SEE WHAT THESE TWO DID TODAY...

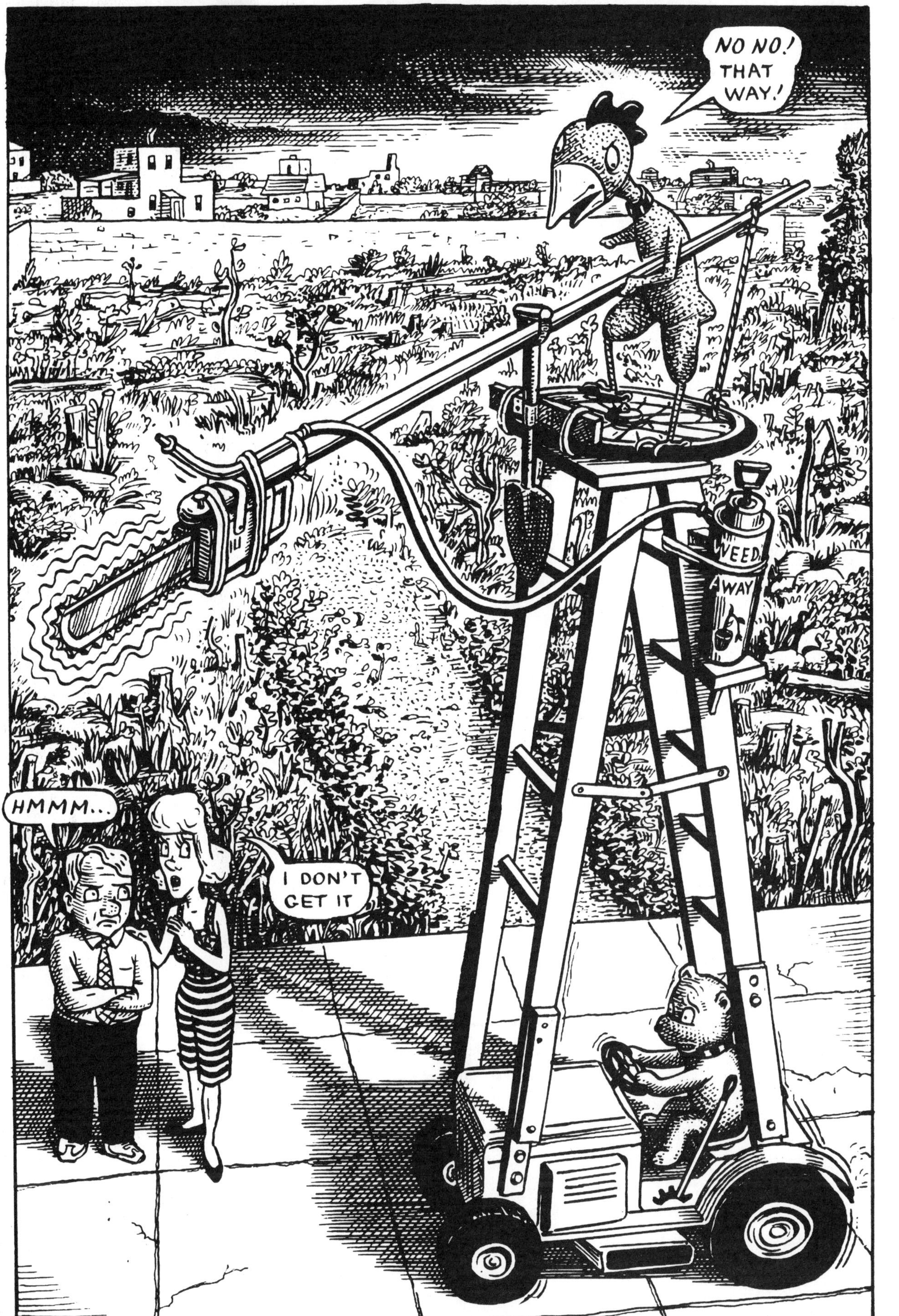
NO NO! THAT WAY!
WEED AWAY
HMMM...
I DON'T GET IT

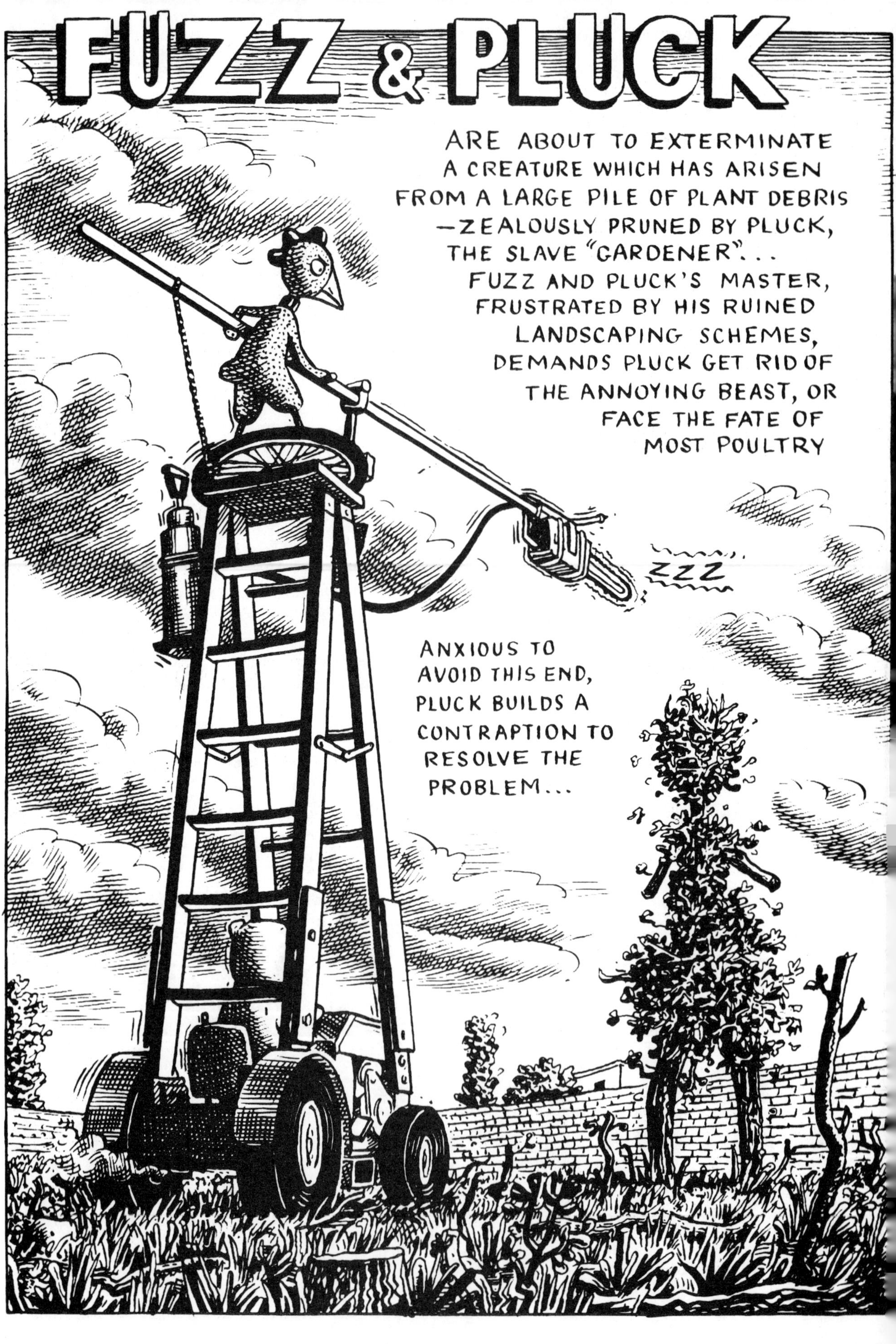
FUZZ & PLUCK
ARE ABOUT TO EXTERMINATE A CREATURE WHICH HAS ARISEN FROM A LARGE PILE OF PLANT DEBRIS —ZEALOUSLY PRUNED BY PLUCK, THE SLAVE "GARDENER"... FUZZ AND PLUCK'S MASTER, FRUSTRATED BY HIS RUINED LANDSCAPING SCHEMES, DEMANDS PLUCK GET RID OF THE ANNOYING BEAST, OR FACE THE FATE OF MOST POULTRY
ZZZ
ANXIOUS TO AVOID THIS END, PLUCK BUILDS A CONTRAPTION TO RESOLVE THE PROBLEM...

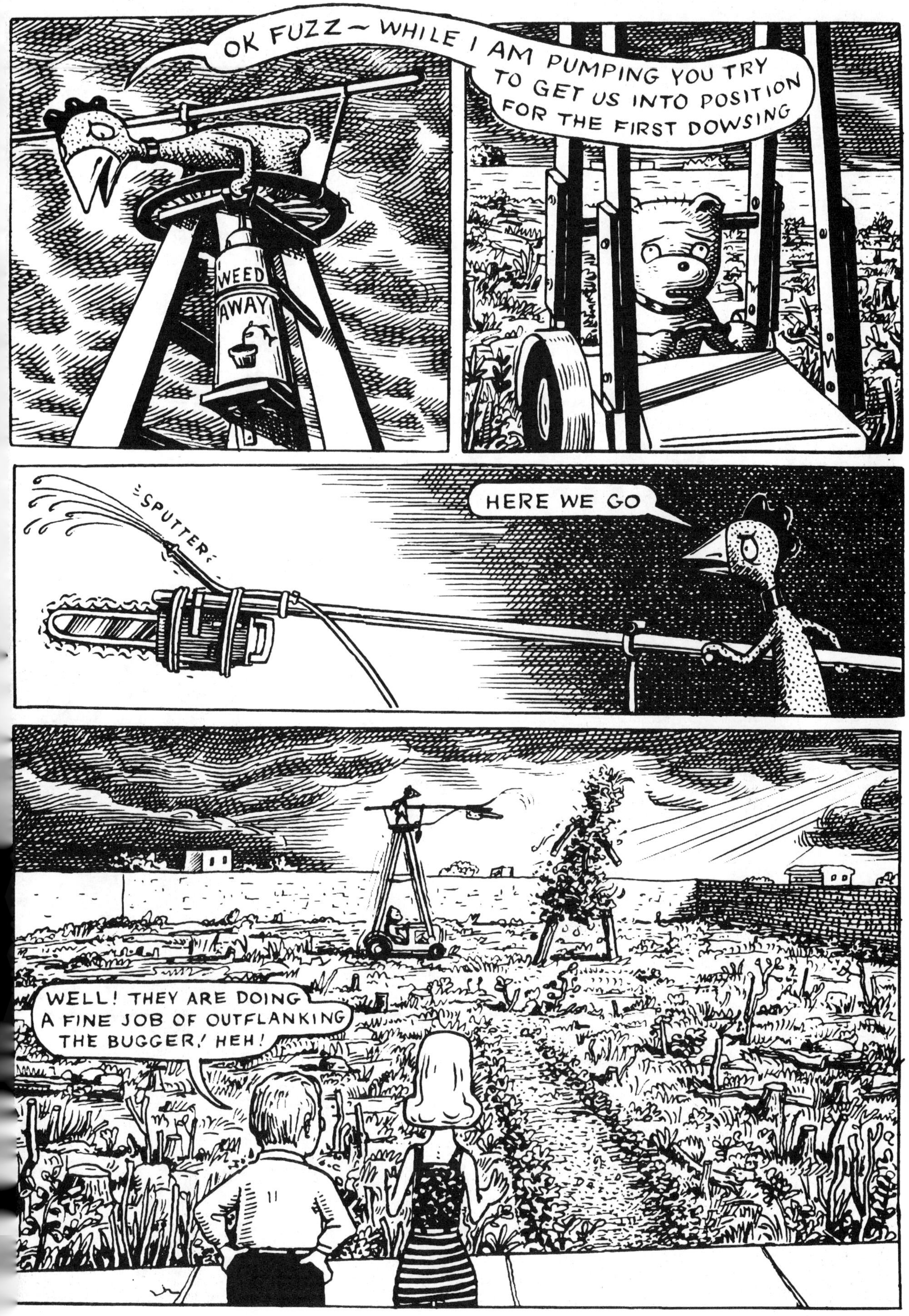
OK FUZZ ~ WHILE I AM PUMPING YOU TRY TO GET US INTO POSITION FOR THE FIRST DOWSING
WEED AWAY
SPUTTER
HERE WE GO
WELL! THEY ARE DOING A FINE JOB OF OUTFLANKING THE BUGGER! HEH!

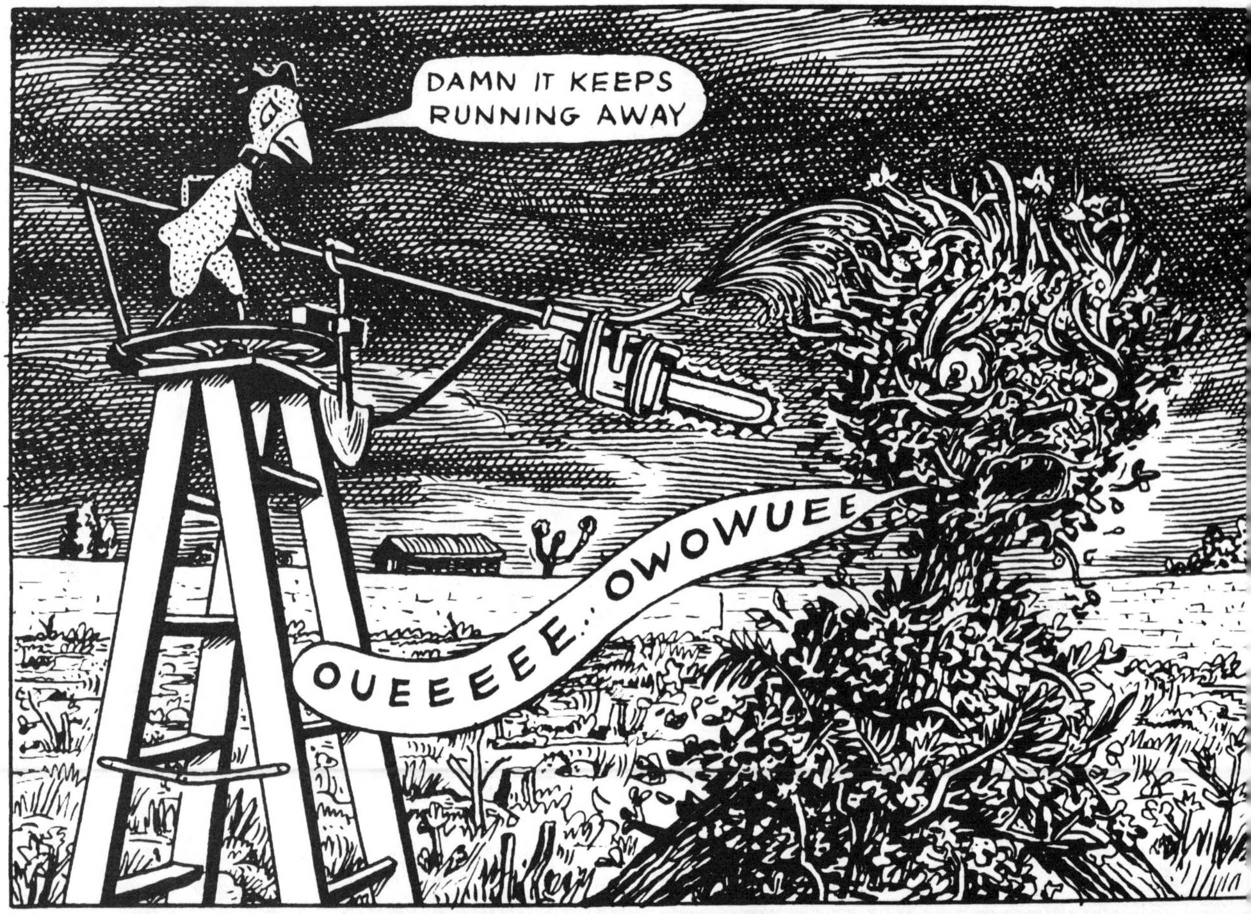
DAMN IT KEEPS RUNNING AWAY
OUEEEEE...OWOWUEE

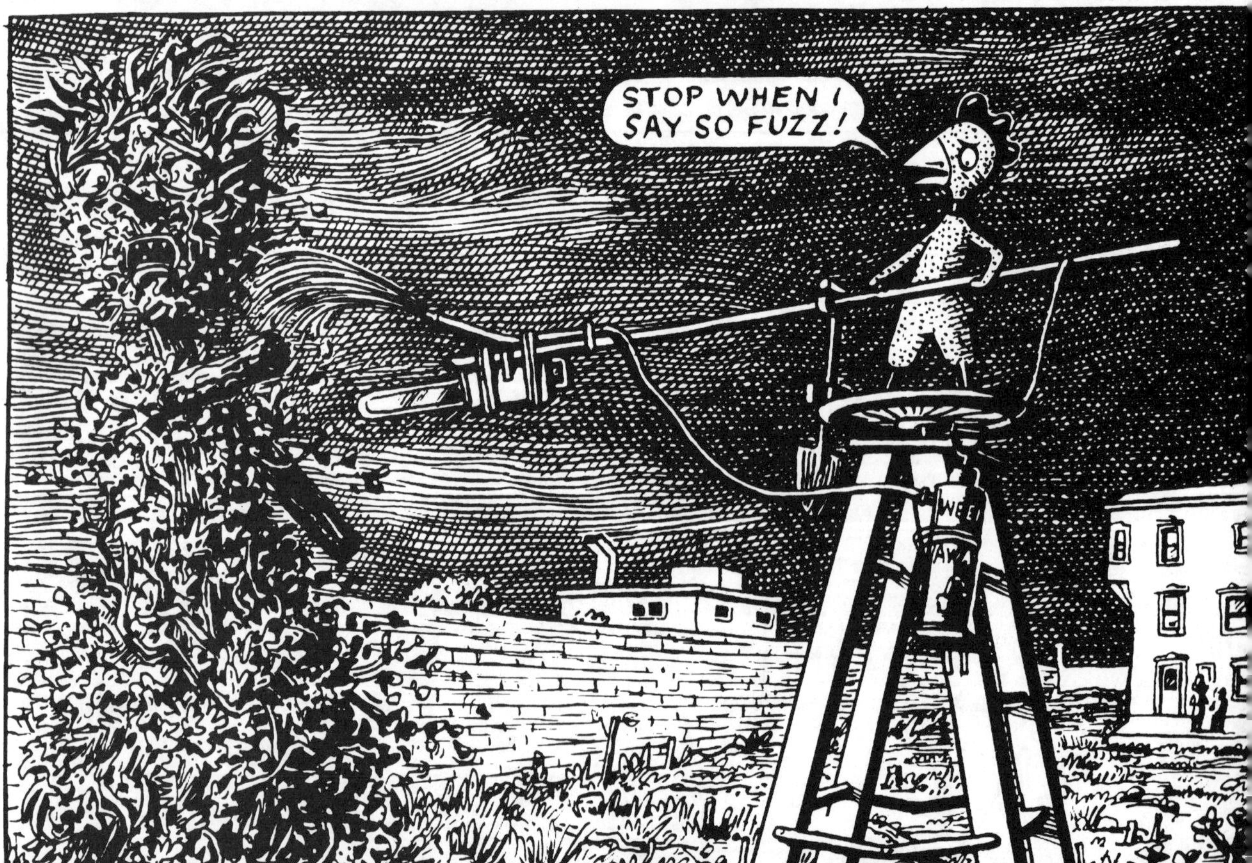
STOP WHEN I SAY SO FUZZ!

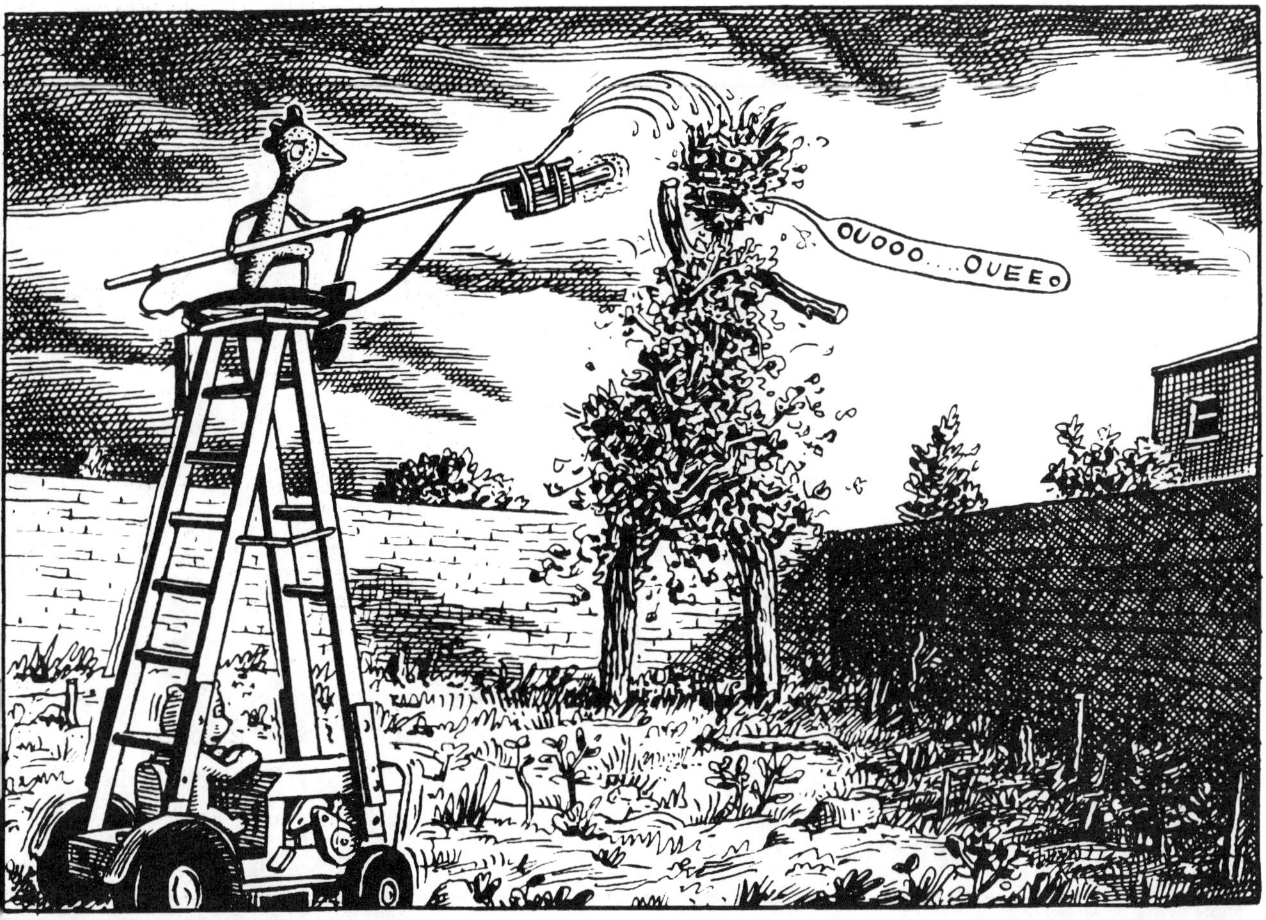
OUOOO....OUEEO

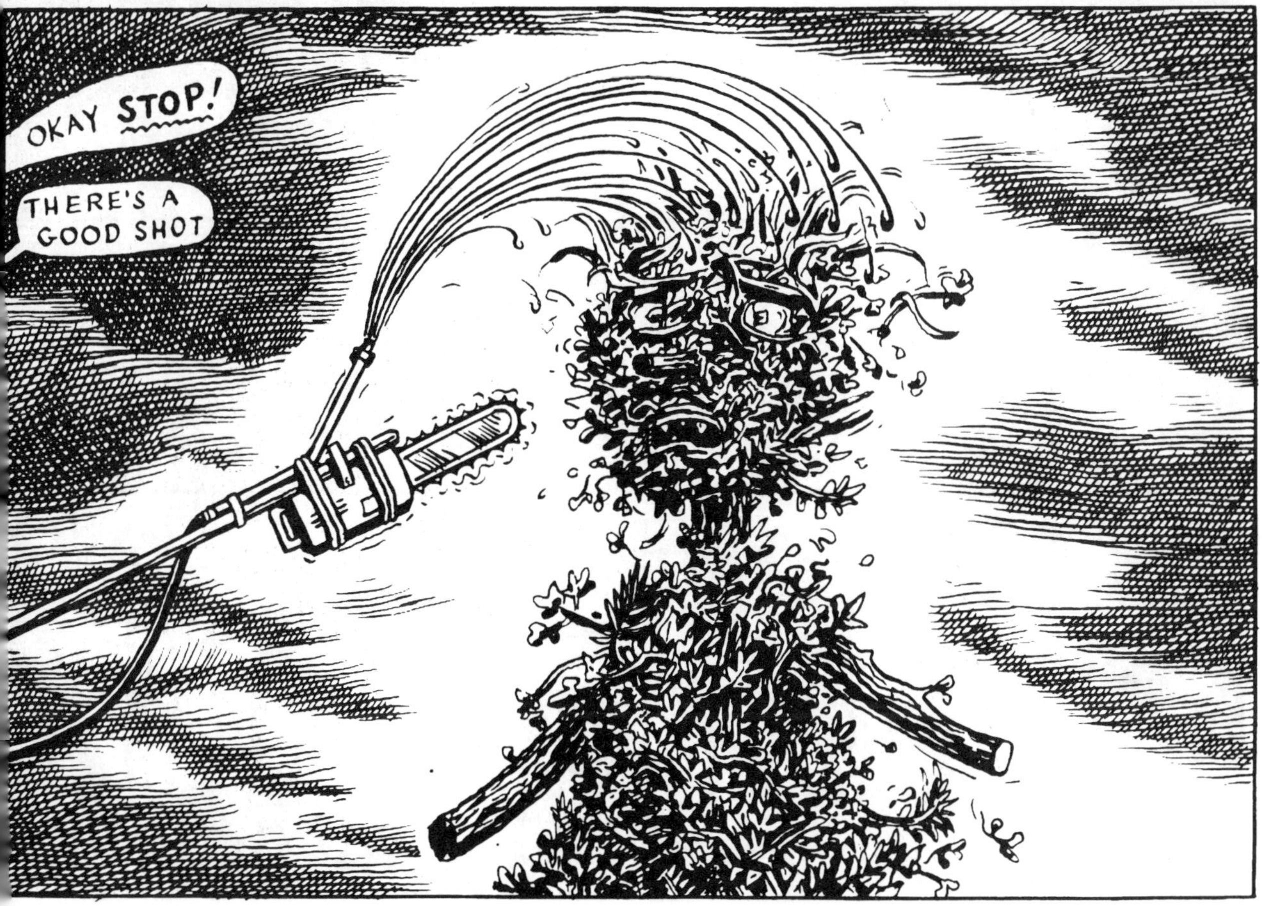
OKAY STOP!
THERE'S A GOOD SHOT

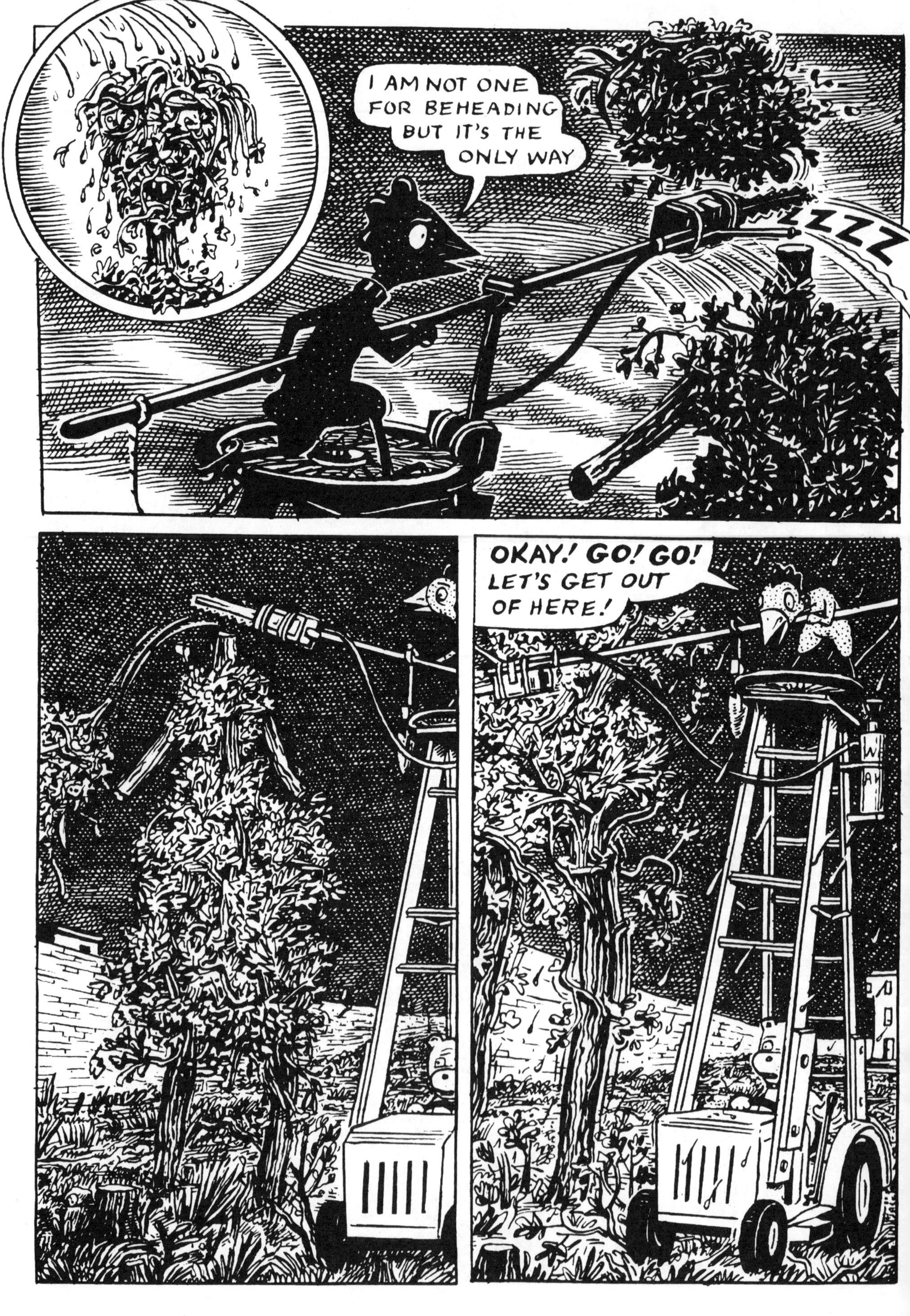
I AM NOT ONE FOR BEHEADING BUT IT'S THE ONLY WAY
ZZZZ
OKAY! GO! GO! LET'S GET OUT OF HERE!

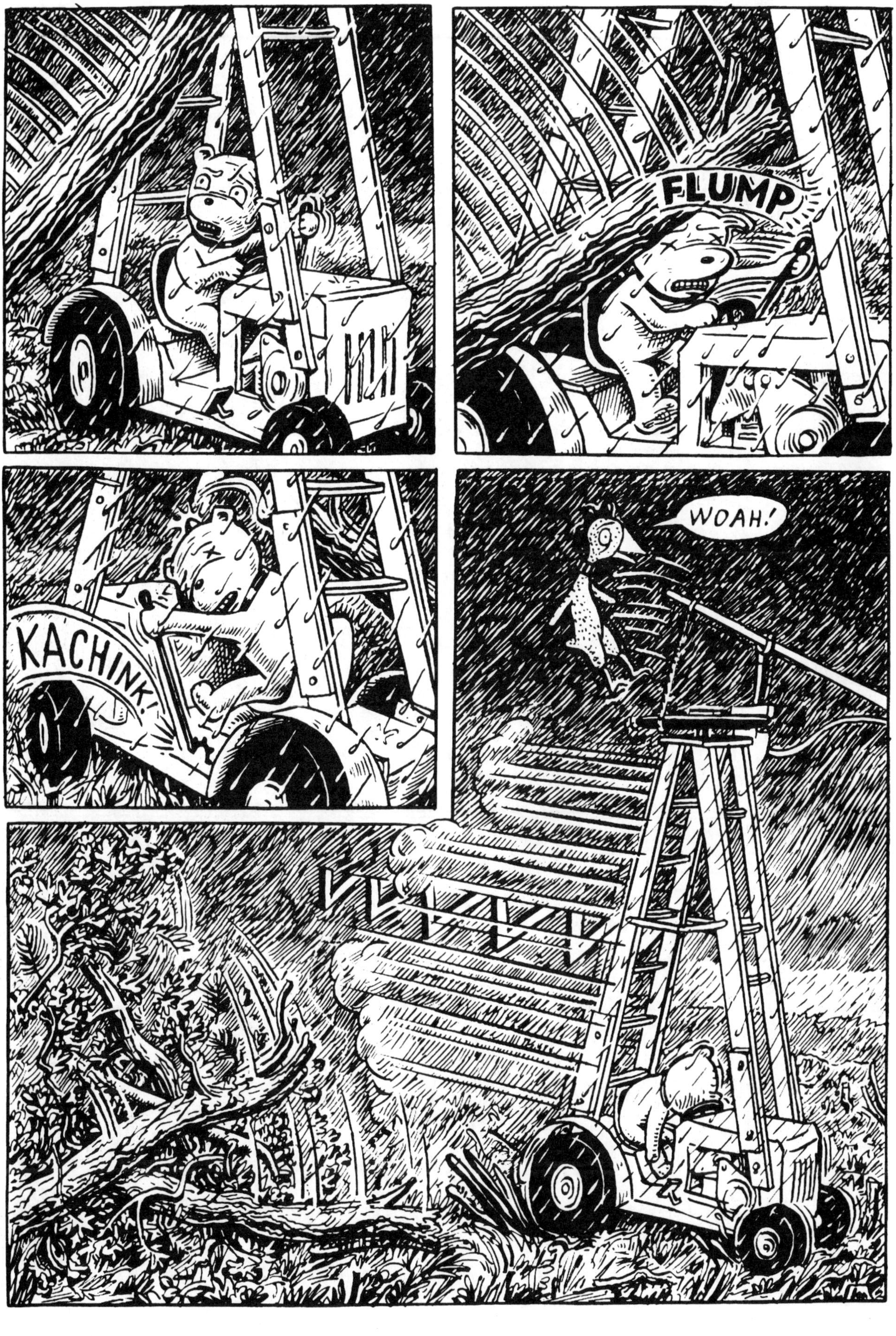
FLUMP
KACHINK!
WOAH!

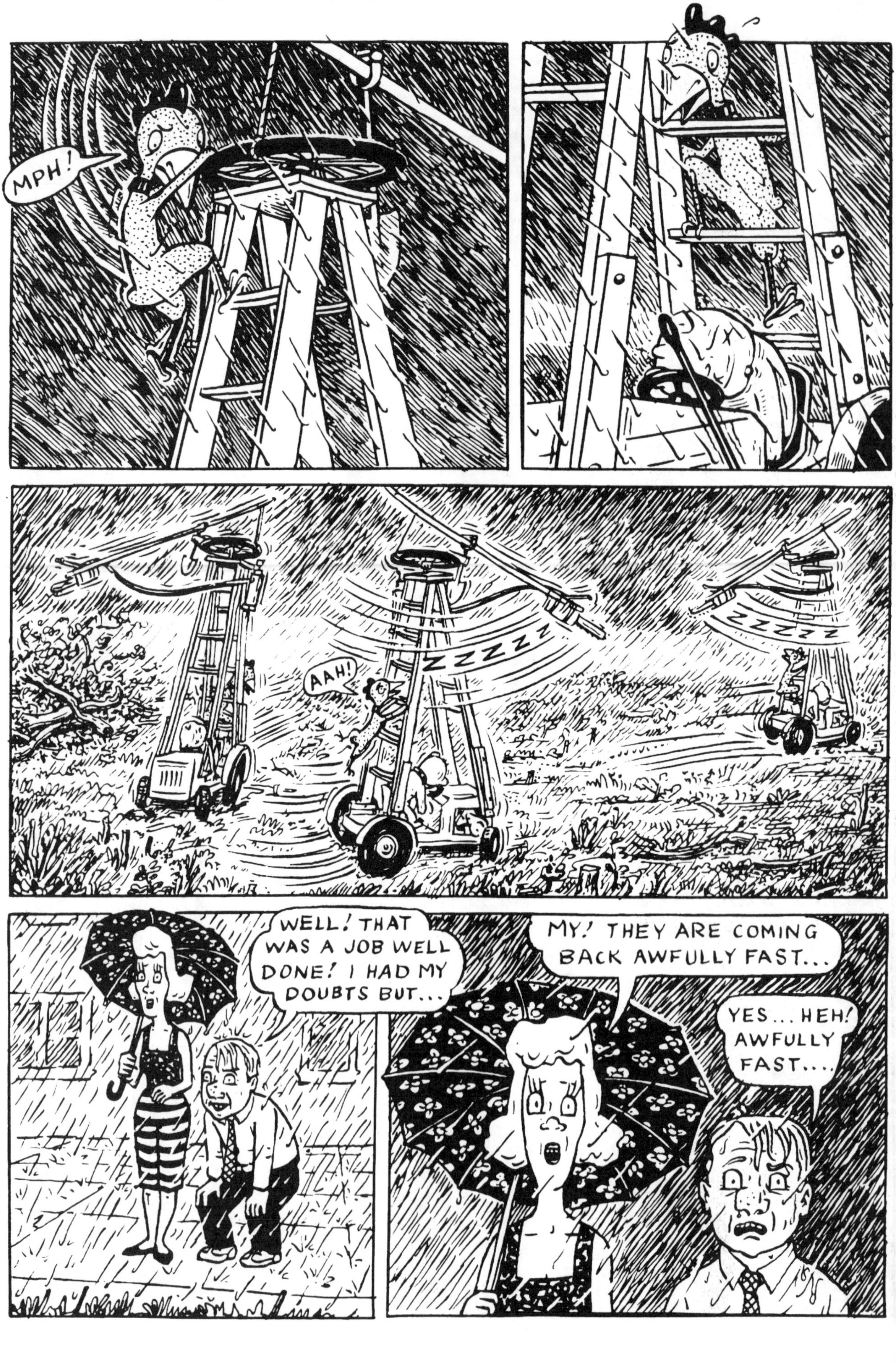
MPH!
AAH!
ZZZZZZ
ZZZZZZ
WELL! THAT WAS A JOB WELL DONE! I HAD MY DOUBTS BUT...
MY! THEY ARE COMING BACK AWFULLY FAST...
YES... HEH! AWFULLY FAST...

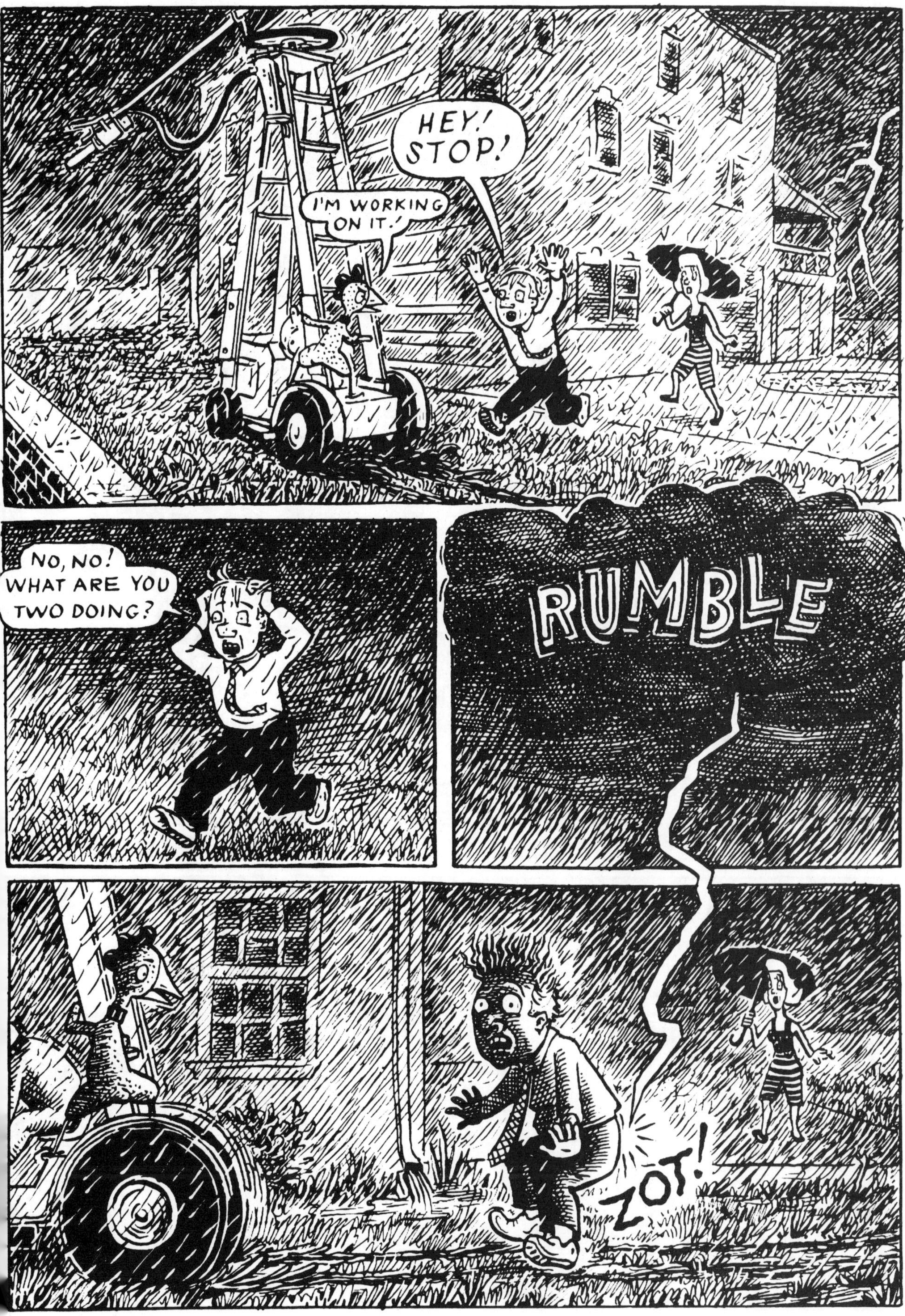
HEY! STOP!
I'M WORKING ON IT!
NO, NO! WHAT ARE YOU TWO DOING?
RUMBLE
ZOT!

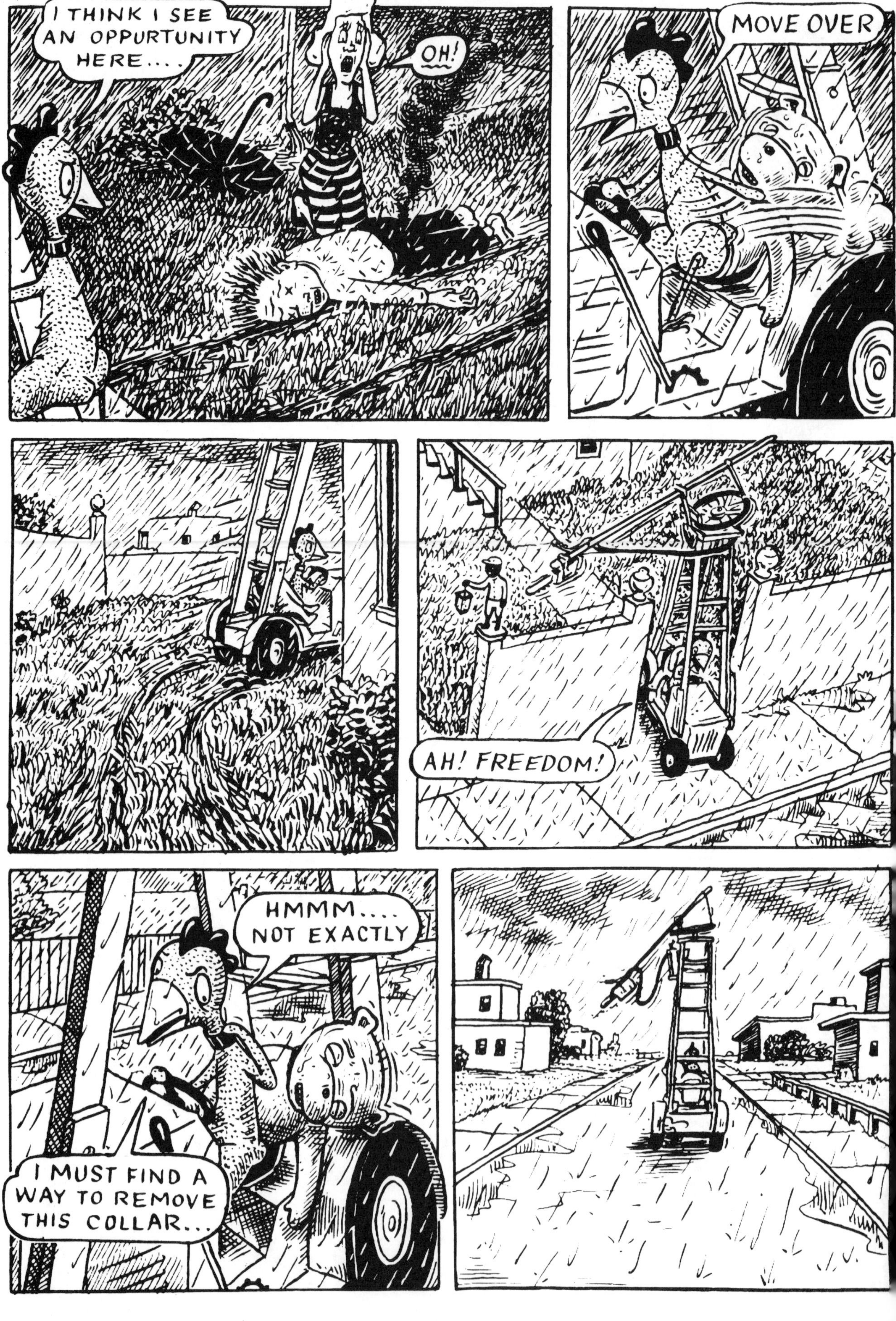
I THINK I SEE AN OPPURTUNITY HERE....
OH!
MOVE OVER
AH! FREEDOM!
HMMM.... NOT EXACTLY
I MUST FIND A WAY TO REMOVE THIS COLLAR...

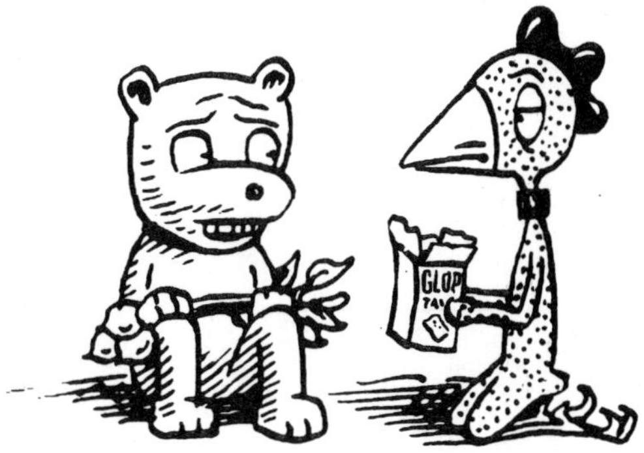
GLOP

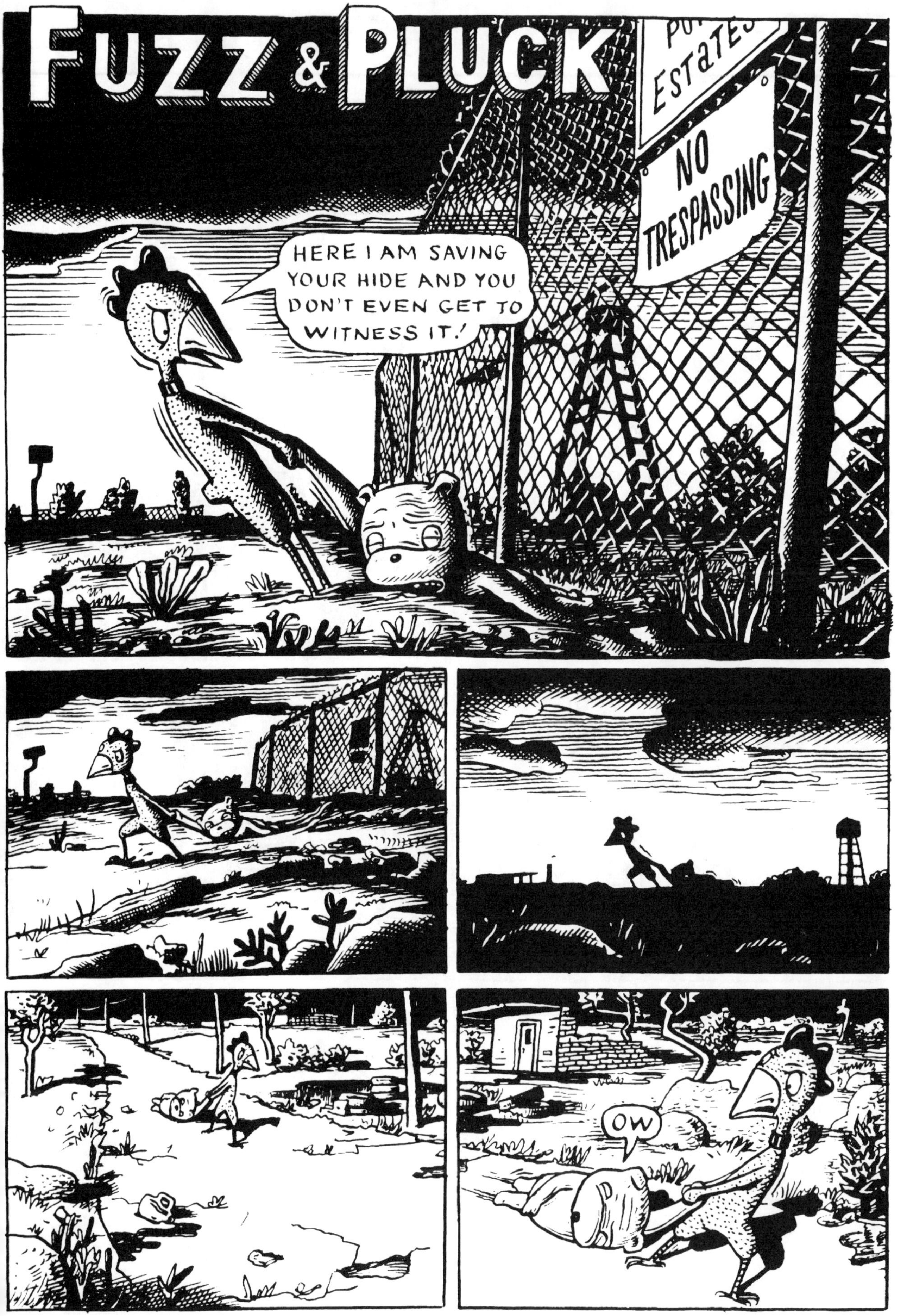
FUZZ & PLUCK
ESTATES
NO TRESPASSING
HERE I AM SAVING YOUR HIDE AND YOU DON'T EVEN GET TO WITNESS IT!
OW

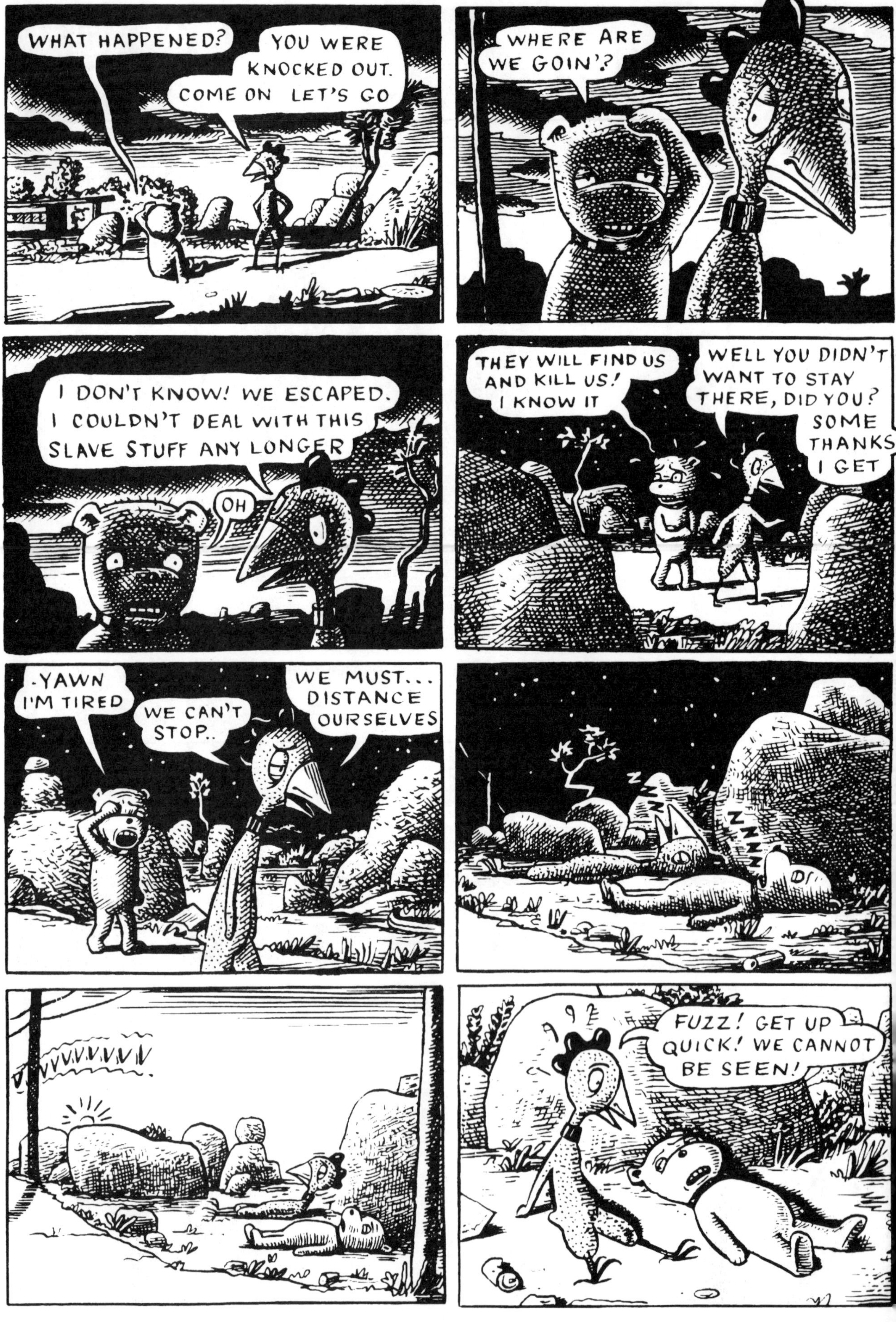
WHAT HAPPENED?
YOU WERE KNOCKED OUT. COME ON LET'S GO
WHERE ARE WE GOIN'?
I DON'T KNOW! WE ESCAPED. I COULDN'T DEAL WITH THIS SLAVE STUFF ANY LONGER
OH
THEY WILL FIND US AND KILL US! I KNOW IT
WELL YOU DIDN'T WANT TO STAY THERE, DID YOU? SOME THANKS I GET
-YAWN I'M TIRED
WE CAN'T STOP..
WE MUST... DISTANCE OURSELVES
VVVVVVVVV
FUZZ! GET UP QUICK! WE CANNOT BE SEEN!

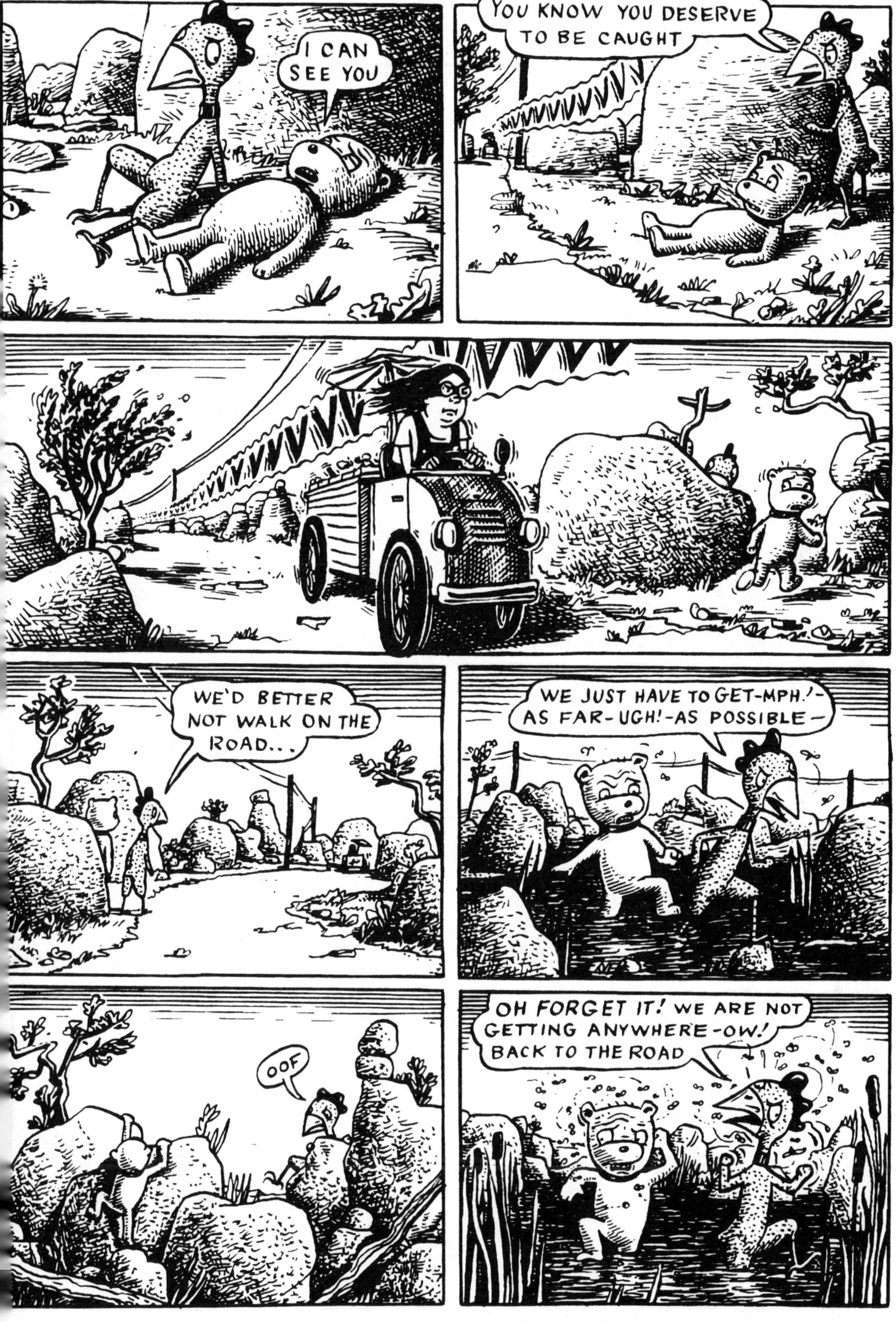
I CAN SEE YOU
YOU KNOW YOU DESERVE TO BE CAUGHT
WE'D BETTER NOT WALK ON THE ROAD...
WE JUST HAVE TO GET-MPH!- AS FAR-UGH!-AS POSSIBLE-
OOF
OH FORGET IT! WE ARE NOT GETTING ANYWHERE-OW! BACK TO THE ROAD

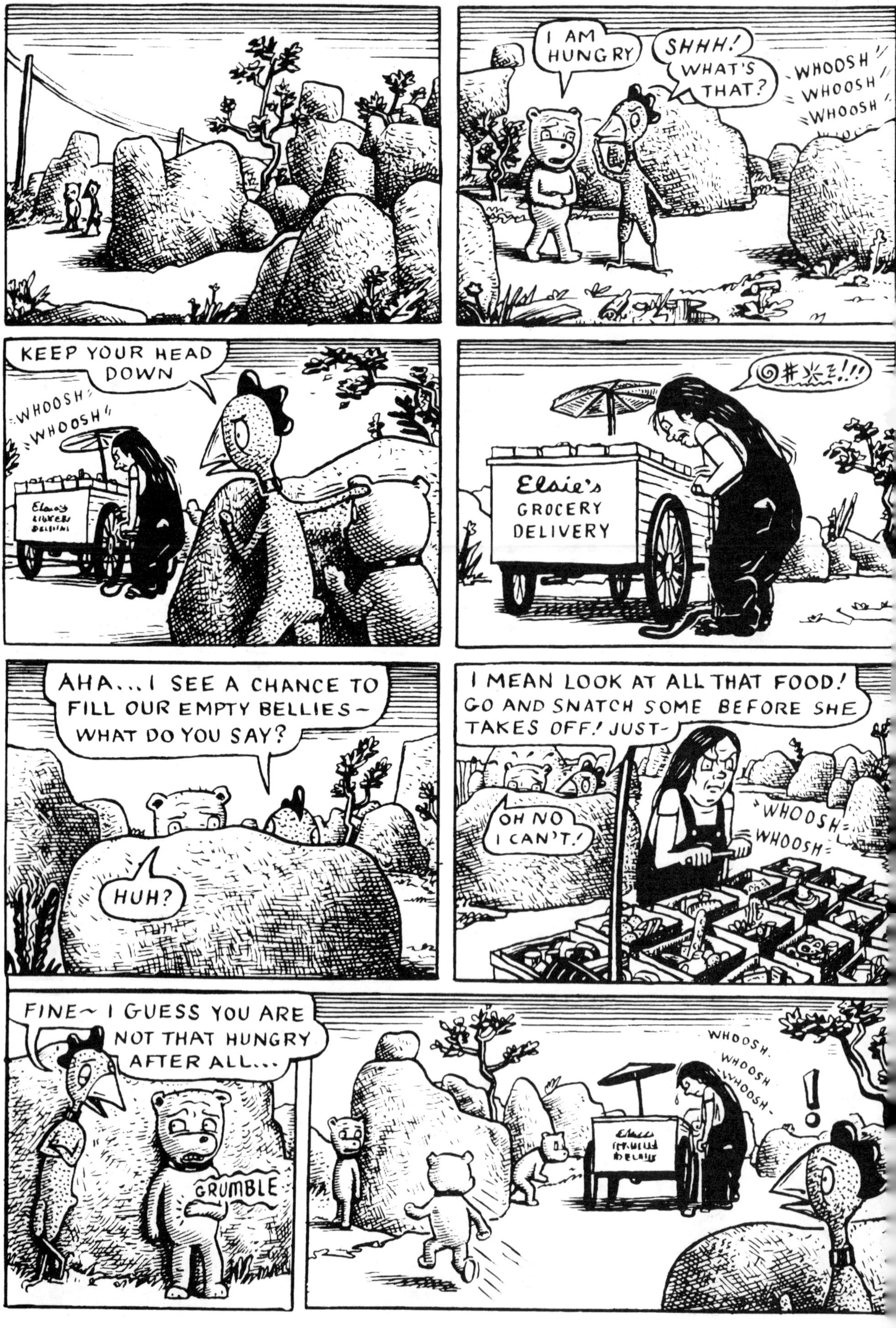
I AM HUNGRY
SHHH! WHAT'S THAT?
WHOOSH WHOOSH WHOOSH
KEEP YOUR HEAD DOWN
WHOOSH WHOOSH
Elsie's GROCERY DELIVERY
AHA... I SEE A CHANCE TO FILL OUR EMPTY BELLIES - WHAT DO YOU SAY?
HUH?
I MEAN LOOK AT ALL THAT FOOD! GO AND SNATCH SOME BEFORE SHE TAKES OFF! JUST-
OH NO I CAN'T!
WHOOSH WHOOSH
FINE~ I GUESS YOU ARE NOT THAT HUNGRY AFTER ALL...
GRUMBLE
WHOOSH WHOOSH WHOOSH
!

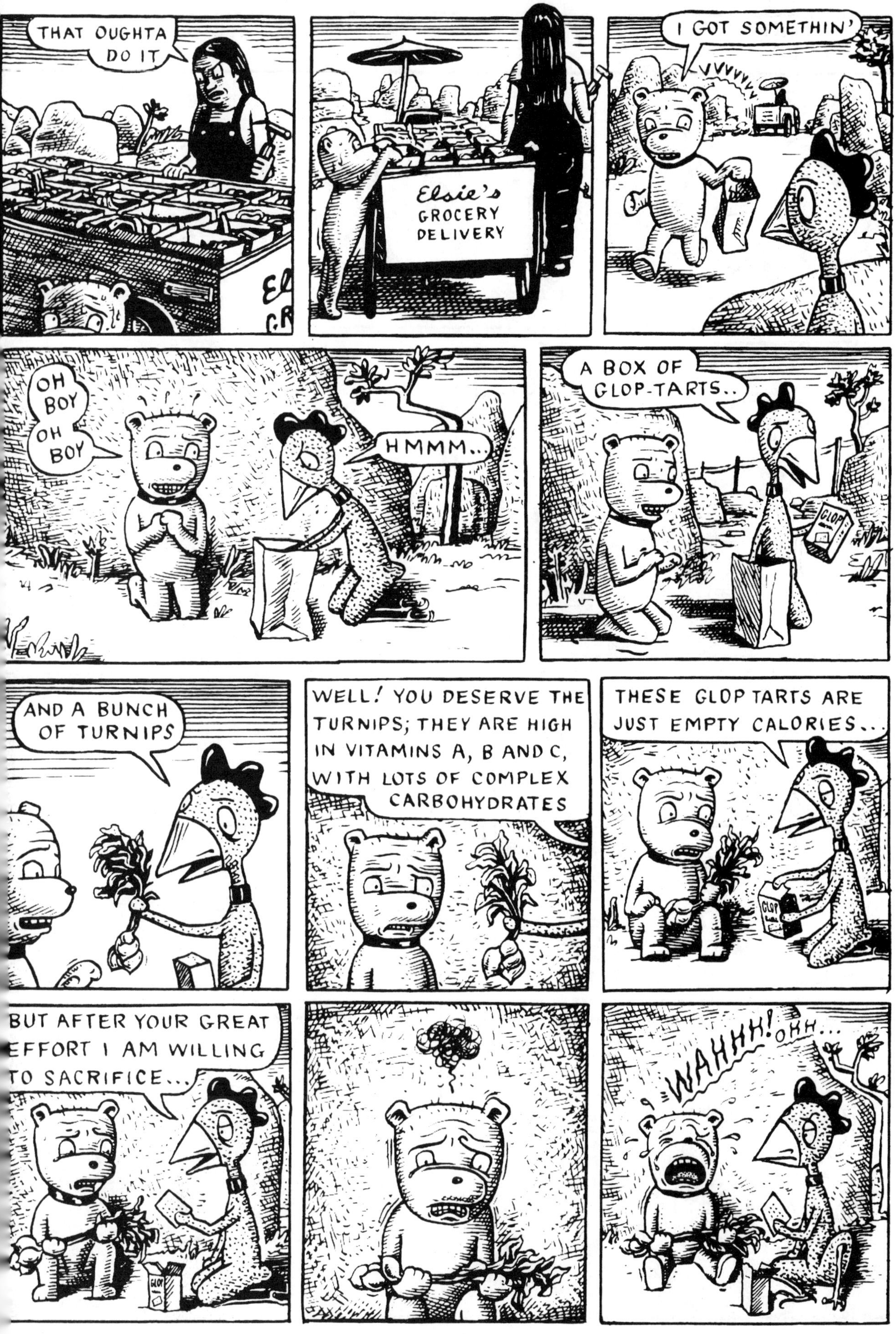
THAT OUGHTA DO IT
Elsie's GROCERY DELIVERY
I GOT SOMETHIN'
VVVVVVV
OH BOY OH BOY
HMMM..
A BOX OF GLOP-TARTS..
GLOP
AND A BUNCH OF TURNIPS
WELL! YOU DESERVE THE TURNIPS; THEY ARE HIGH IN VITAMINS A, B AND C, WITH LOTS OF COMPLEX CARBOHYDRATES
THESE GLOP TARTS ARE JUST EMPTY CALORIES..
GLOP
BUT AFTER YOUR GREAT EFFORT I AM WILLING TO SACRIFICE...
WAHHH! OHH...

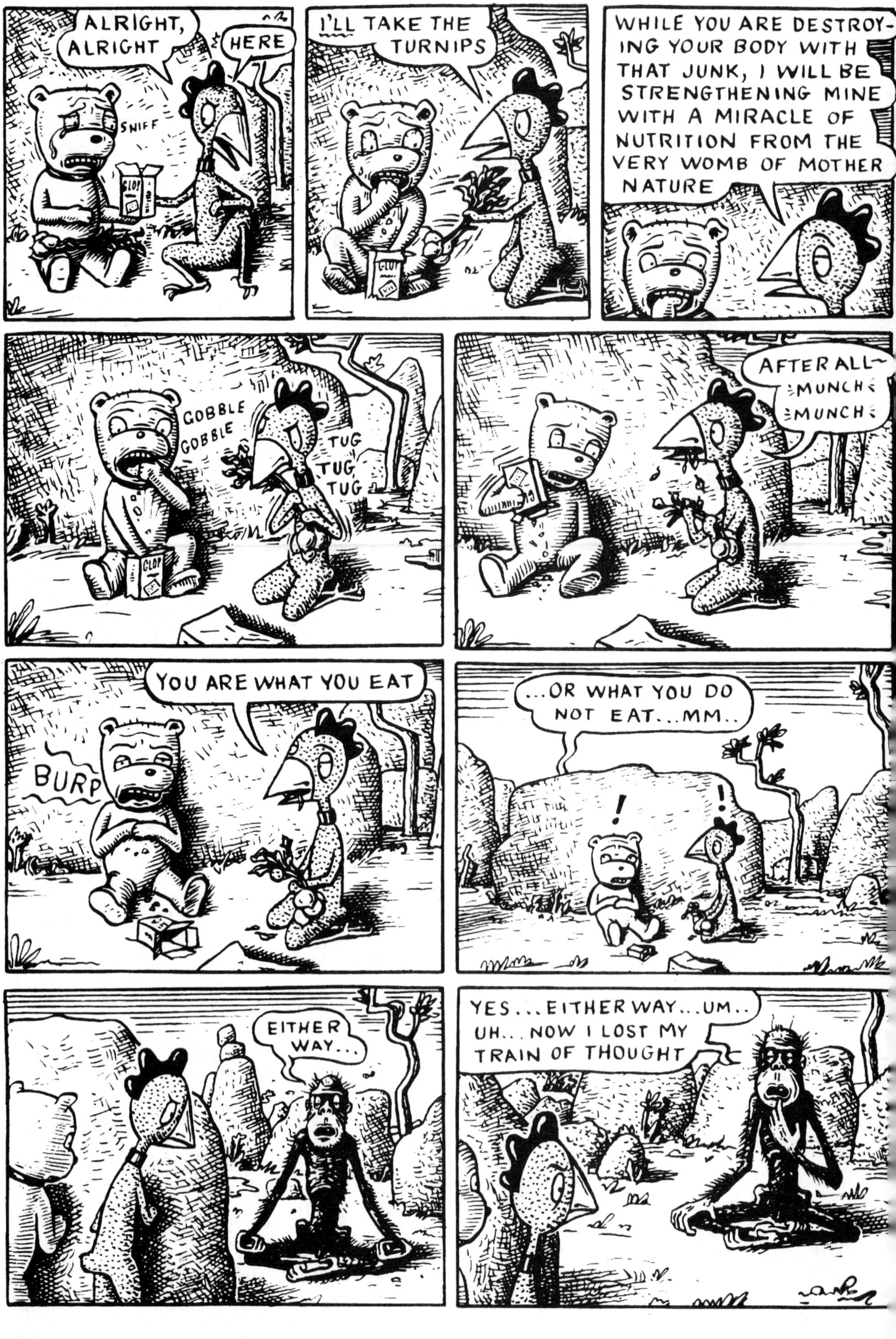
ALRIGHT, ALRIGHT
HERE
SNIFF
CLOP
I'LL TAKE THE TURNIPS
CLOP
WHILE YOU ARE DESTROYING YOUR BODY WITH THAT JUNK, I WILL BE STRENGTHENING MINE WITH A MIRACLE OF NUTRITION FROM THE VERY WOMB OF MOTHER NATURE
GOBBLE GOBBLE
TUG TUG TUG
CLOP
AFTER ALL
MUNCH MUNCH
YOU ARE WHAT YOU EAT
BURP
...OR WHAT YOU DO NOT EAT...MM..
!
!
EITHER WAY...
YES...EITHER WAY...UM.. UH...NOW I LOST MY TRAIN OF THOUGHT

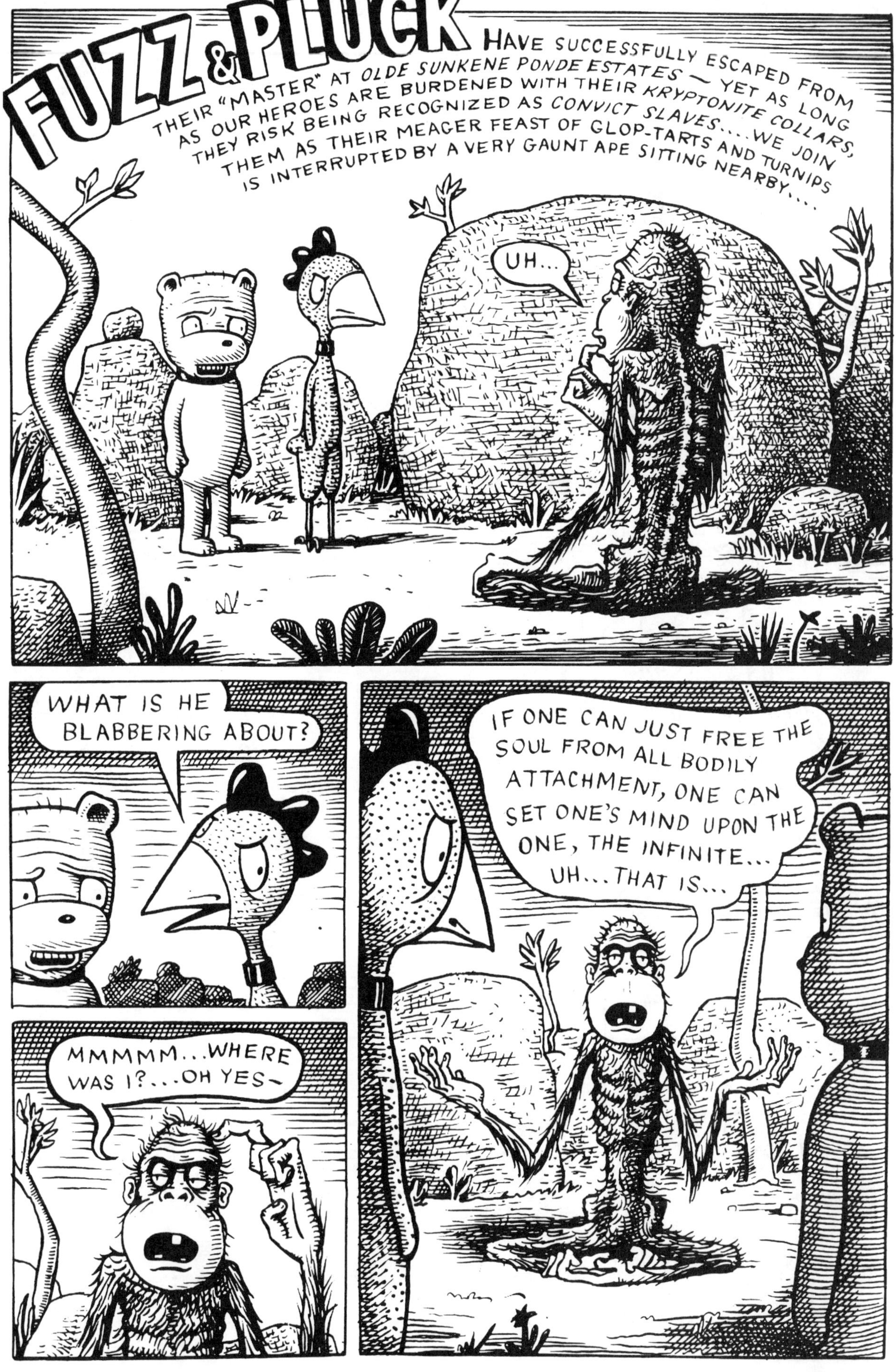
FUZZ & PLUCK
HAVE SUCCESSFULLY ESCAPED FROM THEIR "MASTER" AT OLDE SUNKENE PONDE ESTATES — YET AS LONG AS OUR HEROES ARE BURDENED WITH THEIR KRYPTONITE COLLARS, THEY RISK BEING RECOGNIZED AS CONVICT SLAVES.... WE JOIN THEM AS THEIR MEAGER FEAST OF GLOP-TARTS AND TURNIPS IS INTERRUPTED BY A VERY GAUNT APE SITTING NEARBY....
UH...
WHAT IS HE BLABBERING ABOUT?
MMMMM...WHERE WAS I?...OH YES-
IF ONE CAN JUST FREE THE SOUL FROM ALL BODILY ATTACHMENT, ONE CAN SET ONE'S MIND UPON THE ONE, THE INFINITE... UH...THAT IS...

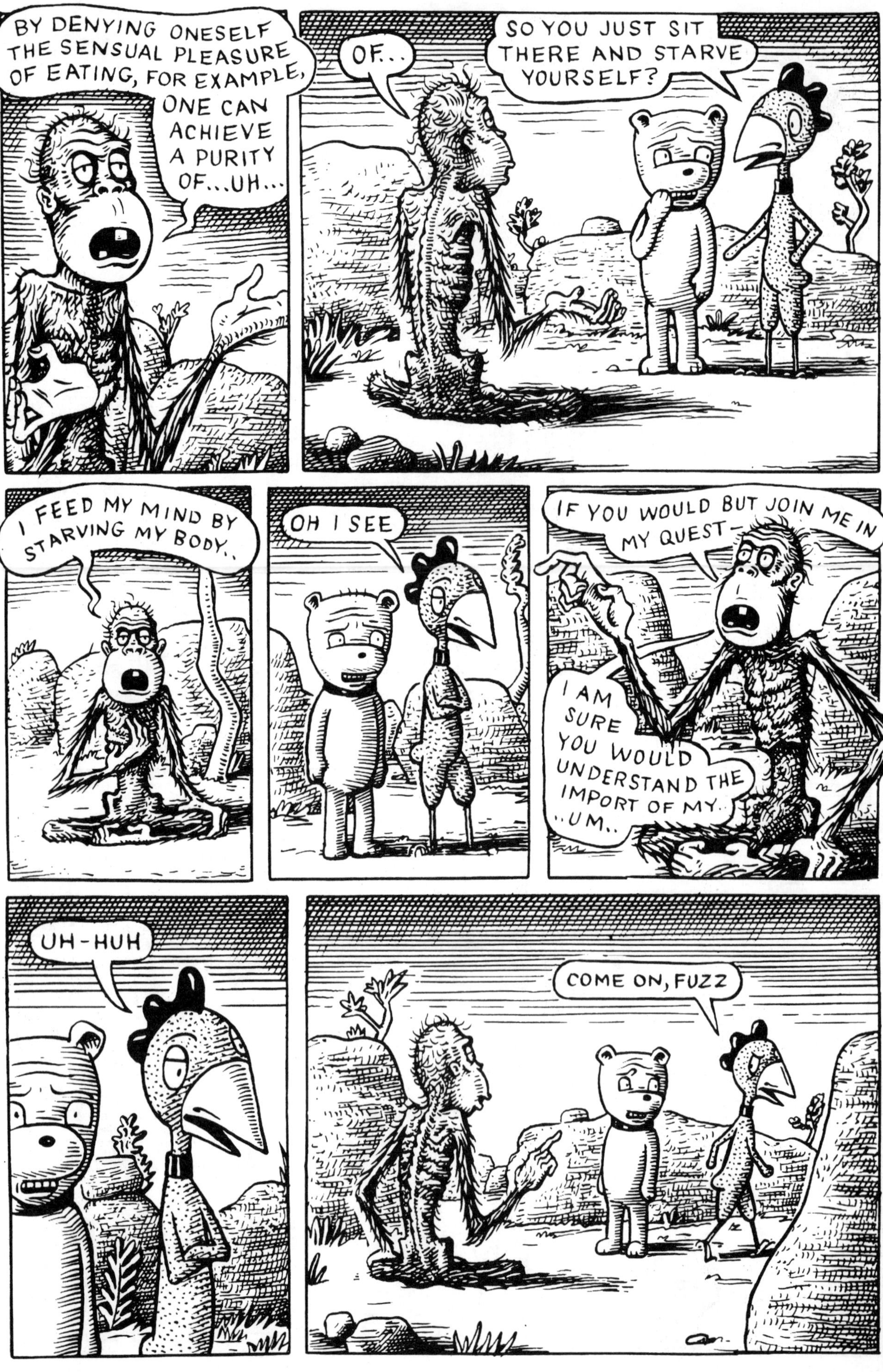
BY DENYING ONESELF THE SENSUAL PLEASURE OF EATING, FOR EXAMPLE,
ONE CAN ACHIEVE A PURITY OF...UH...
OF..
SO YOU JUST SIT THERE AND STARVE YOURSELF?
I FEED MY MIND BY STARVING MY BODY..
OH I SEE
IF YOU WOULD BUT JOIN ME IN MY QUEST—
I AM SURE YOU WOULD UNDERSTAND THE IMPORT OF MY.. ..UM..
UH-HUH
COME ON, FUZZ

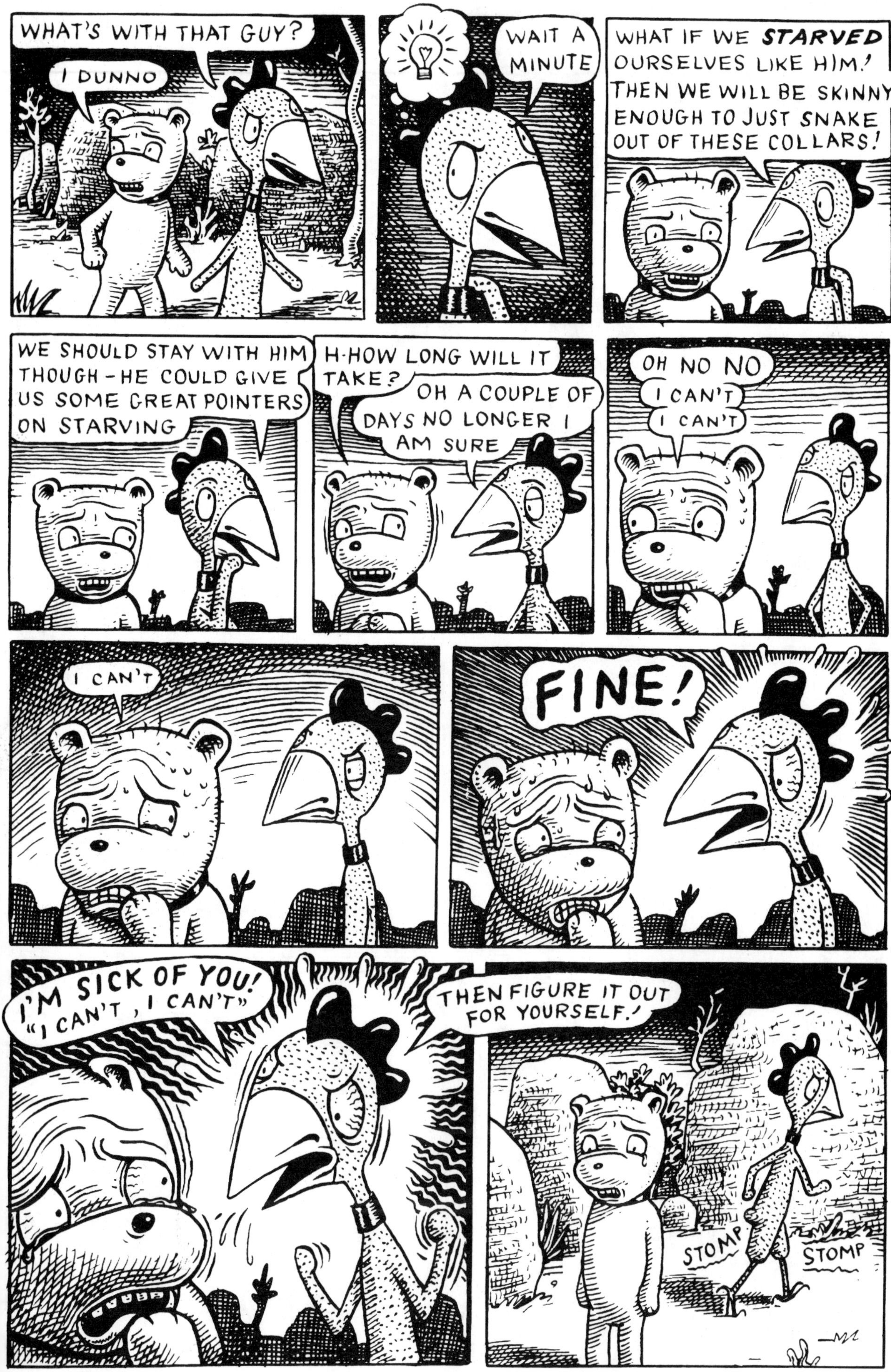
WHAT'S WITH THAT GUY?
I DUNNO
WAIT A MINUTE
WHAT IF WE **STARVED** OURSELVES LIKE HIM! THEN WE WILL BE SKINNY ENOUGH TO JUST SNAKE OUT OF THESE COLLARS!
WE SHOULD STAY WITH HIM THOUGH - HE COULD GIVE US SOME GREAT POINTERS ON STARVING
H-HOW LONG WILL IT TAKE?
OH A COUPLE OF DAYS NO LONGER I AM SURE
OH NO NO I CAN'T I CAN'T
I CAN'T
FINE!
I'M SICK OF YOU! "I CAN'T, I CAN'T"
THEN FIGURE IT OUT FOR YOURSELF!
STOMP
STOMP

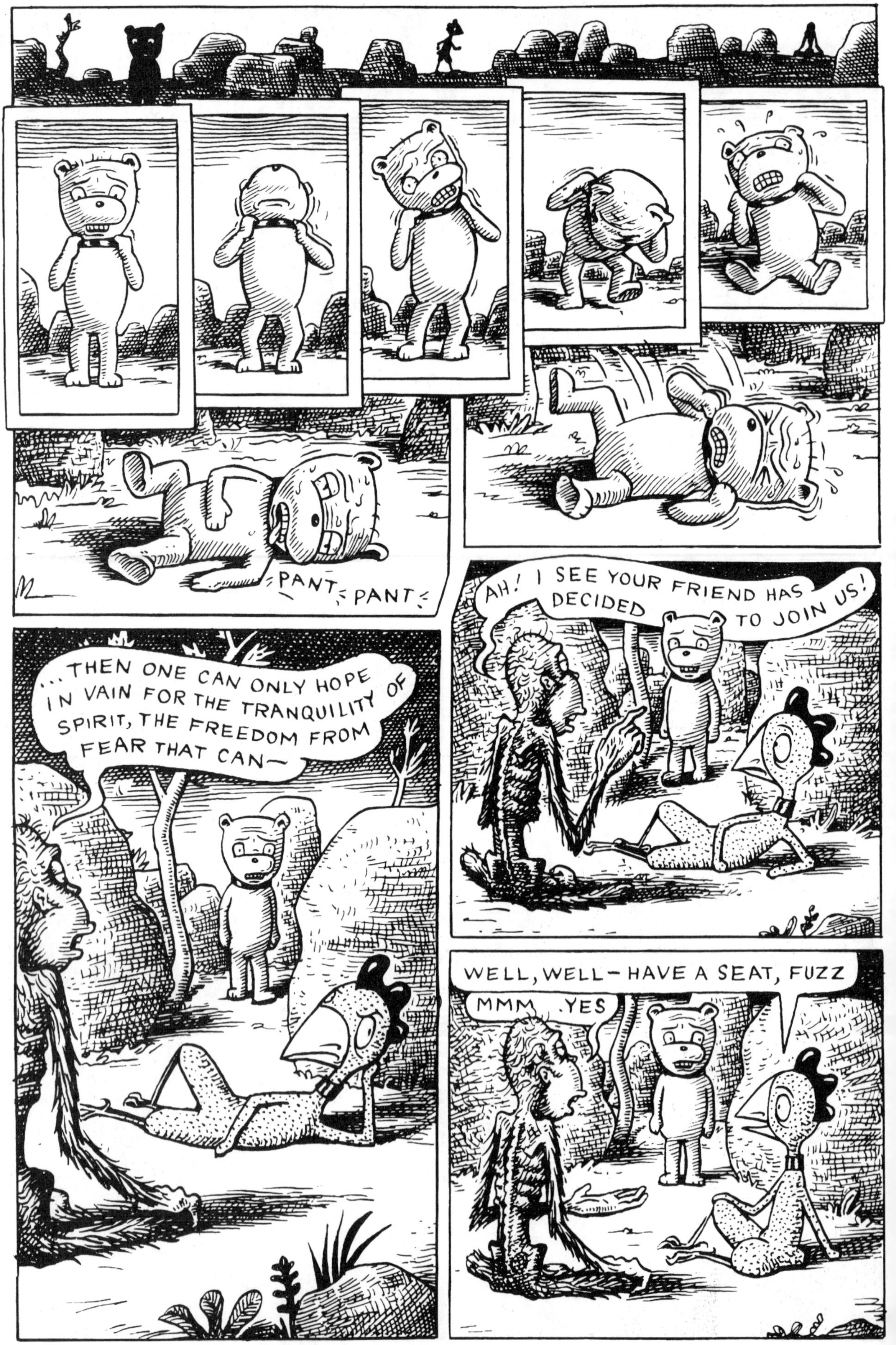
PANT PANT
AH! I SEE YOUR FRIEND HAS DECIDED TO JOIN US!
...THEN ONE CAN ONLY HOPE IN VAIN FOR THE TRANQUILITY OF SPIRIT, THE FREEDOM FROM FEAR THAT CAN—
WELL, WELL—HAVE A SEAT, FUZZ
MMM .YES

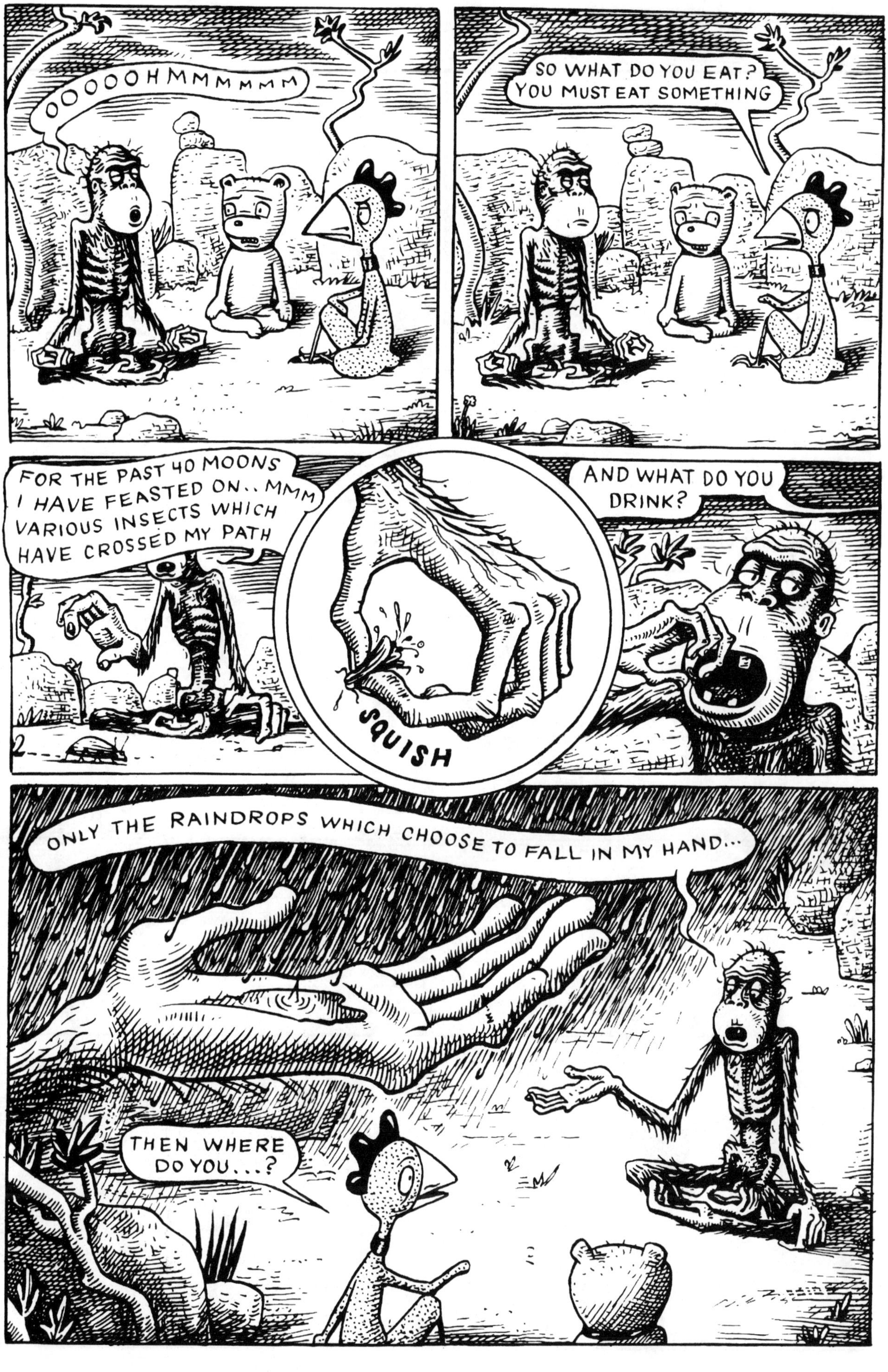
OOOOOHMMMMMMM
SO WHAT DO YOU EAT? YOU MUST EAT SOMETHING
FOR THE PAST 40 MOONS I HAVE FEASTED ON.. MMM VARIOUS INSECTS WHICH HAVE CROSSED MY PATH
SQUISH
AND WHAT DO YOU DRINK?
ONLY THE RAINDROPS WHICH CHOOSE TO FALL IN MY HAND...
THEN WHERE DO YOU...?

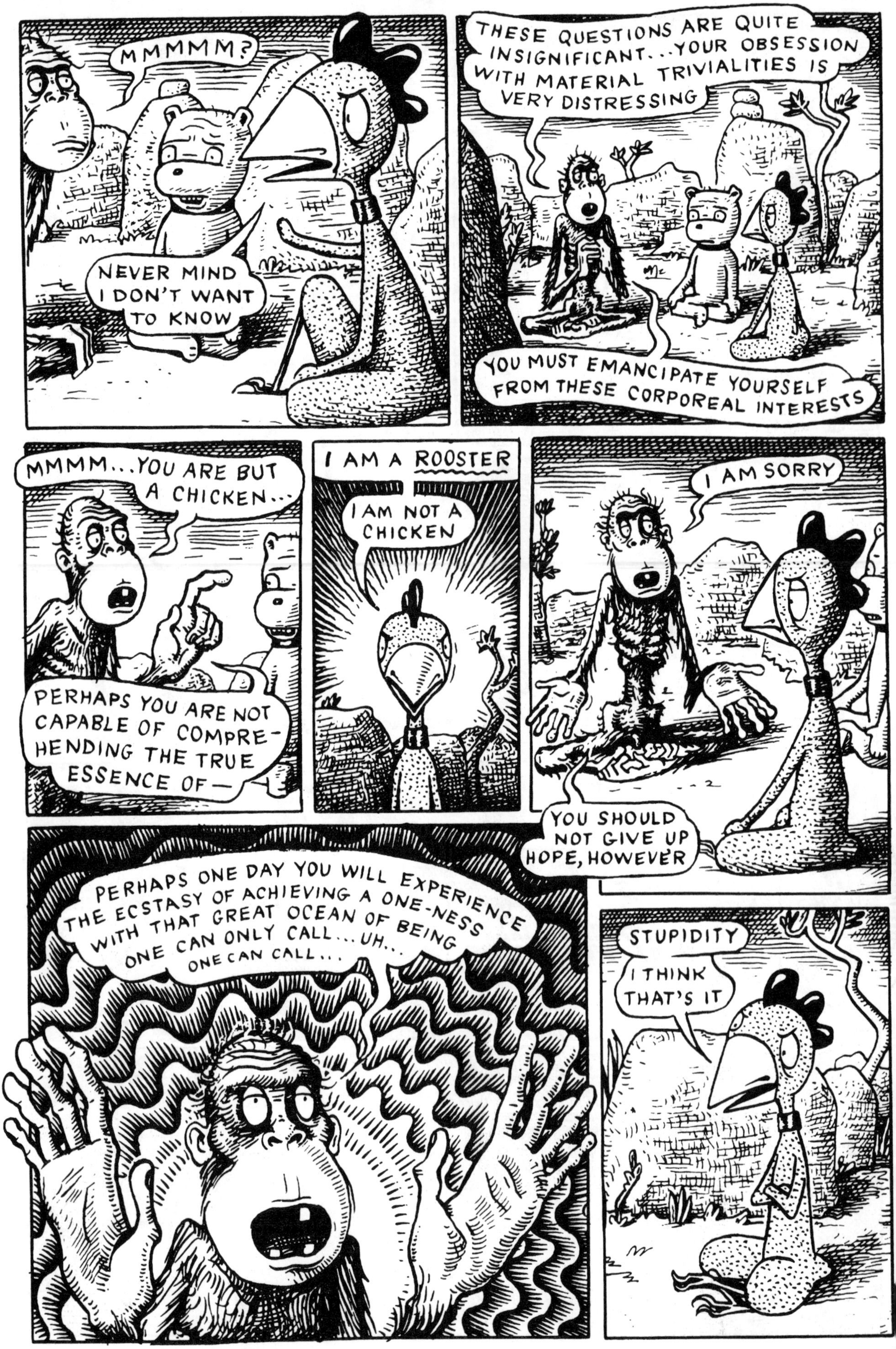
MMMMM?
NEVER MIND I DON'T WANT TO KNOW
THESE QUESTIONS ARE QUITE INSIGNIFICANT... YOUR OBSESSION WITH MATERIAL TRIVIALITIES IS VERY DISTRESSING
YOU MUST EMANCIPATE YOURSELF FROM THESE CORPOREAL INTERESTS
MMMM... YOU ARE BUT A CHICKEN...
PERHAPS YOU ARE NOT CAPABLE OF COMPRE-HENDING THE TRUE ESSENCE OF—
I AM A ROOSTER
I AM NOT A CHICKEN
I AM SORRY
YOU SHOULD NOT GIVE UP HOPE, HOWEVER
PERHAPS ONE DAY YOU WILL EXPERIENCE THE ECSTASY OF ACHIEVING A ONE-NESS WITH THAT GREAT OCEAN OF BEING ONE CAN ONLY CALL... UH... ONE CAN CALL...
STUPIDITY
I THINK THAT'S IT

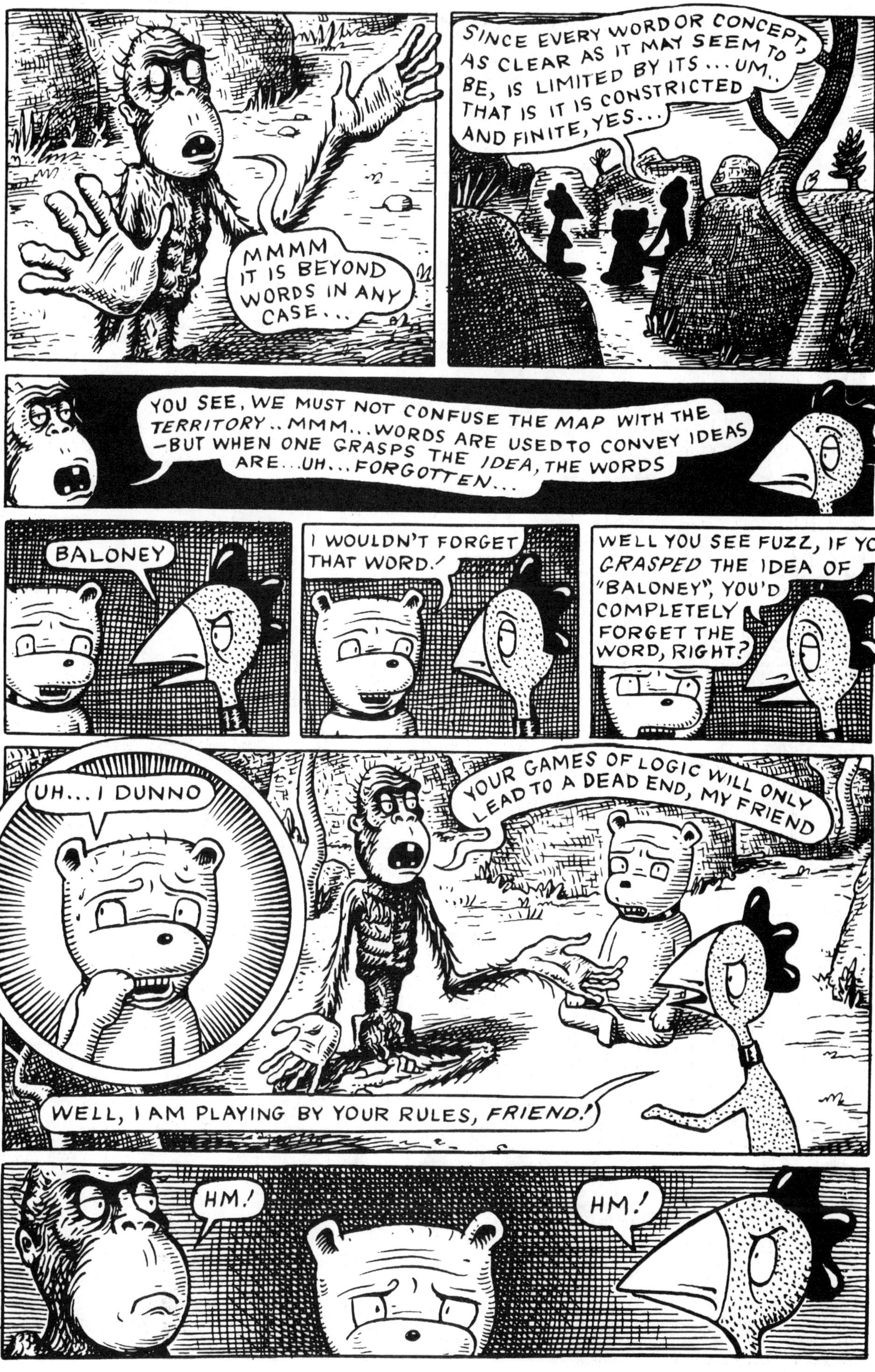
MMMM IT IS BEYOND WORDS IN ANY CASE...
SINCE EVERY WORD OR CONCEPT, AS CLEAR AS IT MAY SEEM TO BE, IS LIMITED BY ITS... UM.. THAT IS IT IS CONSTRICTED AND FINITE, YES...
YOU SEE, WE MUST NOT CONFUSE THE *MAP* WITH THE *TERRITORY*.. MMM... WORDS ARE USED TO CONVEY IDEAS —BUT WHEN ONE GRASPS THE *IDEA*, THE WORDS ARE...UH... *FORGOTTEN*...
BALONEY
I WOULDN'T FORGET THAT WORD!
WELL YOU SEE FUZZ, IF YOU *GRASPED* THE IDEA OF "BALONEY", YOU'D COMPLETELY FORGET THE WORD, RIGHT?
UH... I DUNNO
YOUR GAMES OF LOGIC WILL ONLY LEAD TO A DEAD END, MY FRIEND
WELL, I AM PLAYING BY YOUR RULES, *FRIEND!*
HM!
HM!

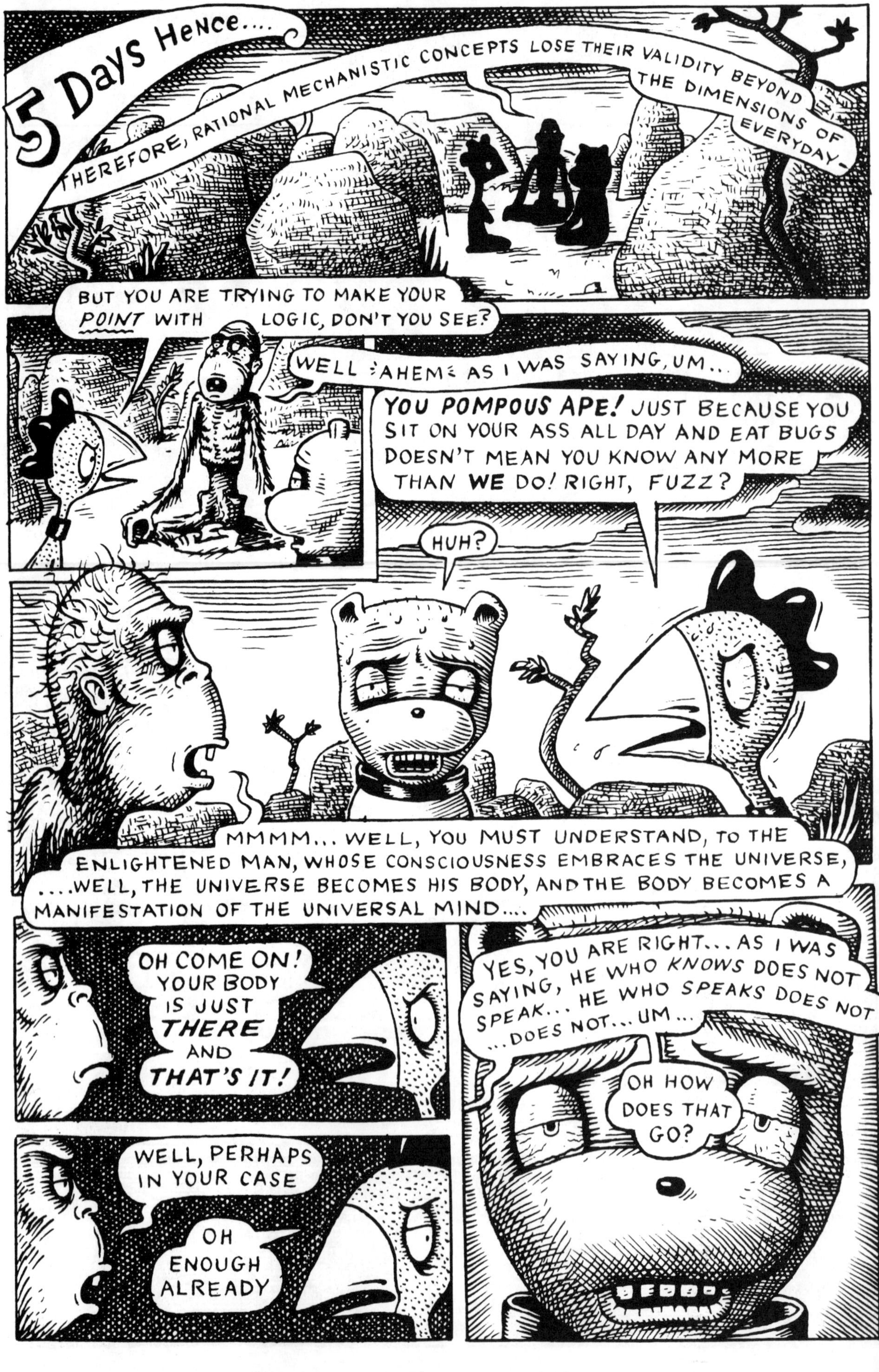
5 Days Hence....
THEREFORE, RATIONAL MECHANISTIC CONCEPTS LOSE THEIR VALIDITY BEYOND THE DIMENSIONS OF EVERYDAY-
BUT YOU ARE TRYING TO MAKE YOUR POINT WITH LOGIC, DON'T YOU SEE?
WELL :AHEM: AS I WAS SAYING, UM...
YOU POMPOUS APE! JUST BECAUSE YOU SIT ON YOUR ASS ALL DAY AND EAT BUGS DOESN'T MEAN YOU KNOW ANY MORE THAN WE DO! RIGHT, FUZZ?
HUH?
MMMM... WELL, YOU MUST UNDERSTAND, TO THE ENLIGHTENED MAN, WHOSE CONSCIOUSNESS EMBRACES THE UNIVERSE, ...WELL, THE UNIVERSE BECOMES HIS BODY, AND THE BODY BECOMES A MANIFESTATION OF THE UNIVERSAL MIND....
OH COME ON! YOUR BODY IS JUST THERE AND THAT'S IT!
WELL, PERHAPS IN YOUR CASE
OH ENOUGH ALREADY
YES, YOU ARE RIGHT... AS I WAS SAYING, HE WHO KNOWS DOES NOT SPEAK... HE WHO SPEAKS DOES NOT ...DOES NOT... UM...
OH HOW DOES THAT GO?

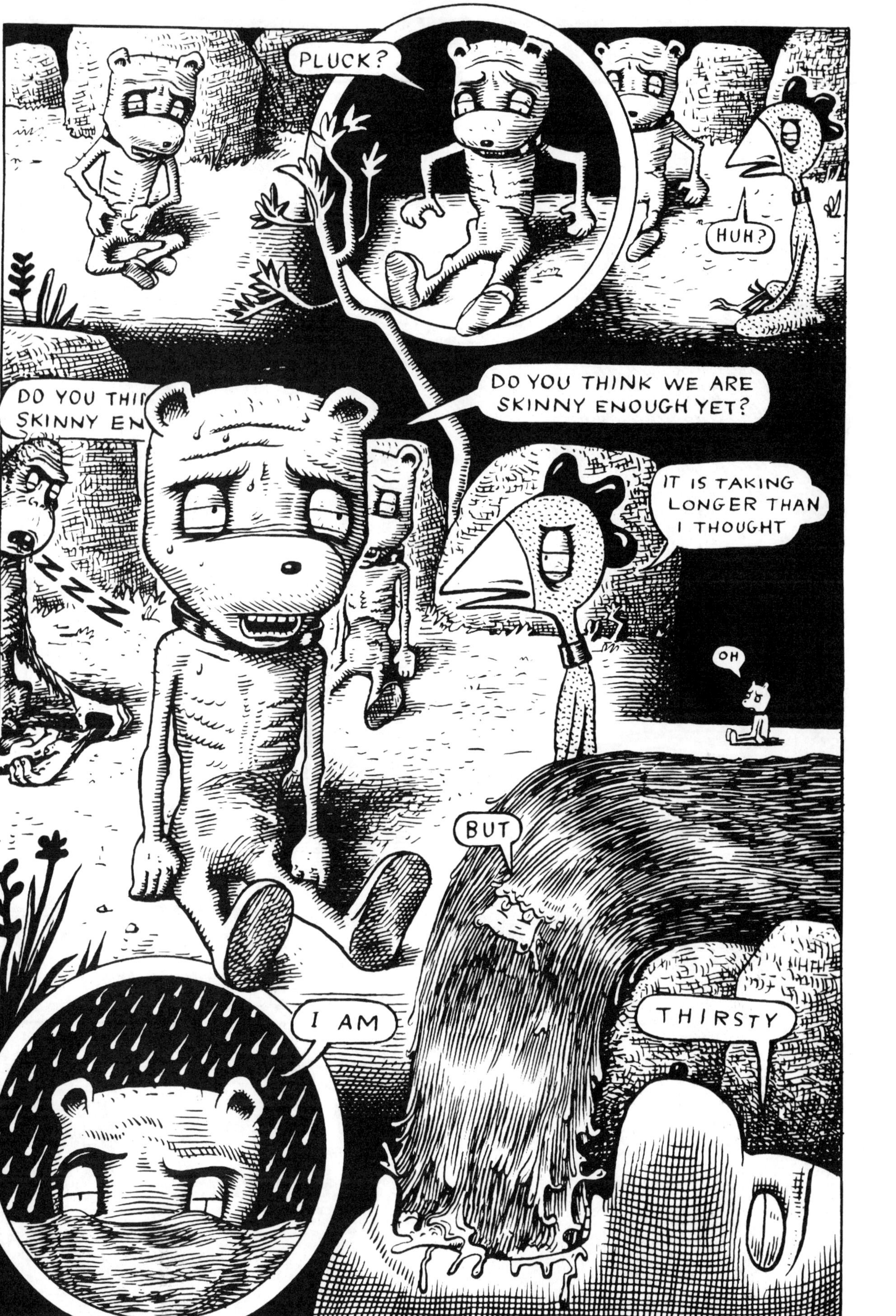

PLUCK?
HUH?
DO YOU THI
SKINNY EN
DO YOU THINK WE ARE SKINNY ENOUGH YET?
ZZZ
IT IS TAKING LONGER THAN I THOUGHT
OH
BUT
I AM
THIRSTY

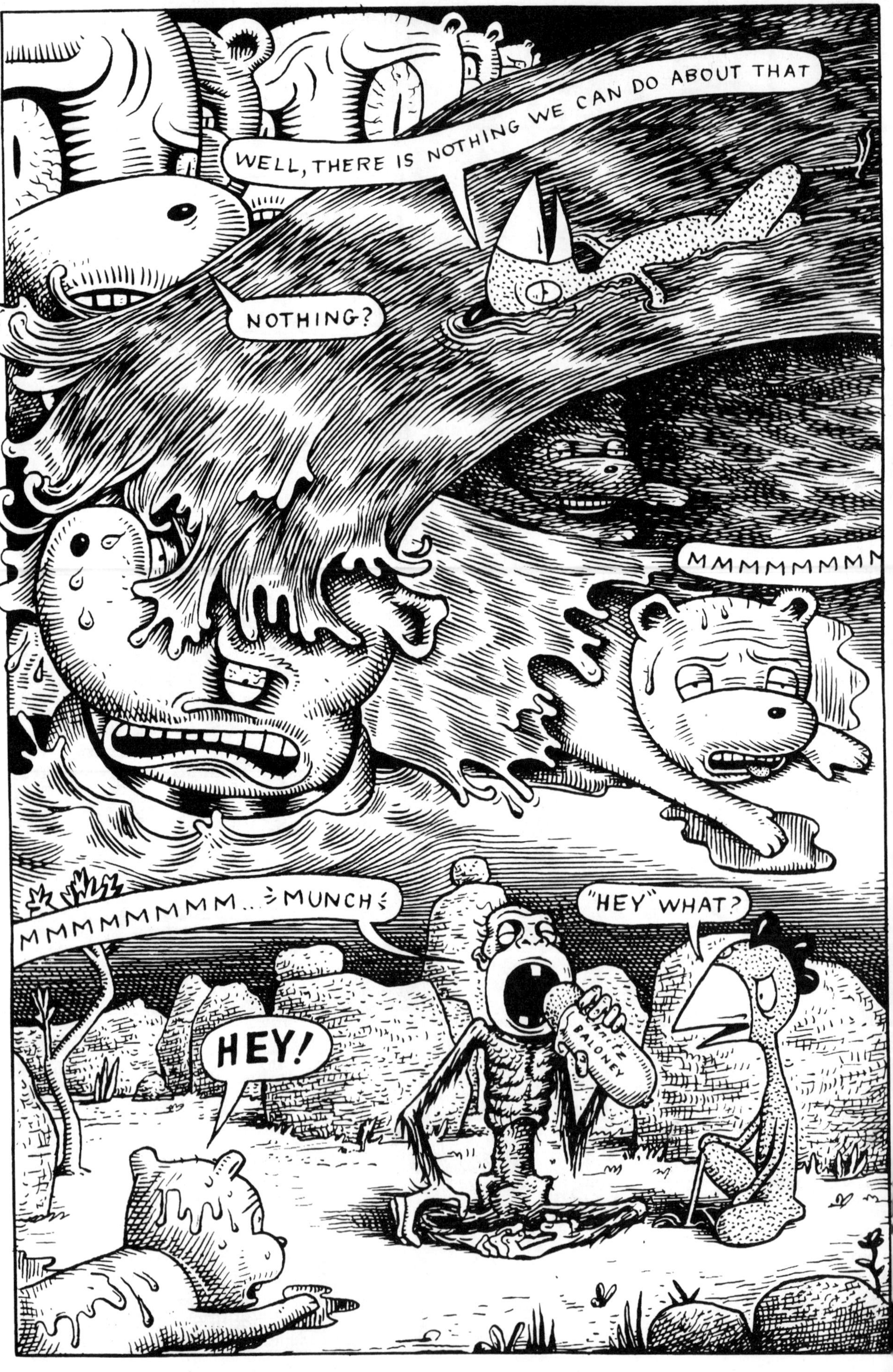
WELL, THERE IS NOTHING WE CAN DO ABOUT THAT
NOTHING?
MMMMMMMM
MMMMMMMM... MUNCH
"HEY" WHAT?
HEY!
BALONEY

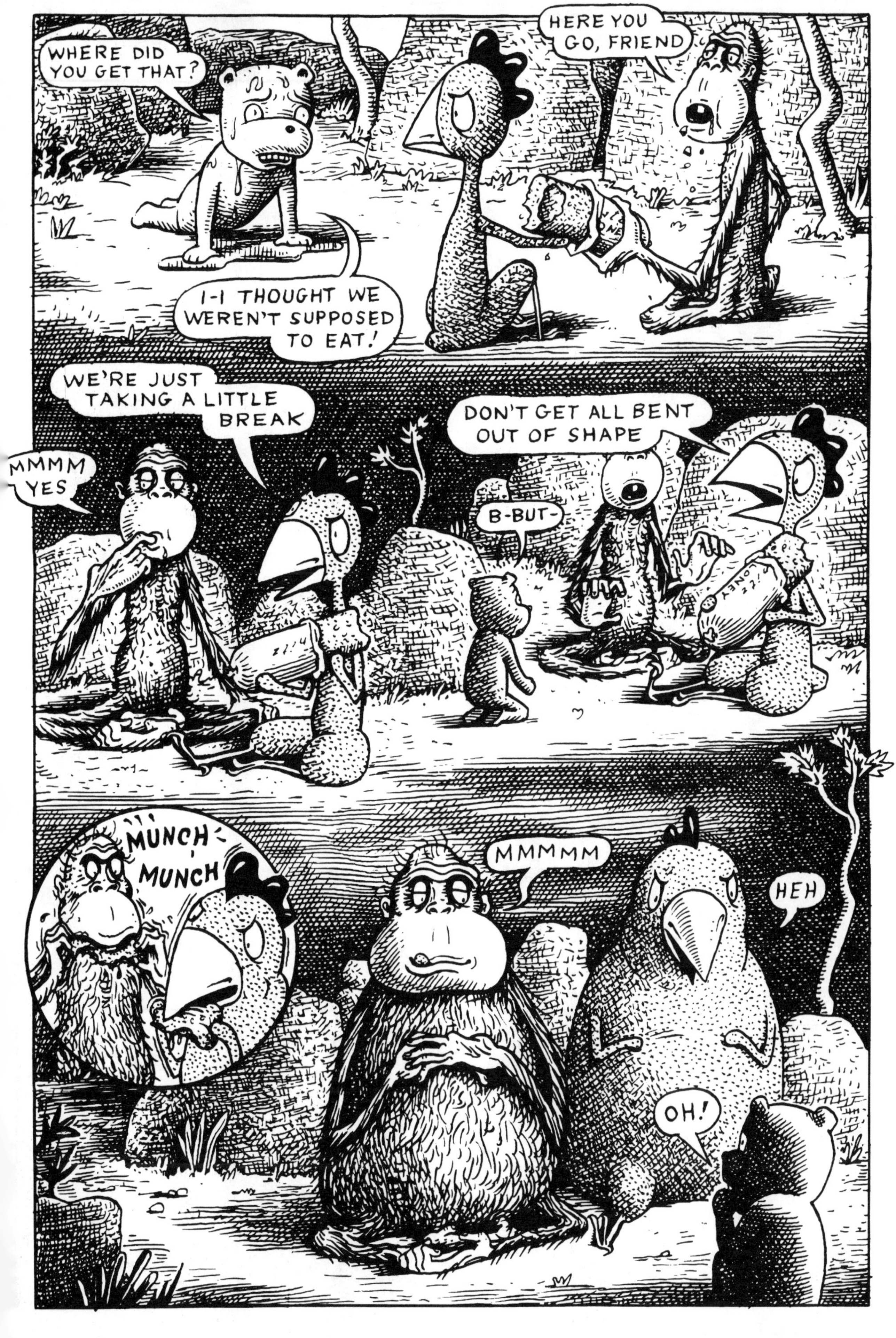
WHERE DID YOU GET THAT?
HERE YOU GO, FRIEND
I-I THOUGHT WE WEREN'T SUPPOSED TO EAT!
WE'RE JUST TAKING A LITTLE BREAK
MMMM YES
DON'T GET ALL BENT OUT OF SHAPE
B-BUT-
MUNCH MUNCH
MMMMM
HEH
OH!

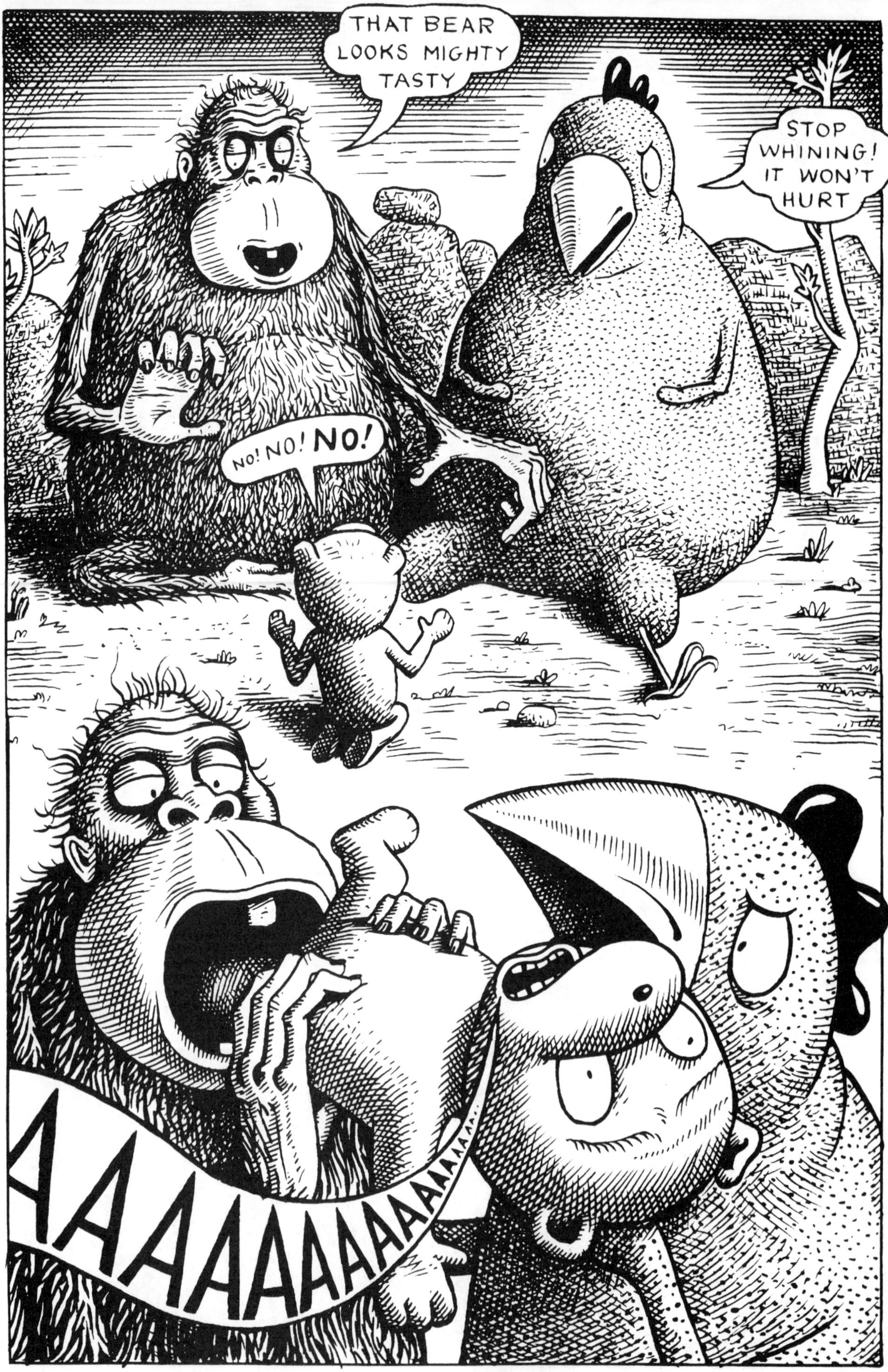

THAT BEAR LOOKS MIGHTY TASTY
STOP WHINING! IT WON'T HURT
NO! NO! NO!
AAAAAAAAAAAAAAA...

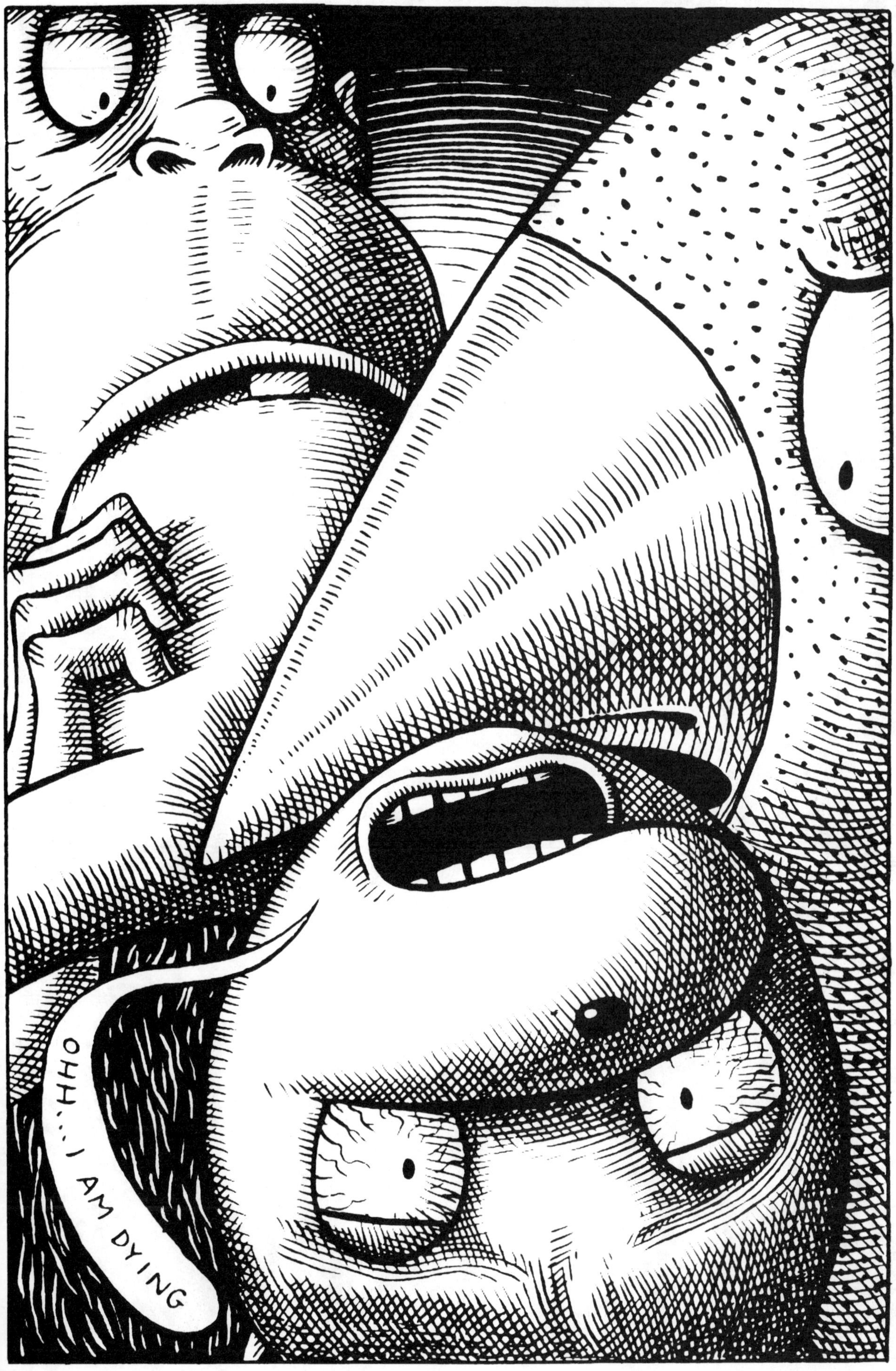
OHH... I AM DYING

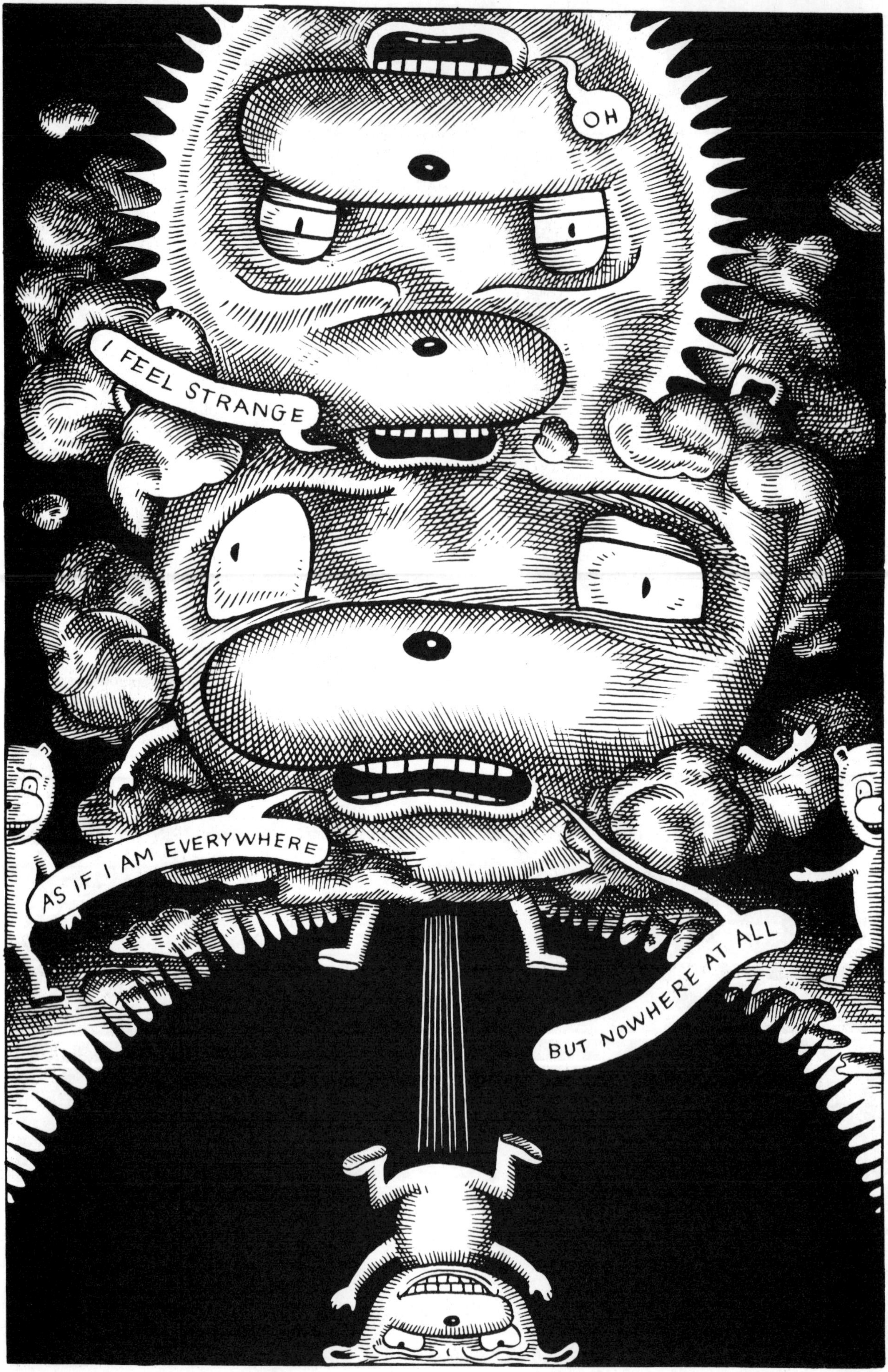
OH
I FEEL STRANGE
AS IF I AM EVERYWHERE
BUT NOWHERE AT ALL

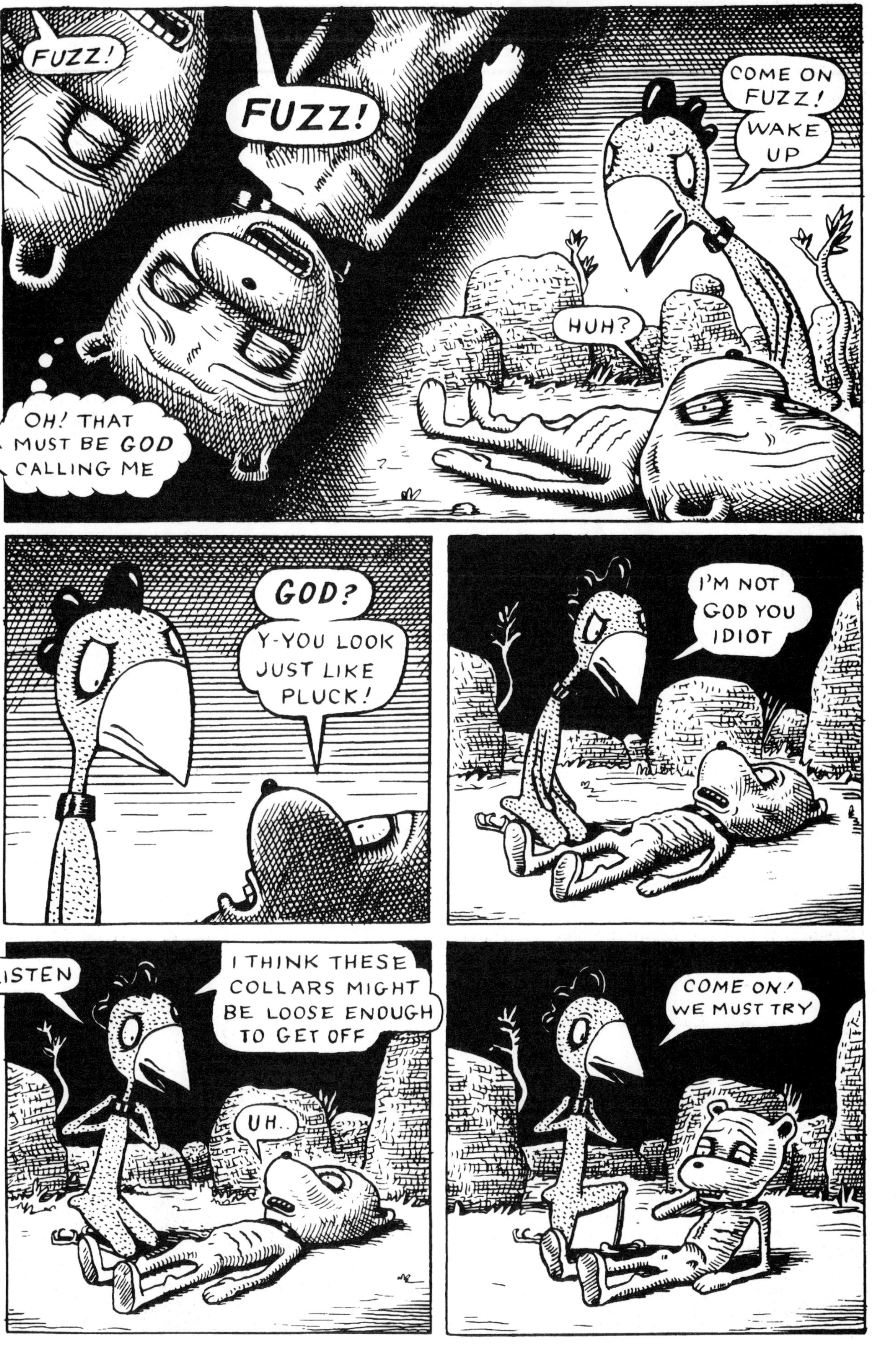
FUZZ!
FUZZ!
COME ON FUZZ! WAKE UP
HUH?
OH! THAT MUST BE GOD CALLING ME
GOD?
Y-YOU LOOK JUST LIKE PLUCK!
I'M NOT GOD YOU IDIOT
LISTEN
I THINK THESE COLLARS MIGHT BE LOOSE ENOUGH TO GET OFF
UH..
COME ON! WE MUST TRY

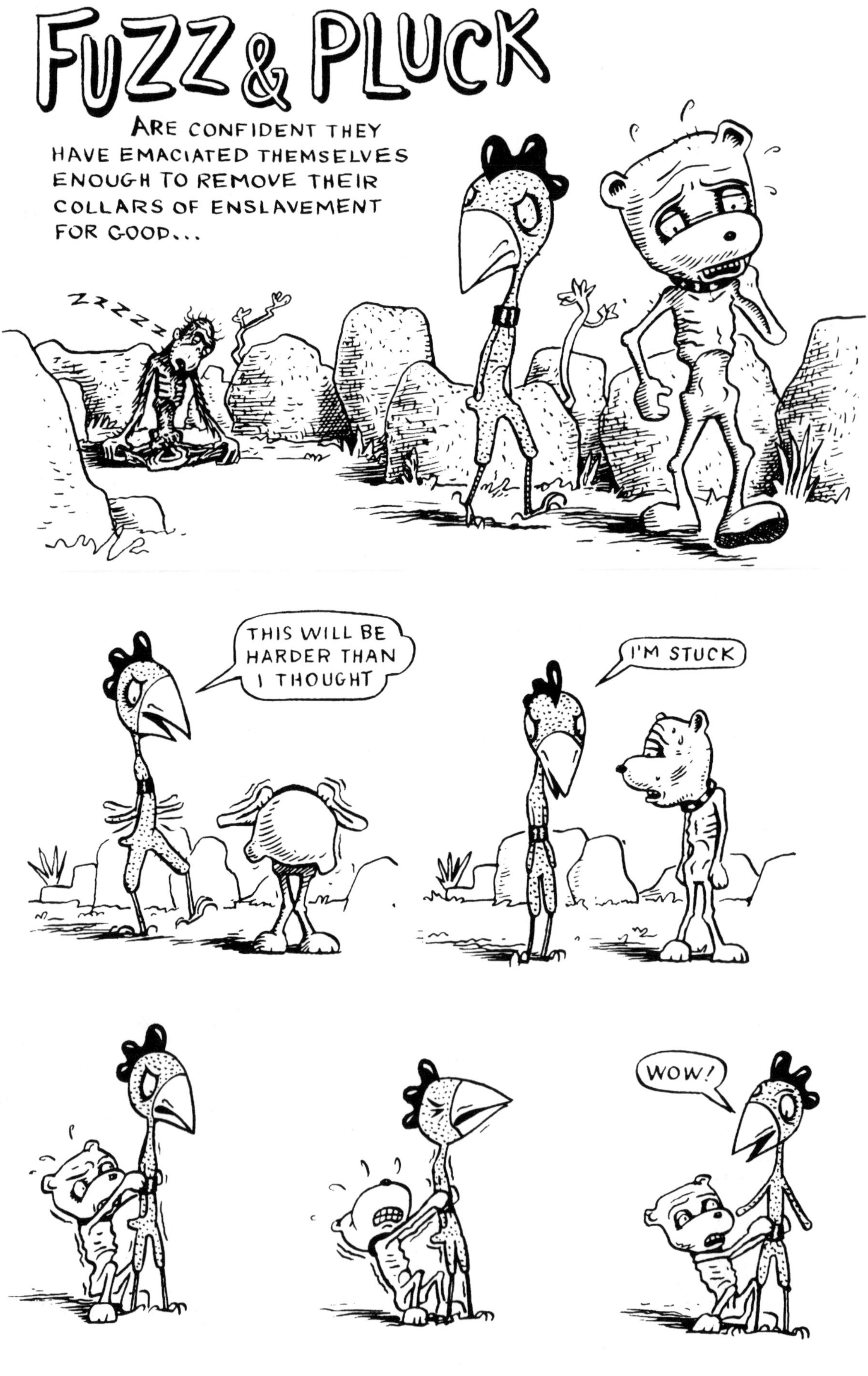
FUZZ & PLUCK
ARE CONFIDENT THEY HAVE EMACIATED THEMSELVES ENOUGH TO REMOVE THEIR COLLARS OF ENSLAVEMENT FOR GOOD...
ZZZZZ
THIS WILL BE HARDER THAN I THOUGHT
I'M STUCK
WOW!

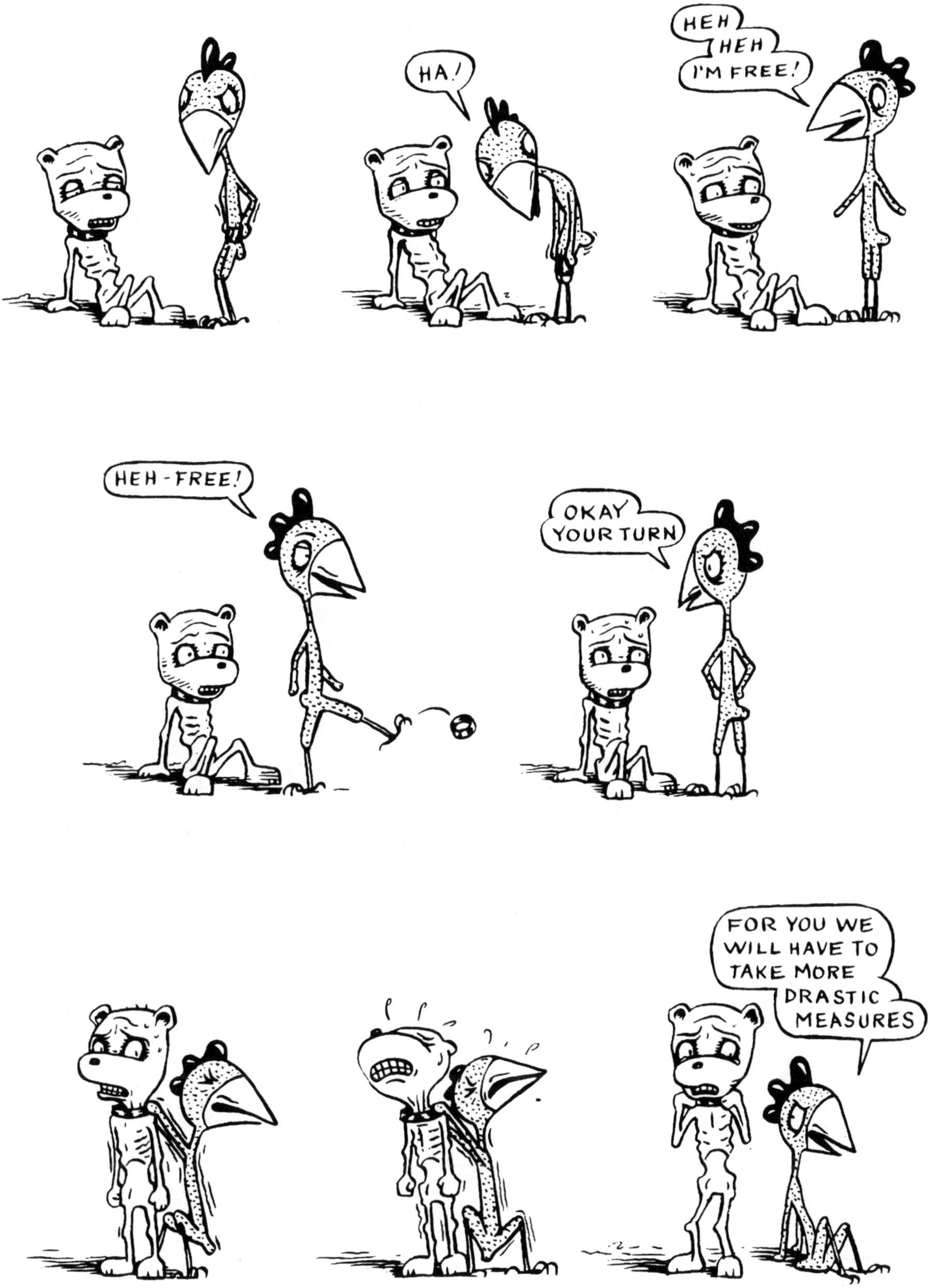
HA!
HEH HEH I'M FREE!
HEH-FREE!
OKAY YOUR TURN
FOR YOU WE WILL HAVE TO TAKE MORE DRASTIC MEASURES

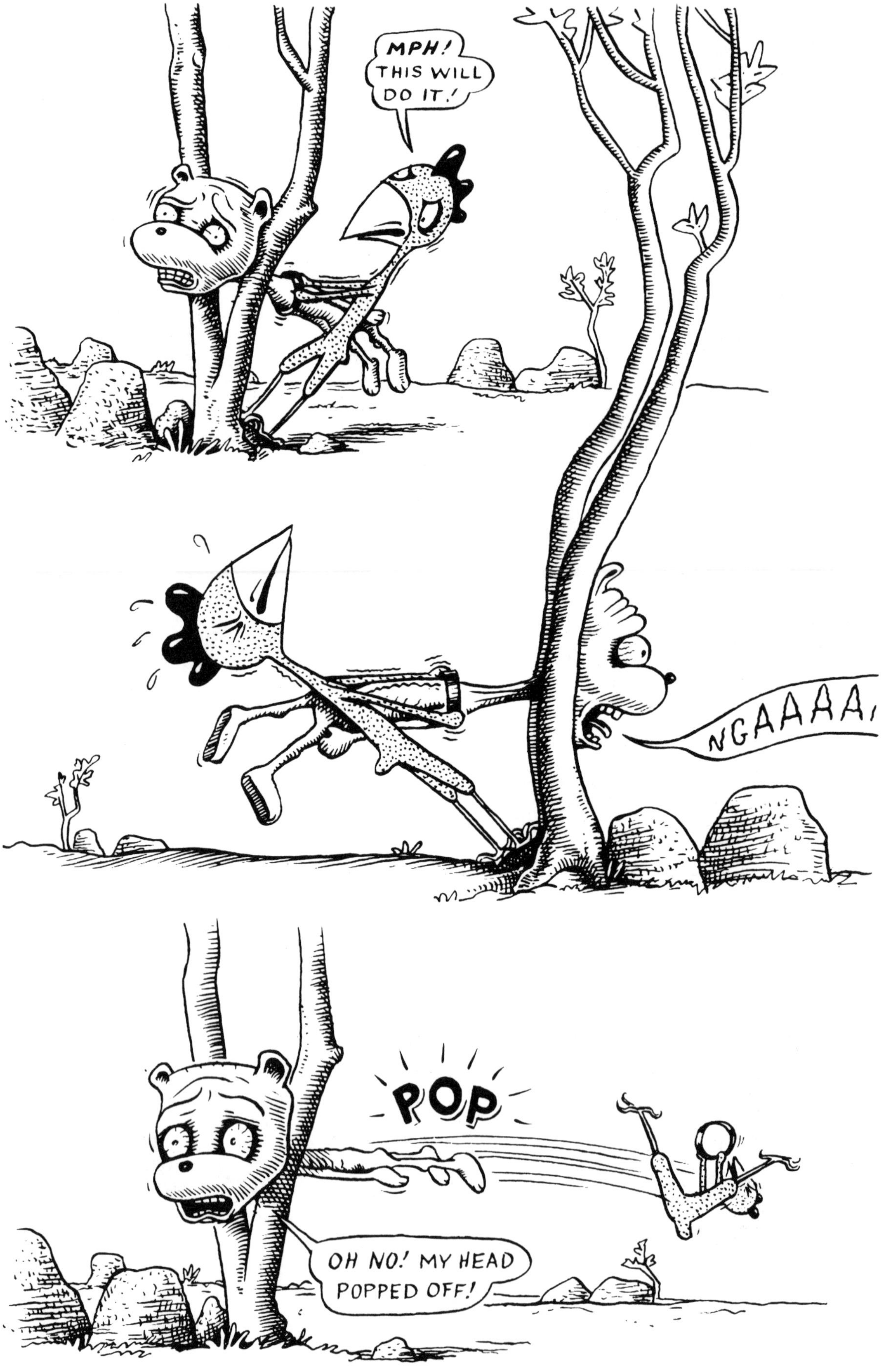
MPH! THIS WILL DO IT!
NGAAAA
POP
OH NO! MY HEAD POPPED OFF!

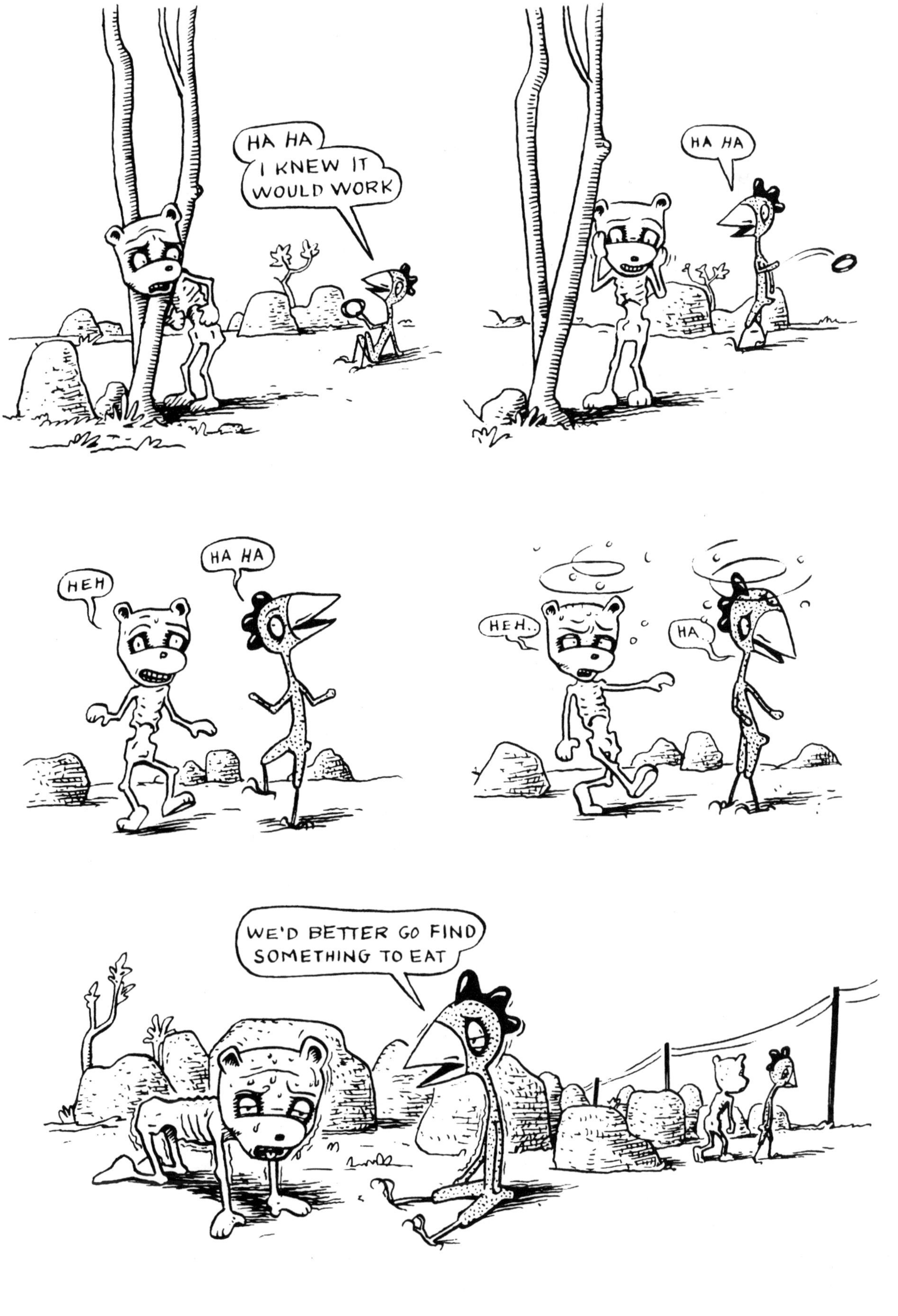
HA HA I KNEW IT WOULD WORK
HA HA
HEH
HA HA
HEH..
HA
WE'D BETTER GO FIND SOMETHING TO EAT

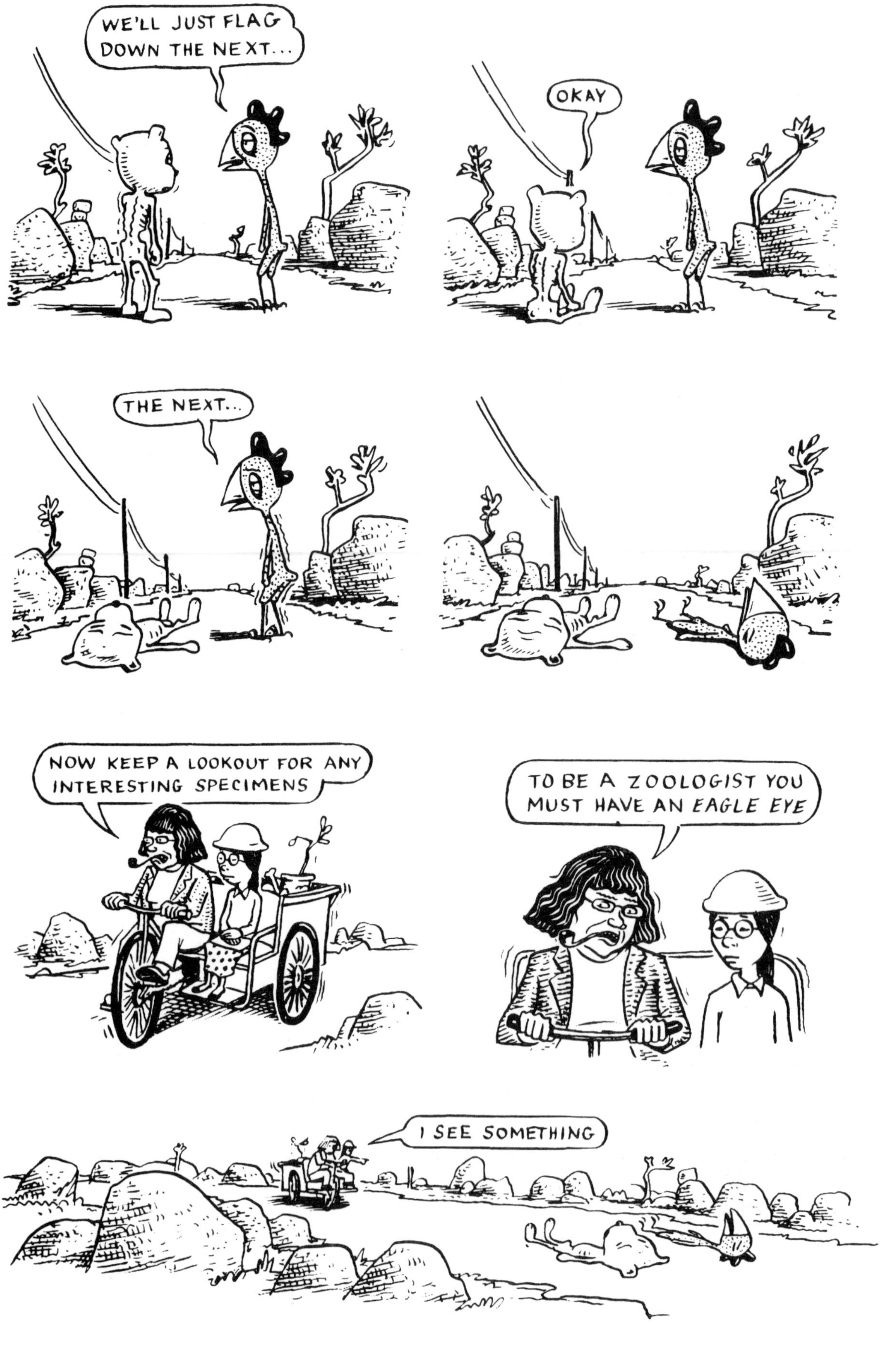
WE'LL JUST FLAG DOWN THE NEXT...
OKAY
THE NEXT...
NOW KEEP A LOOKOUT FOR ANY INTERESTING SPECIMENS
TO BE A ZOOLOGIST YOU MUST HAVE AN *EAGLE EYE*
I SEE SOMETHING

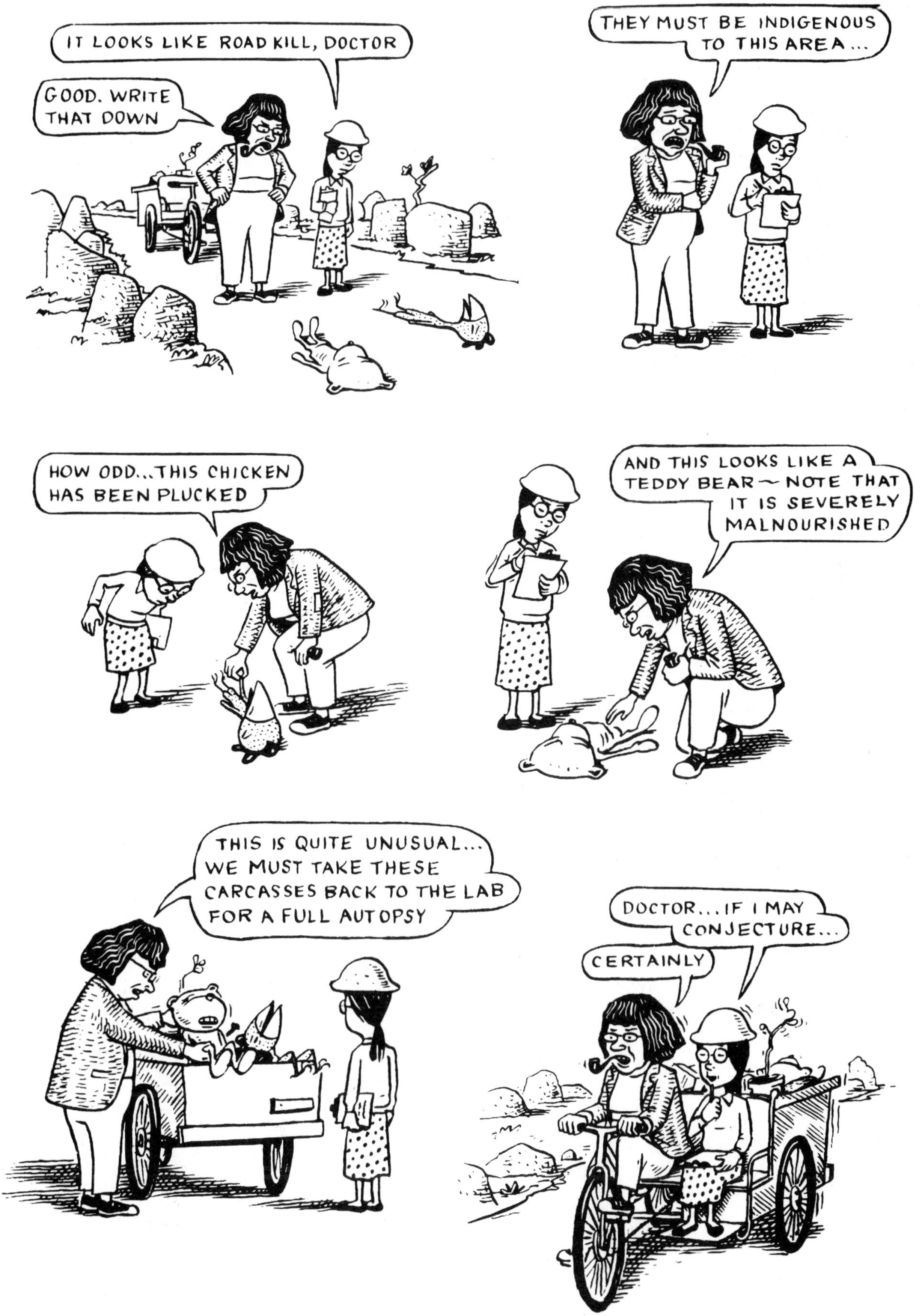
IT LOOKS LIKE ROAD KILL, DOCTOR
GOOD. WRITE THAT DOWN
THEY MUST BE INDIGENOUS TO THIS AREA...
HOW ODD...THIS CHICKEN HAS BEEN PLUCKED
AND THIS LOOKS LIKE A TEDDY BEAR ~ NOTE THAT IT IS SEVERELY MALNOURISHED
THIS IS QUITE UNUSUAL... WE MUST TAKE THESE CARCASSES BACK TO THE LAB FOR A FULL AUTOPSY
DOCTOR... IF I MAY CONJECTURE...
CERTAINLY

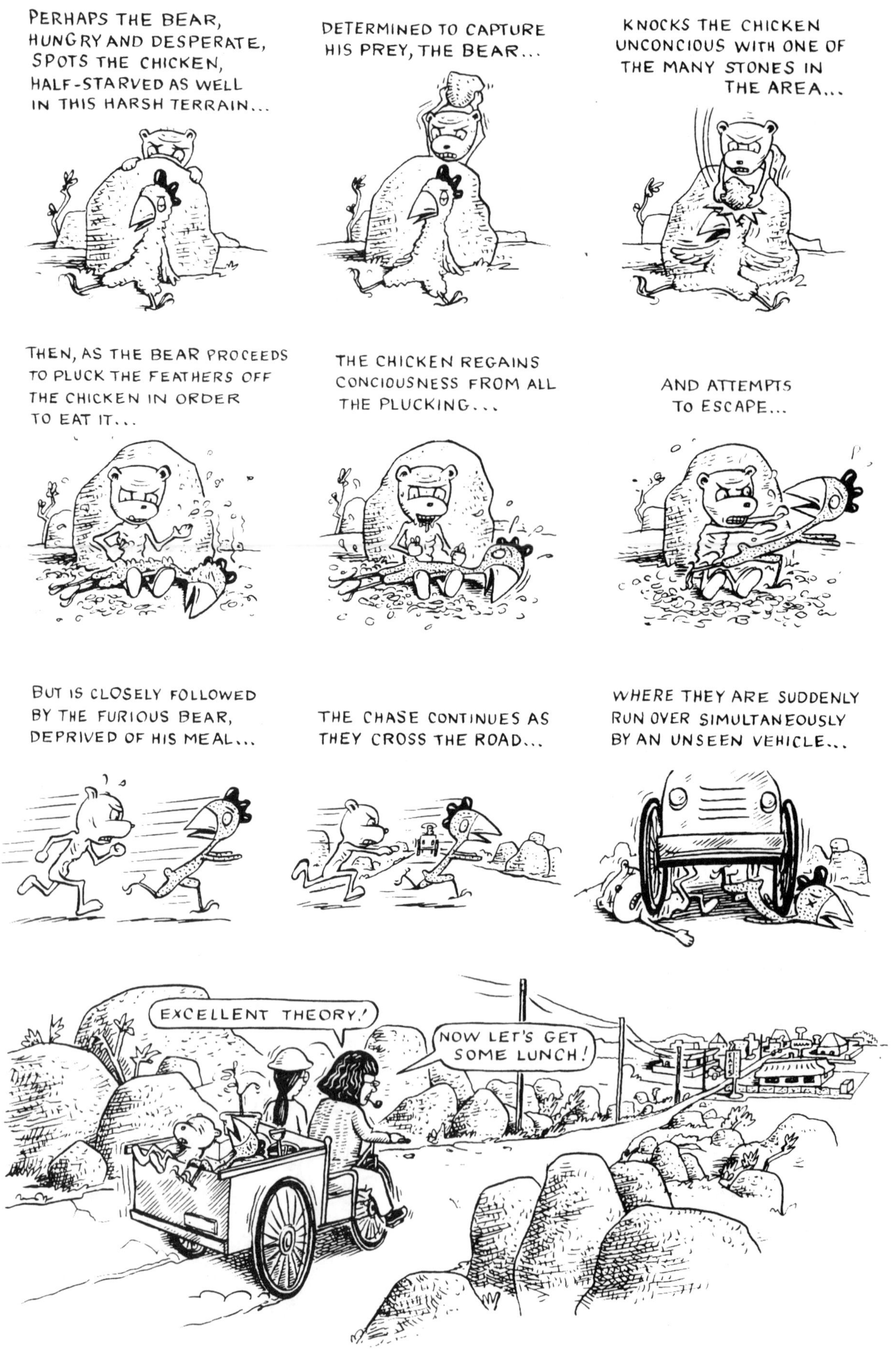
PERHAPS THE BEAR, HUNGRY AND DESPERATE, SPOTS THE CHICKEN, HALF-STARVED AS WELL IN THIS HARSH TERRAIN...
DETERMINED TO CAPTURE HIS PREY, THE BEAR...
KNOCKS THE CHICKEN UNCONCIOUS WITH ONE OF THE MANY STONES IN THE AREA...
THEN, AS THE BEAR PROCEEDS TO PLUCK THE FEATHERS OFF THE CHICKEN IN ORDER TO EAT IT...
THE CHICKEN REGAINS CONCIOUSNESS FROM ALL THE PLUCKING...
AND ATTEMPTS TO ESCAPE...
BUT IS CLOSELY FOLLOWED BY THE FURIOUS BEAR, DEPRIVED OF HIS MEAL...
THE CHASE CONTINUES AS THEY CROSS THE ROAD...
WHERE THEY ARE SUDDENLY RUN OVER SIMULTANEOUSLY BY AN UNSEEN VEHICLE...
EXCELLENT THEORY!
NOW LET'S GET SOME LUNCH!

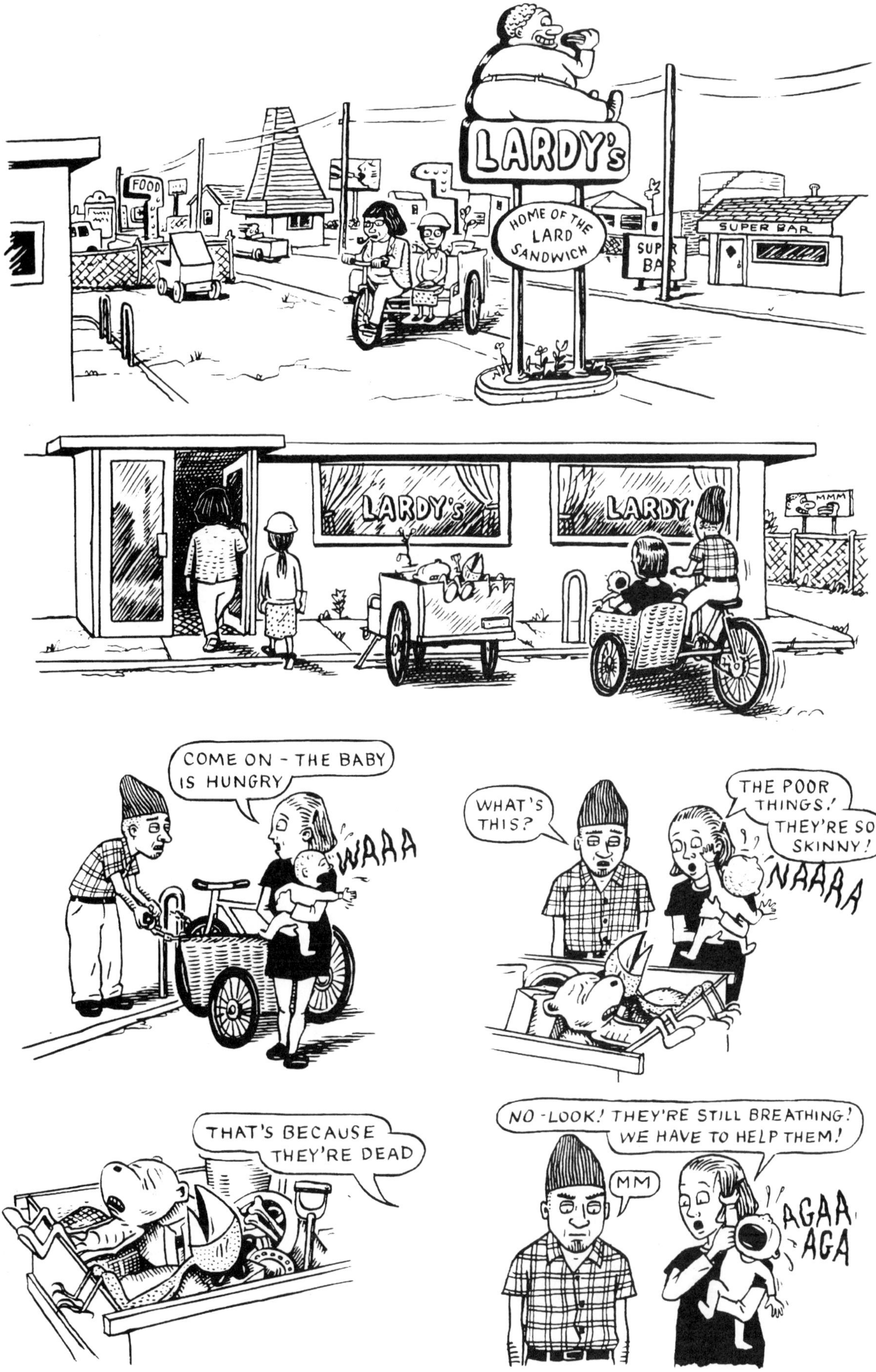
LARDY's
HOME OF THE LARD SANDWICH
FOOD
SUPER BAR
SUPER BAR
LARDY's
LARDY
MMM
COME ON - THE BABY IS HUNGRY
WAAA
WHAT'S THIS?
THE POOR THINGS! THEY'RE SO SKINNY!
NAAAA
THAT'S BECAUSE THEY'RE DEAD
NO - LOOK! THEY'RE STILL BREATHING! WE HAVE TO HELP THEM!
MM
AGAA AGA

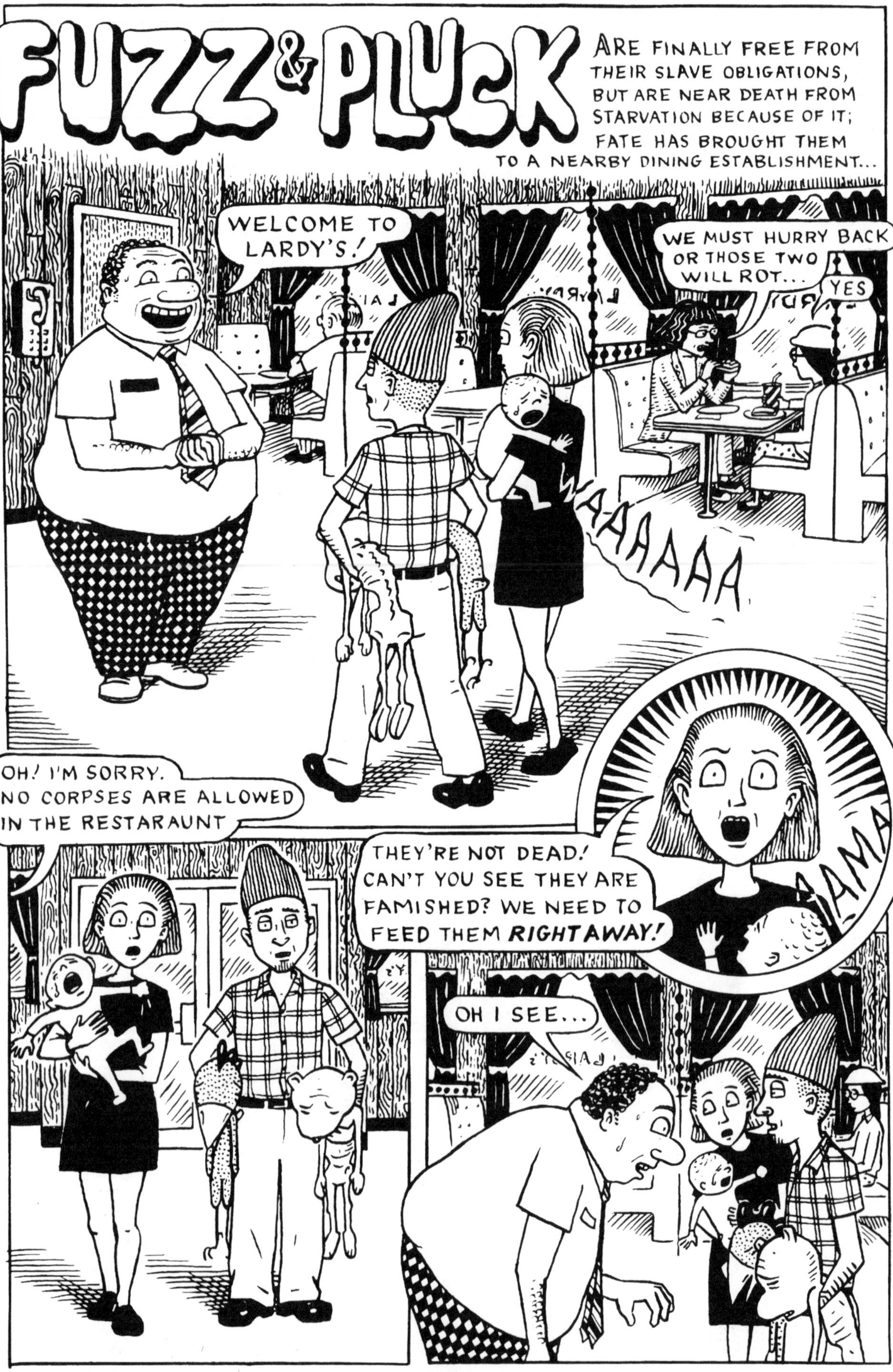
FUZZ & PLUCK
ARE FINALLY FREE FROM THEIR SLAVE OBLIGATIONS, BUT ARE NEAR DEATH FROM STARVATION BECAUSE OF IT; FATE HAS BROUGHT THEM TO A NEARBY DINING ESTABLISHMENT...
WELCOME TO LARDY'S!
WE MUST HURRY BACK OR THOSE TWO WILL ROT...
YES
WAAAAAAA
OH! I'M SORRY. NO CORPSES ARE ALLOWED IN THE RESTARAUNT
THEY'RE NOT DEAD! CAN'T YOU SEE THEY ARE FAMISHED? WE NEED TO FEED THEM RIGHTAWAY!
AAMA
OH I SEE...

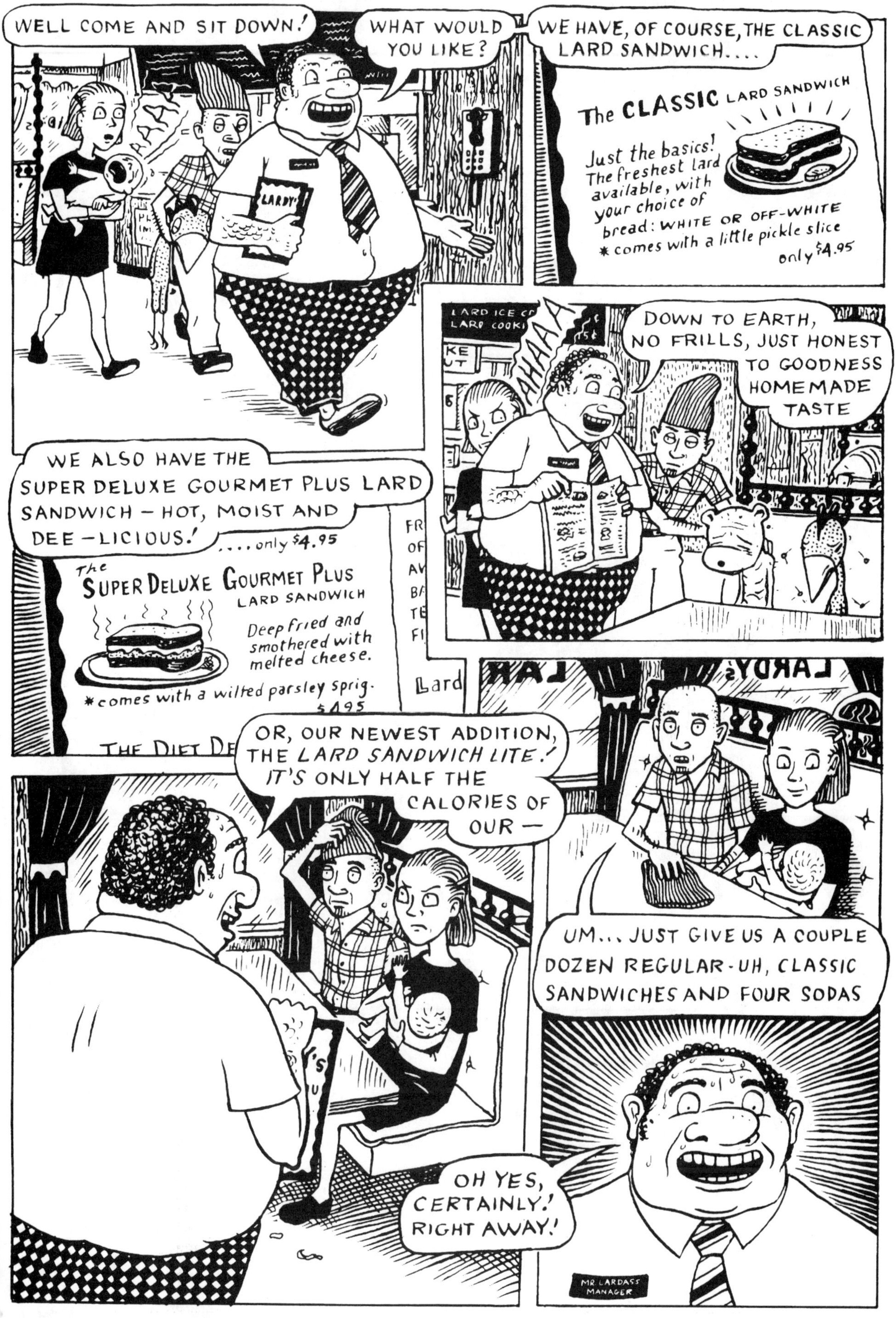
WELL COME AND SIT DOWN!
WHAT WOULD YOU LIKE?
LARDY'S
WE HAVE, OF COURSE, THE CLASSIC LARD SANDWICH....
The CLASSIC LARD SANDWICH
Just the basics! The freshest lard available, with your choice of bread: WHITE OR OFF-WHITE
* comes with a little pickle slice
only $4.95
LARD ICE CR
LARD COOKI
AHAAAA
DOWN TO EARTH, NO FRILLS, JUST HONEST TO GOODNESS HOMEMADE TASTE
WE ALSO HAVE THE SUPER DELUXE GOURMET PLUS LARD SANDWICH - HOT, MOIST AND DEE-LICIOUS!
....only $4.95
The SUPER DELUXE GOURMET PLUS LARD SANDWICH
Deep fried and smothered with melted cheese.
* comes with a wilted parsley sprig.
Lard
LARDY'S
OR, OUR NEWEST ADDITION, THE LARD SANDWICH LITE! IT'S ONLY HALF THE CALORIES OF OUR —
UM... JUST GIVE US A COUPLE DOZEN REGULAR-UH, CLASSIC SANDWICHES AND FOUR SODAS
OH YES, CERTAINLY! RIGHT AWAY!
MR. LARDASS MANAGER

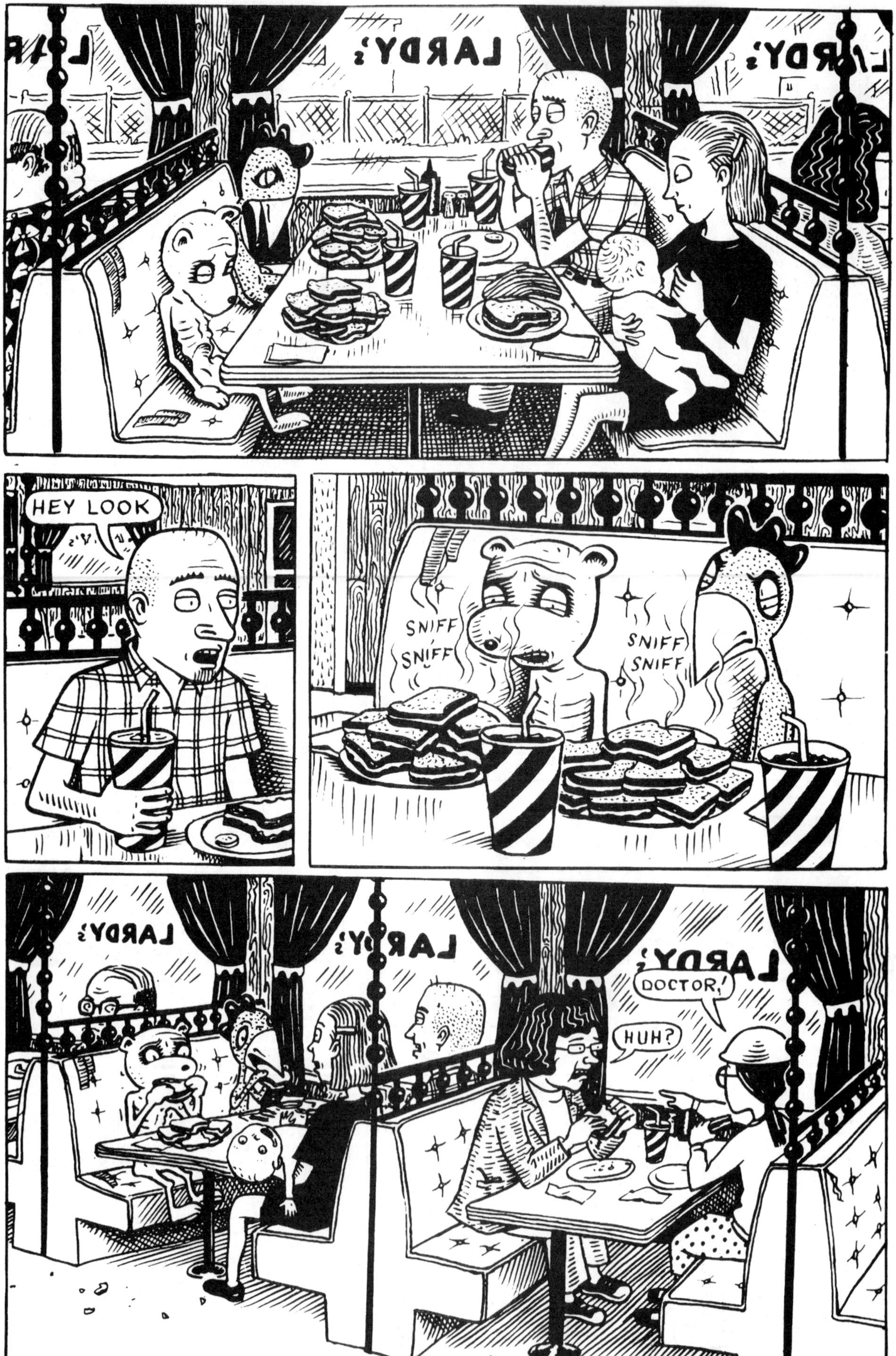
HEY LOOK
SNIFF
SNIFF
SNIFF
SNIFF
DOCTOR!
HUH?

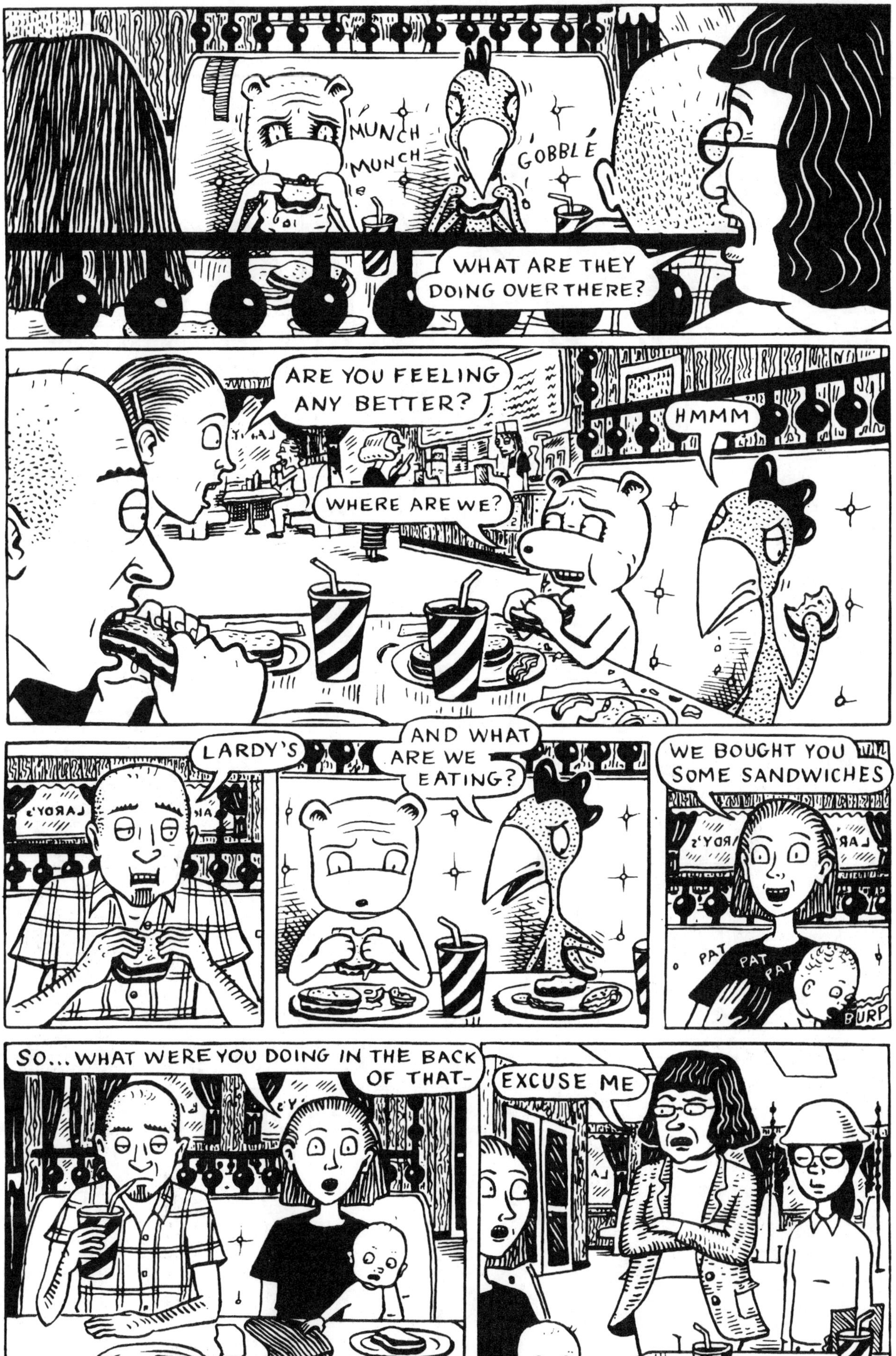
MUNCH
MUNCH
GOBBLE
WHAT ARE THEY DOING OVER THERE?
ARE YOU FEELING ANY BETTER?
HMMM
WHERE ARE WE?
LARDY'S
AND WHAT ARE WE EATING?
WE BOUGHT YOU SOME SANDWICHES
PAT
PAT
PAT
BURP
SO... WHAT WERE YOU DOING IN THE BACK OF THAT-
EXCUSE ME

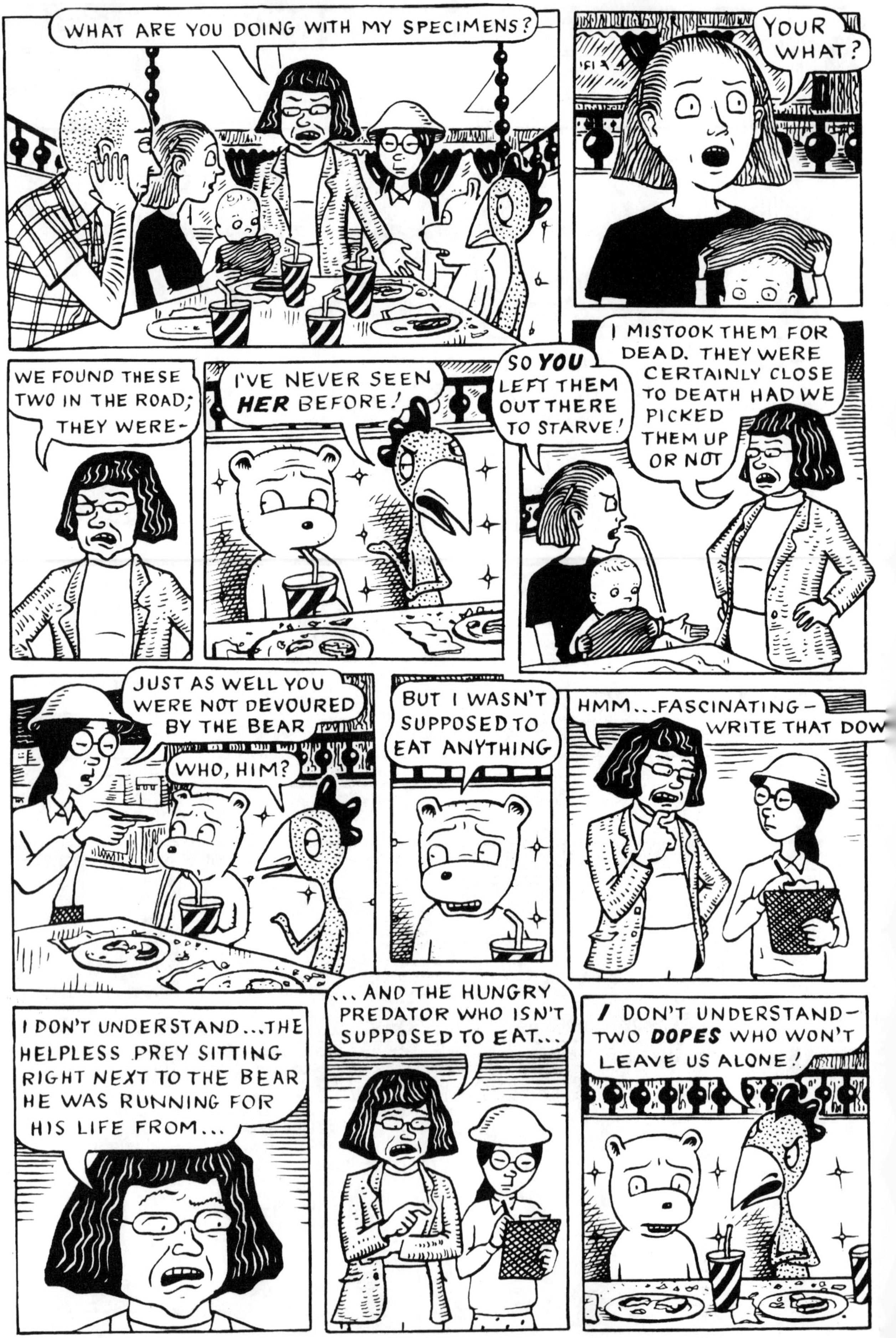
WHAT ARE YOU DOING WITH MY SPECIMENS?
YOUR WHAT?
WE FOUND THESE TWO IN THE ROAD; THEY WERE-
I'VE NEVER SEEN HER BEFORE!
SO YOU LEFT THEM OUT THERE TO STARVE!
I MISTOOK THEM FOR DEAD. THEY WERE CERTAINLY CLOSE TO DEATH HAD WE PICKED THEM UP OR NOT
JUST AS WELL YOU WERE NOT DEVOURED BY THE BEAR
WHO, HIM?
BUT I WASN'T SUPPOSED TO EAT ANYTHING
HMM...FASCINATING- WRITE THAT DOW
I DON'T UNDERSTAND...THE HELPLESS PREY SITTING RIGHT NEXT TO THE BEAR HE WAS RUNNING FOR HIS LIFE FROM...
...AND THE HUNGRY PREDATOR WHO ISN'T SUPPOSED TO EAT...
I DON'T UNDERSTAND- TWO DOPES WHO WON'T LEAVE US ALONE!

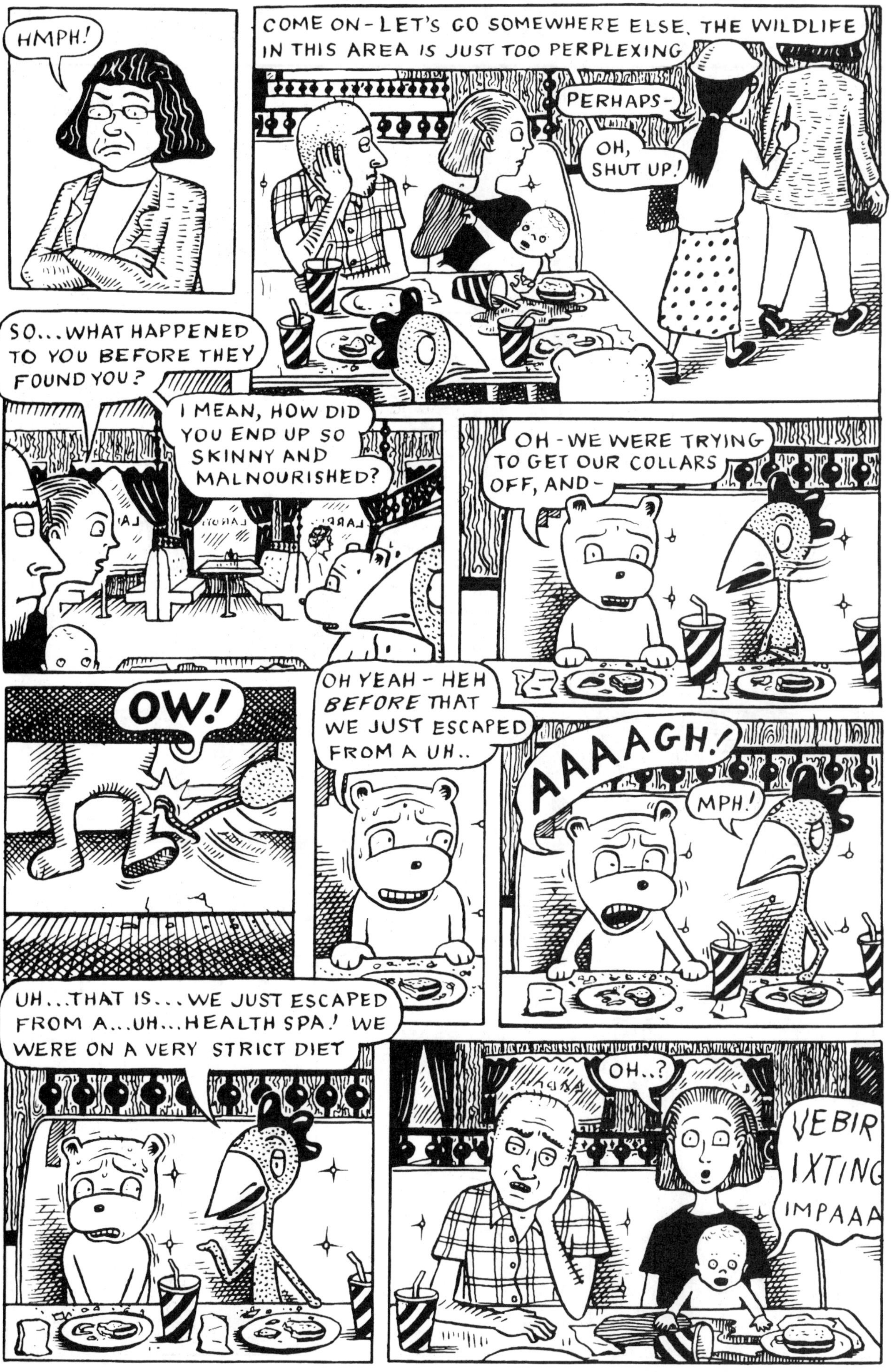
HMPH!
COME ON - LET'S GO SOMEWHERE ELSE. THE WILDLIFE IN THIS AREA IS JUST TOO PERPLEXING
PERHAPS-
OH, SHUT UP!
SO... WHAT HAPPENED TO YOU BEFORE THEY FOUND YOU?
I MEAN, HOW DID YOU END UP SO SKINNY AND MALNOURISHED?
OH - WE WERE TRYING TO GET OUR COLLARS OFF, AND-
OW!
OH YEAH - HEH *BEFORE* THAT WE JUST ESCAPED FROM A UH..
AAAAGH!
MPH!
UH... THAT IS... WE JUST ESCAPED FROM A... UH... HEALTH SPA! WE WERE ON A VERY STRICT DIET
OH..?
VEBIR
IXTING
IMPAAA

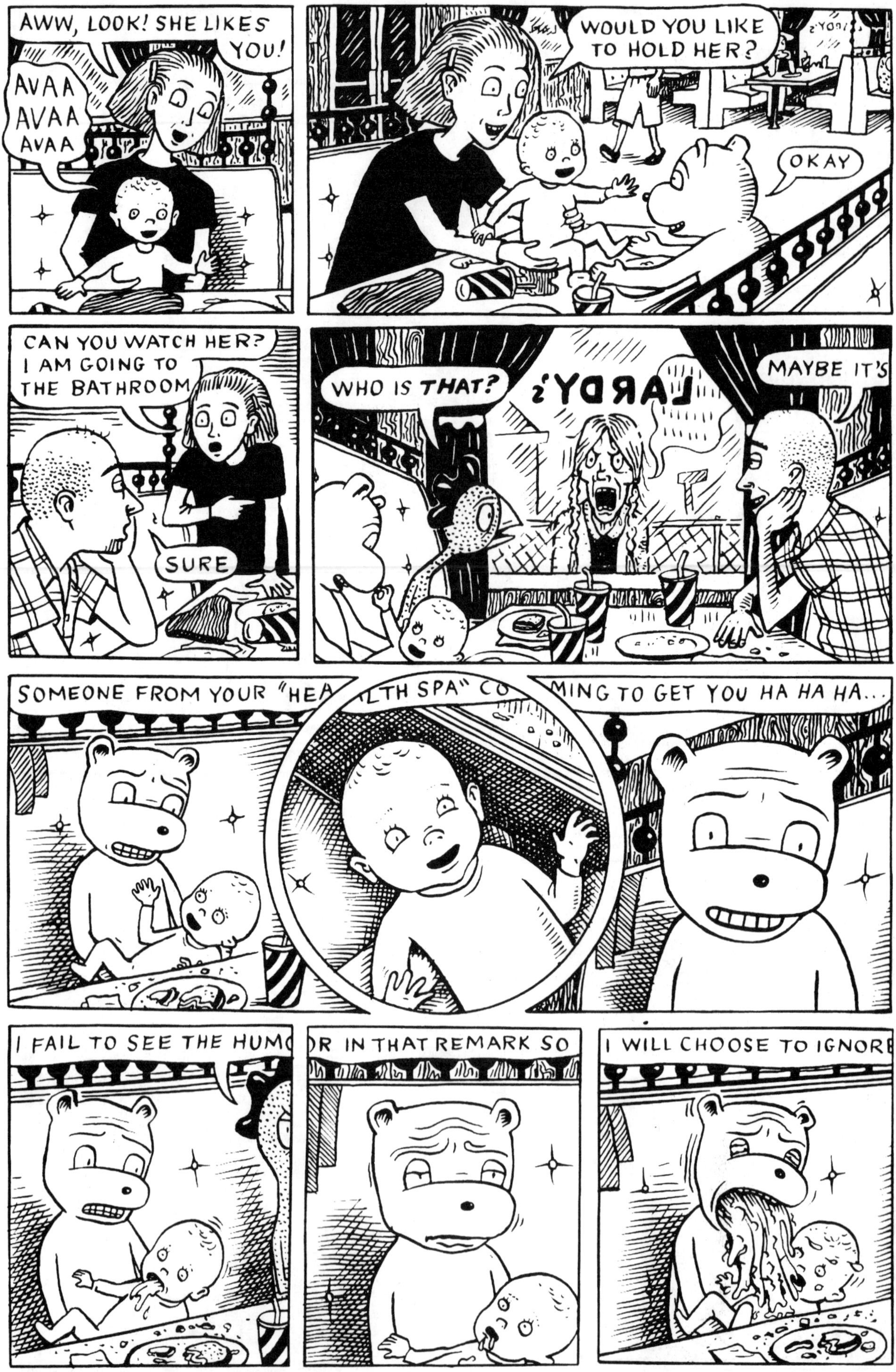
AWW, LOOK! SHE LIKES YOU!
AVAA AVAA AVAA
WOULD YOU LIKE TO HOLD HER?
OKAY
CAN YOU WATCH HER? I AM GOING TO THE BATHROOM
SURE
WHO IS THAT?
LARDY'S
MAYBE IT'S
SOMEONE FROM YOUR "HEALTH SPA" COMING TO GET YOU HA HA HA...
I FAIL TO SEE THE HUMOR IN THAT REMARK SO
I WILL CHOOSE TO IGNORE

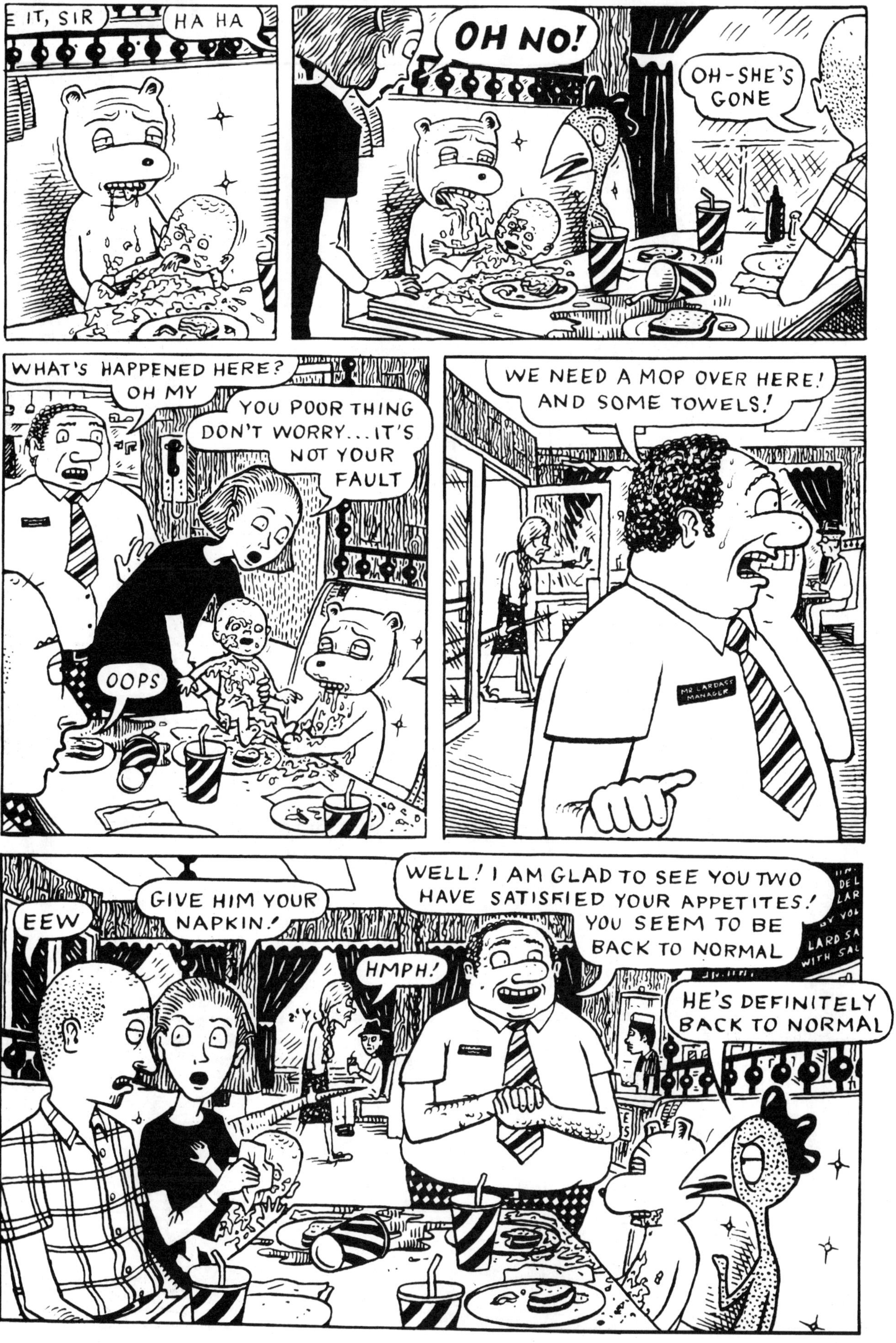
IT, SIR
HA HA
OH NO!
OH-SHE'S GONE
WHAT'S HAPPENED HERE? OH MY
YOU POOR THING DON'T WORRY... IT'S NOT YOUR FAULT
OOPS
WE NEED A MOP OVER HERE! AND SOME TOWELS!
MR LARDASS MANAGER
EEW
GIVE HIM YOUR NAPKIN!
HMPH!
WELL! I AM GLAD TO SEE YOU TWO HAVE SATISFIED YOUR APPETITES! YOU SEEM TO BE BACK TO NORMAL
HE'S DEFINITELY BACK TO NORMAL

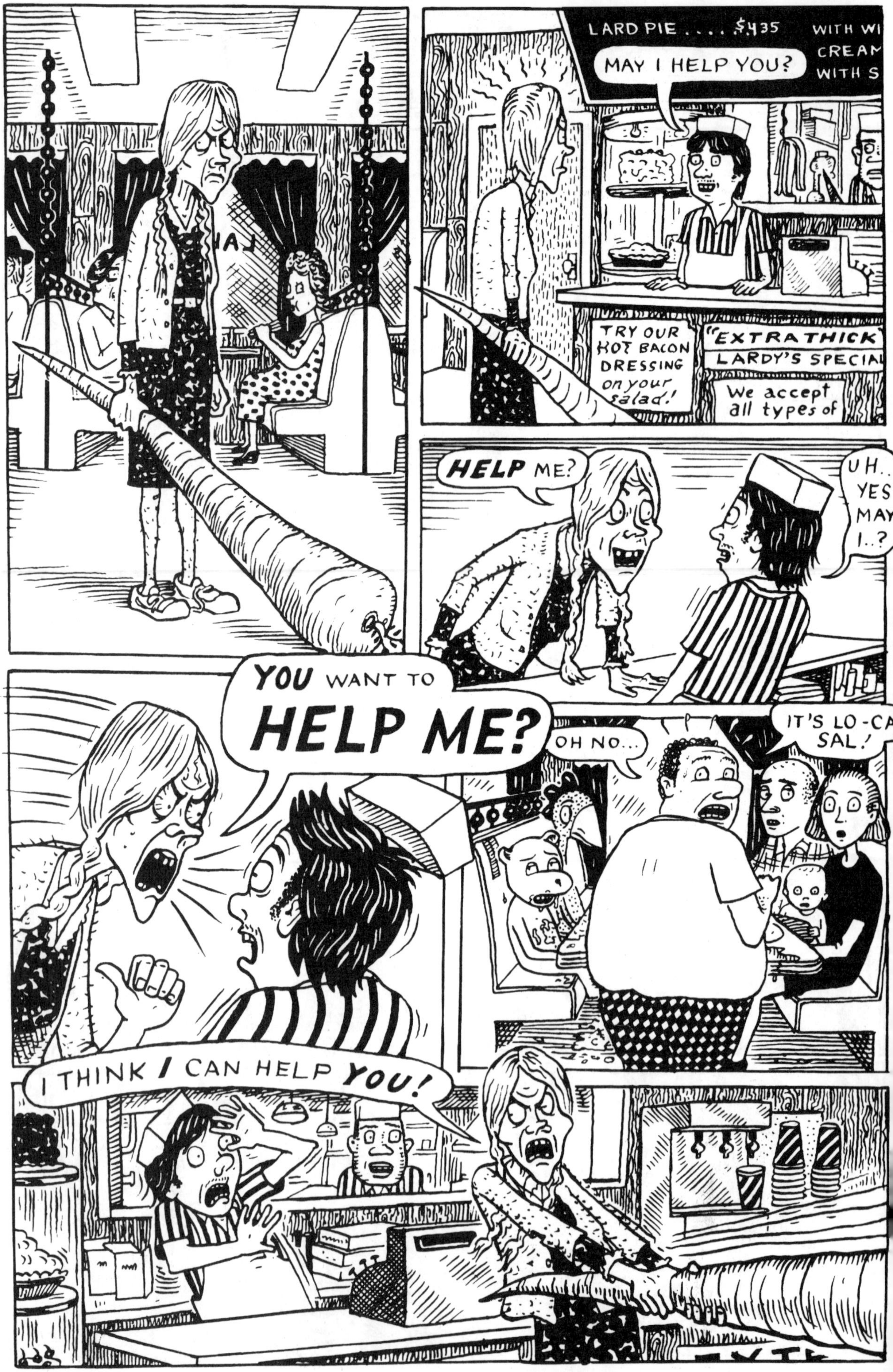

LARD PIE $4.35
WITH WI
CREAM
WITH S
MAY I HELP YOU?
TRY OUR HOT BACON DRESSING on your salad!
"EXTRA THICK"
LARDY'S SPECIAL
We accept all types of
HELP ME?
UH.. YES MAY I..?
YOU WANT TO HELP ME?
OH NO...
IT'S LO-CA SAL!
I THINK I CAN HELP YOU!

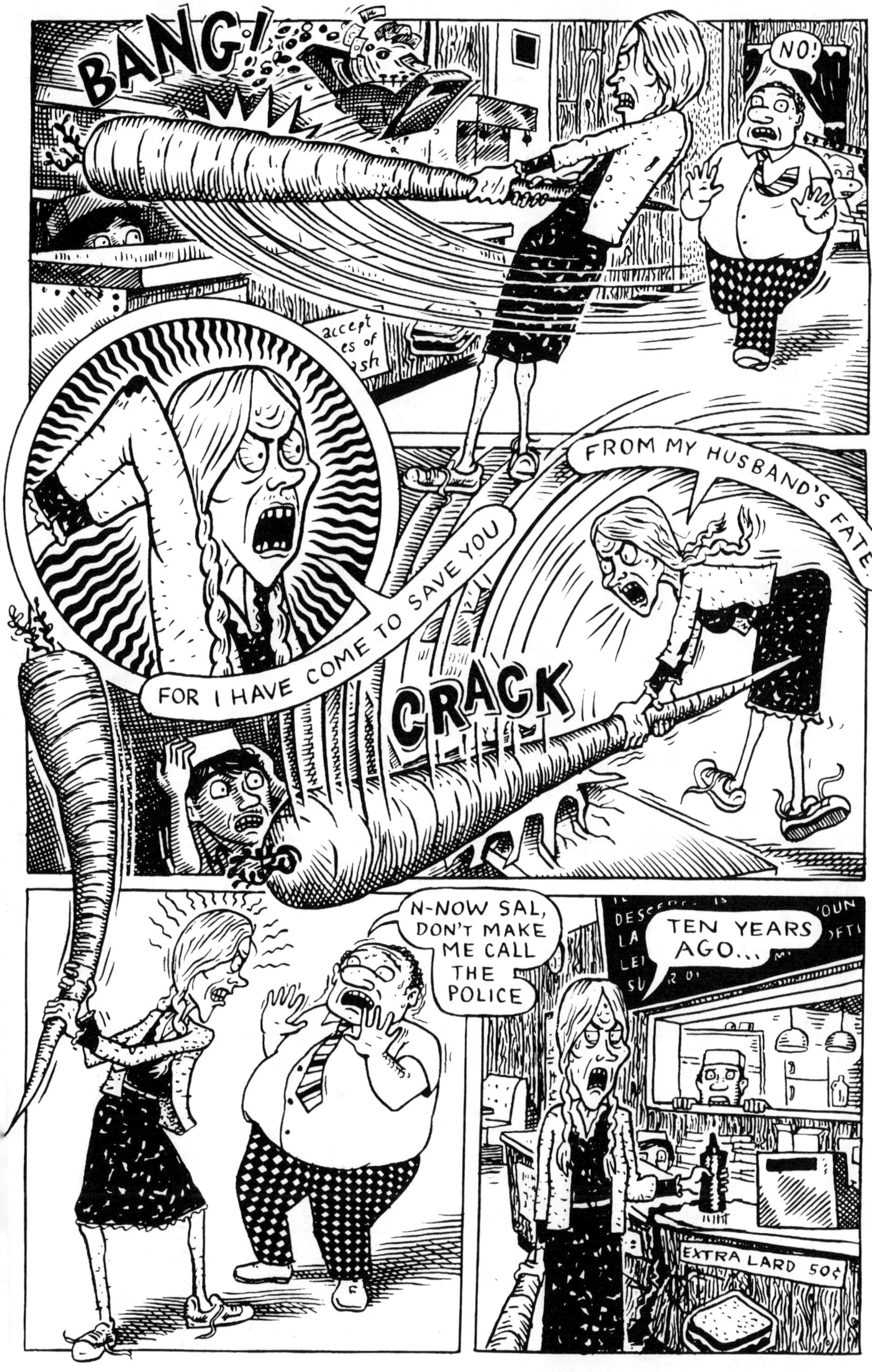
BANG!
NO!
FOR I HAVE COME TO SAVE YOU
FROM MY HUSBAND'S FATE!
CRACK
N-NOW SAL, DON'T MAKE ME CALL THE POLICE
TEN YEARS AGO...
EXTRA LARD 50¢

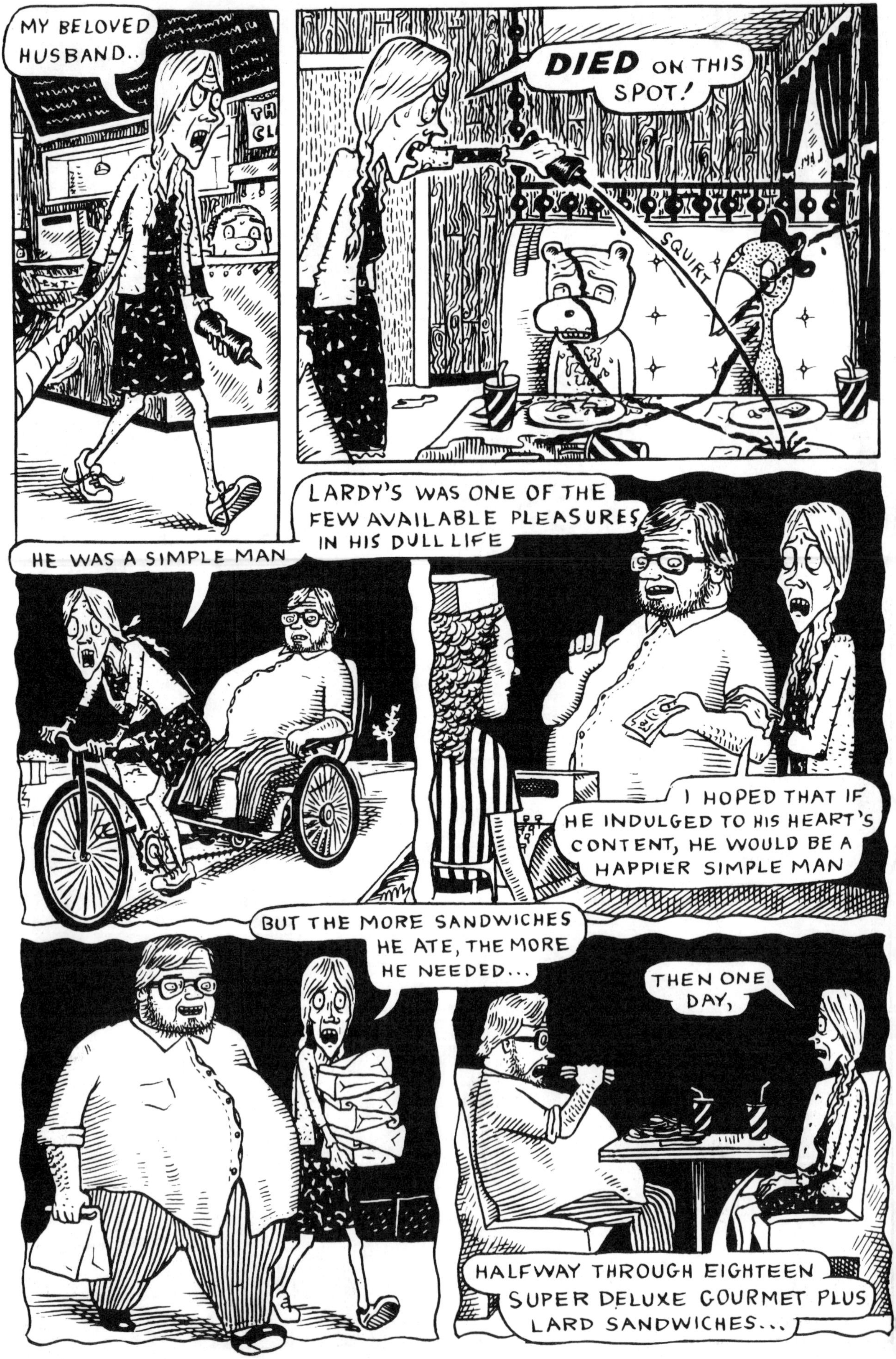

MY BELOVED HUSBAND..
DIED ON THIS SPOT!
SQUIRT
LARDY'S WAS ONE OF THE FEW AVAILABLE PLEASURES IN HIS DULL LIFE
HE WAS A SIMPLE MAN
I HOPED THAT IF HE INDULGED TO HIS HEART'S CONTENT, HE WOULD BE A HAPPIER SIMPLE MAN
BUT THE MORE SANDWICHES HE ATE, THE MORE HE NEEDED...
THEN ONE DAY,
HALFWAY THROUGH EIGHTEEN SUPER DELUXE GOURMET PLUS LARD SANDWICHES...

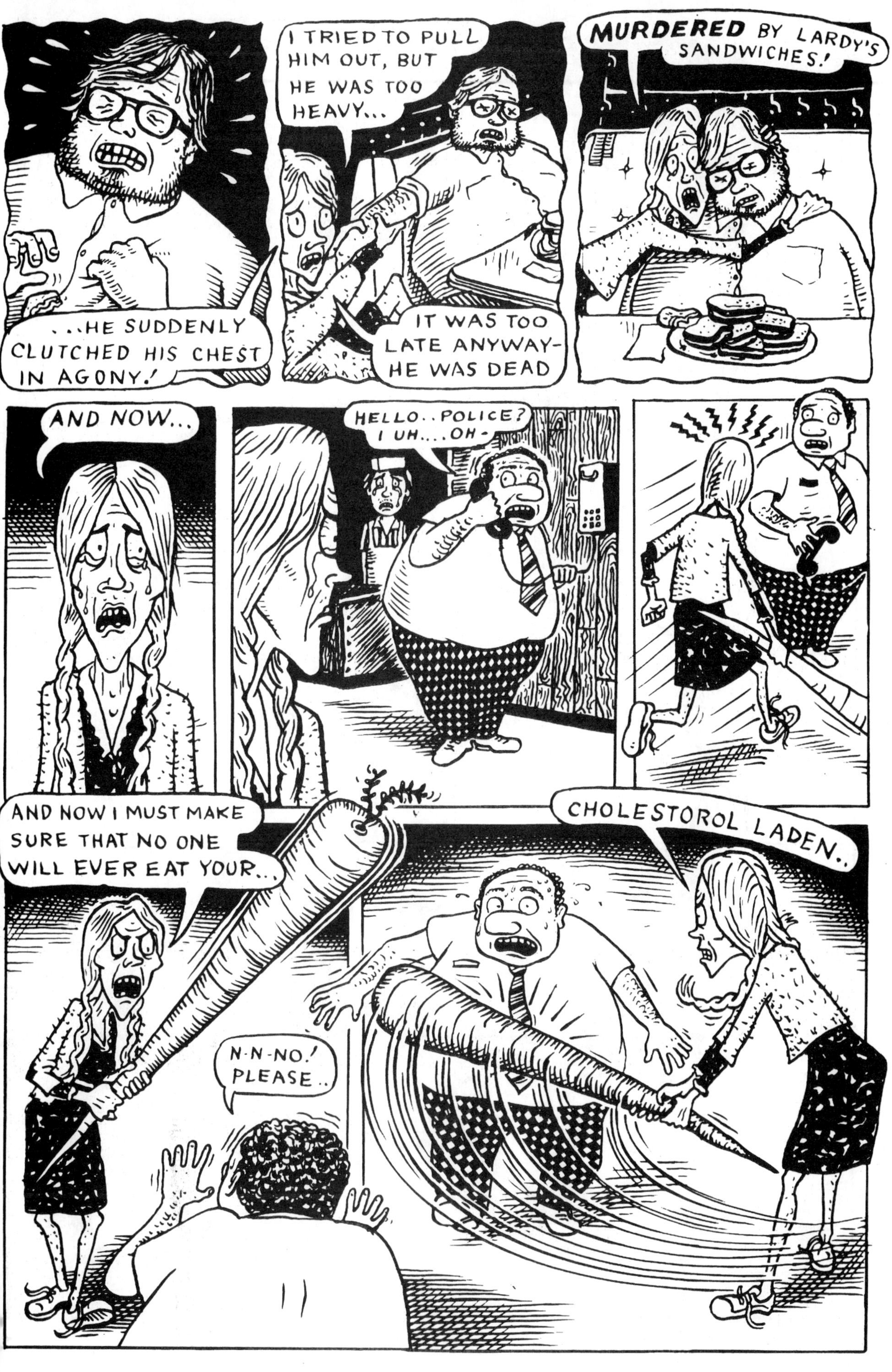
...HE SUDDENLY CLUTCHED HIS CHEST IN AGONY!
I TRIED TO PULL HIM OUT, BUT HE WAS TOO HEAVY...
IT WAS TOO LATE ANYWAY- HE WAS DEAD
MURDERED BY LARDY'S SANDWICHES!
AND NOW...
HELLO..POLICE? I UH....OH-
AND NOW I MUST MAKE SURE THAT NO ONE WILL EVER EAT YOUR..
N-N-NO! PLEASE..
CHOLESTOROL LADEN..

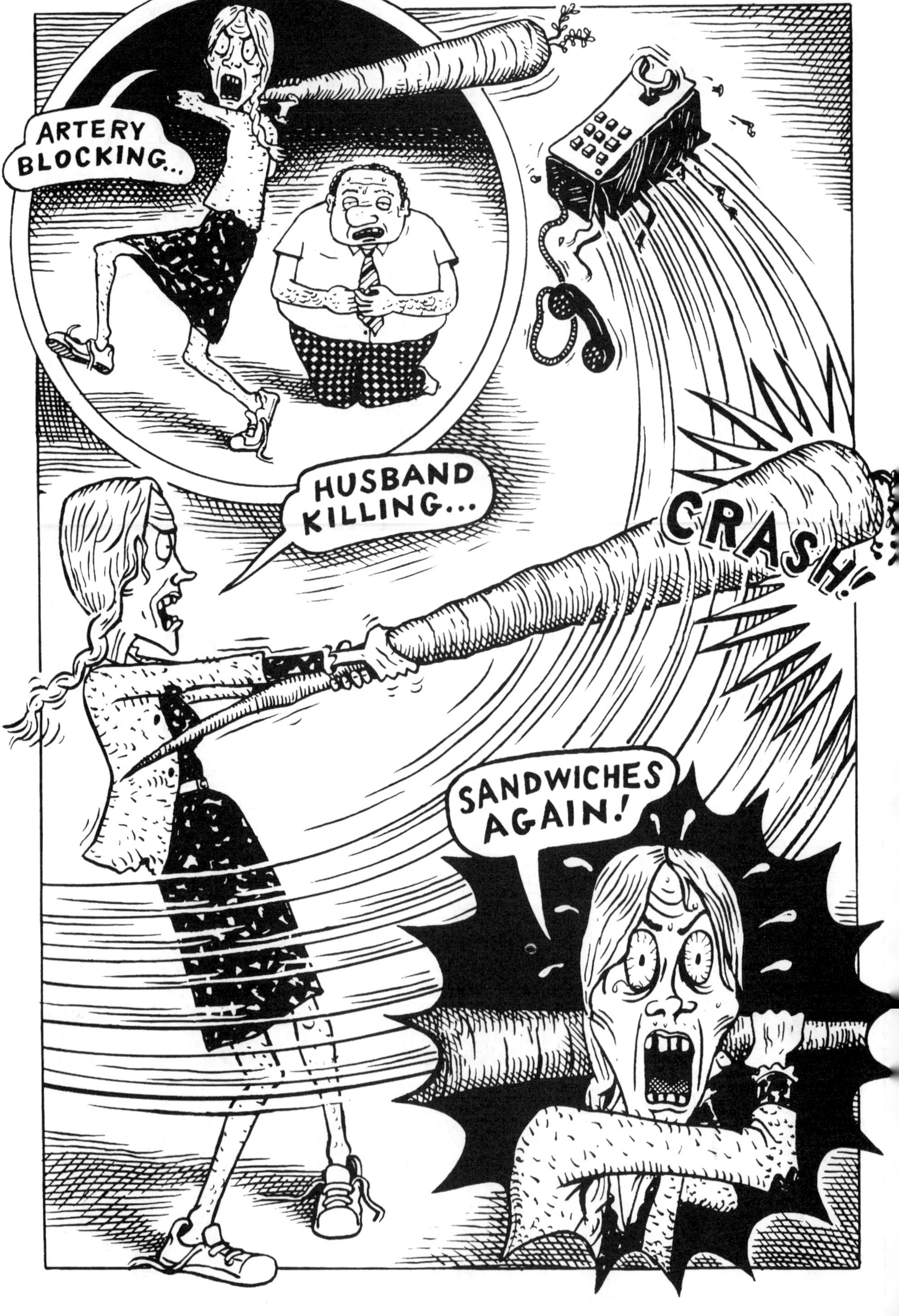
ARTERY BLOCKING...
HUSBAND KILLING...
CRASH!
SANDWICHES AGAIN!

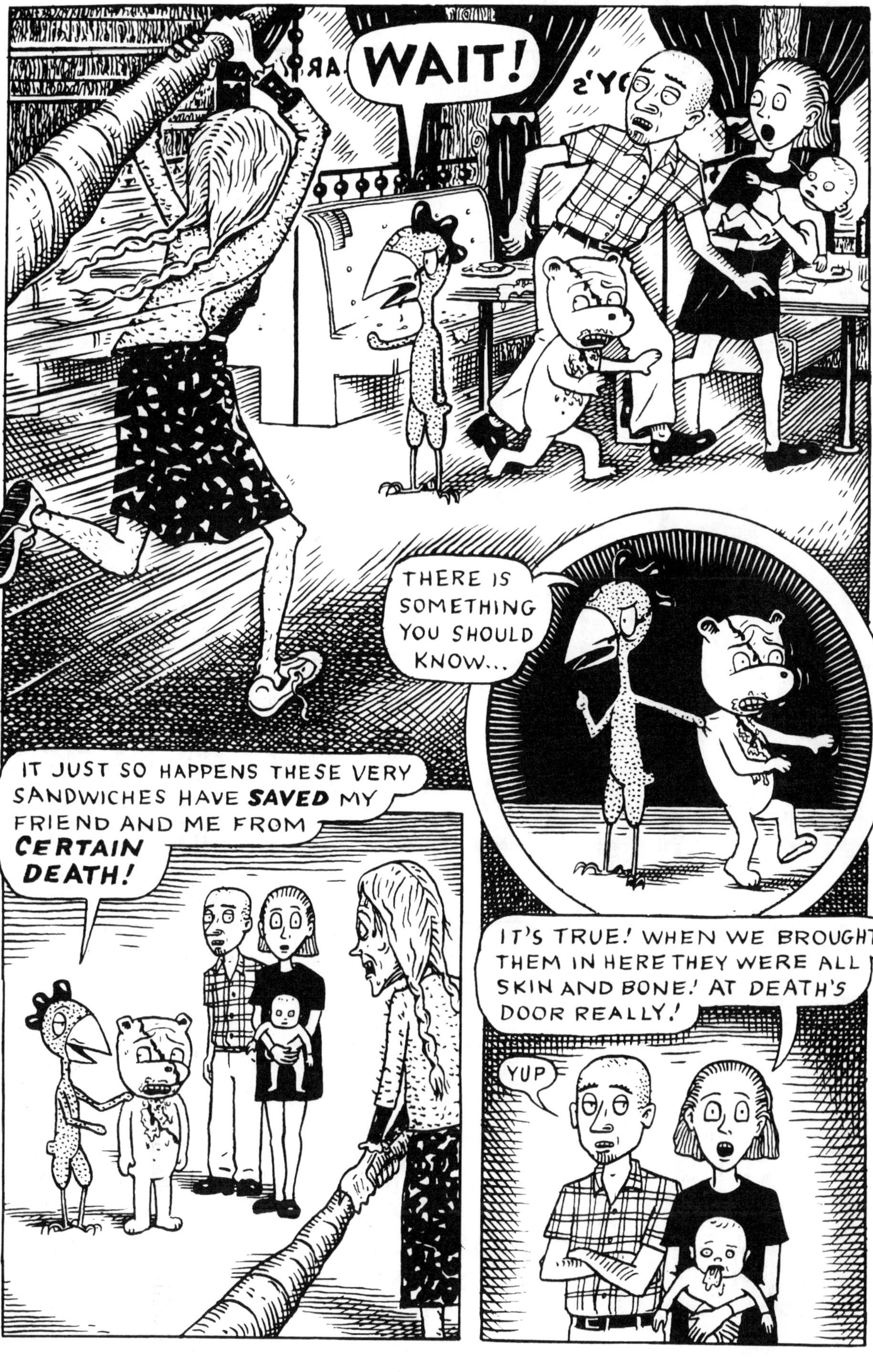
WAIT!
THERE IS SOMETHING YOU SHOULD KNOW...
IT JUST SO HAPPENS THESE VERY SANDWICHES HAVE **SAVED** MY FRIEND AND ME FROM **CERTAIN DEATH!**
IT'S TRUE! WHEN WE BROUGHT THEM IN HERE THEY WERE ALL SKIN AND BONE! AT DEATH'S DOOR REALLY!
YUP

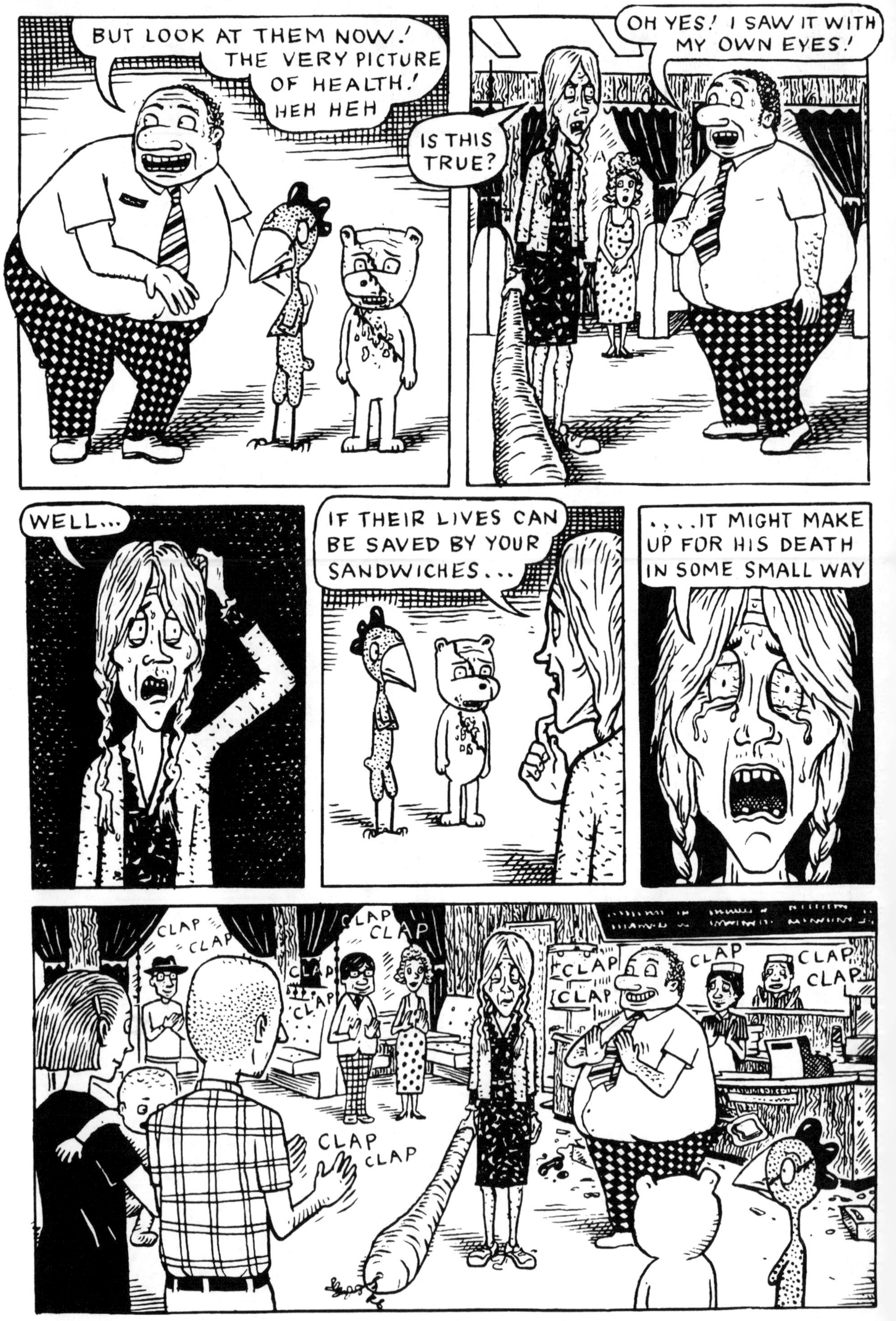

BUT LOOK AT THEM NOW! THE VERY PICTURE OF HEALTH! HEH HEH
IS THIS TRUE?
OH YES! I SAW IT WITH MY OWN EYES!
WELL...
IF THEIR LIVES CAN BE SAVED BY YOUR SANDWICHES...
....IT MIGHT MAKE UP FOR HIS DEATH IN SOME SMALL WAY
CLAP CLAP
CLAP CLAP
CLAP CLAP
CLAP CLAP
CLAP
CLAP CLAP
CLAP CLAP

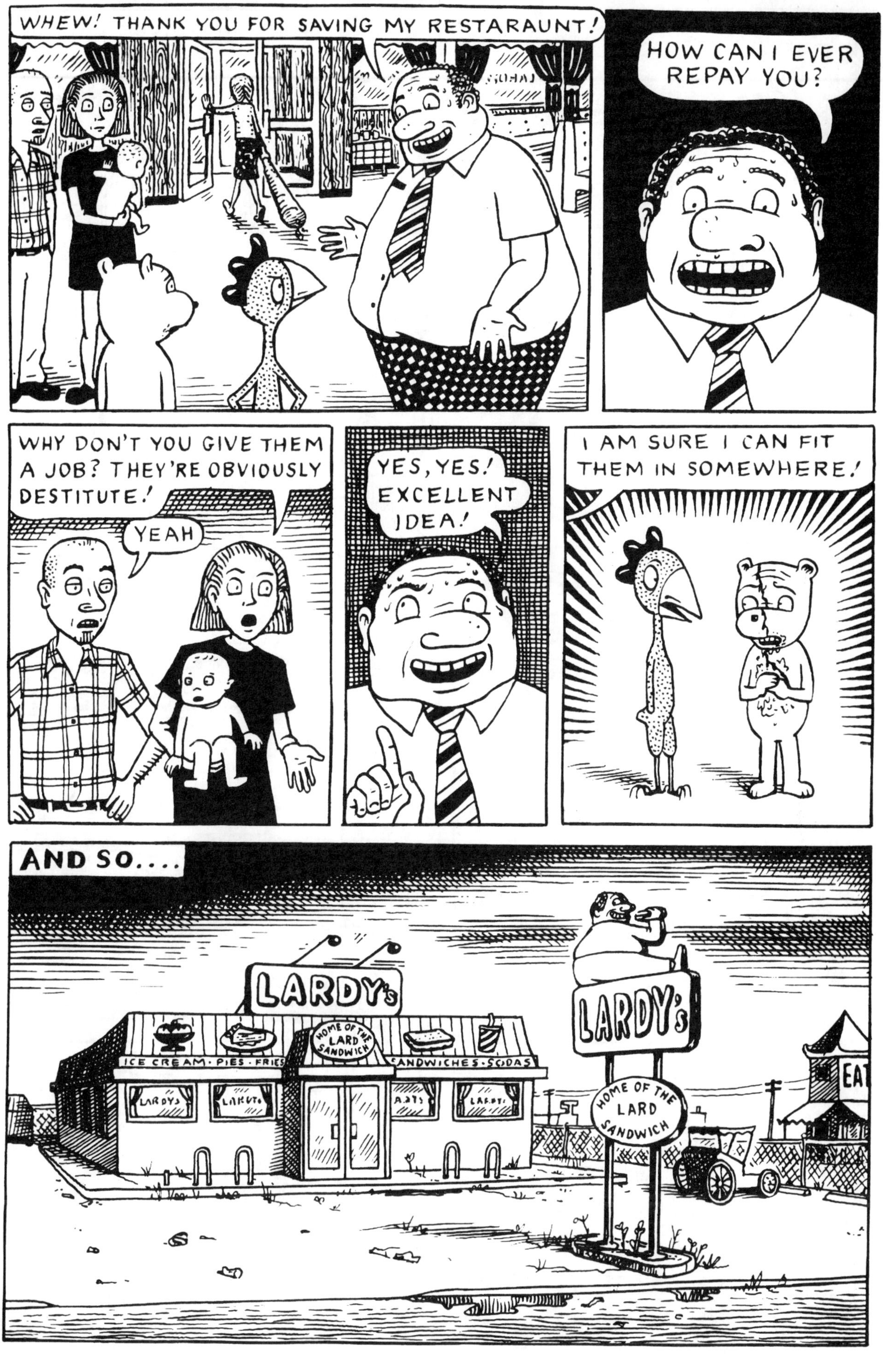

WHEW! THANK YOU FOR SAVING MY RESTARAUNT!
HOW CAN I EVER REPAY YOU?
WHY DON'T YOU GIVE THEM A JOB? THEY'RE OBVIOUSLY DESTITUTE!
YEAH
YES, YES! EXCELLENT IDEA!
I AM SURE I CAN FIT THEM IN SOMEWHERE!
AND SO....
LARDY's
LARDY's
HOME OF THE LARD SANDWICH
ICE CREAM · PIES · FRIES
SANDWICHES · SODAS
HOME OF THE LARD SANDWICH

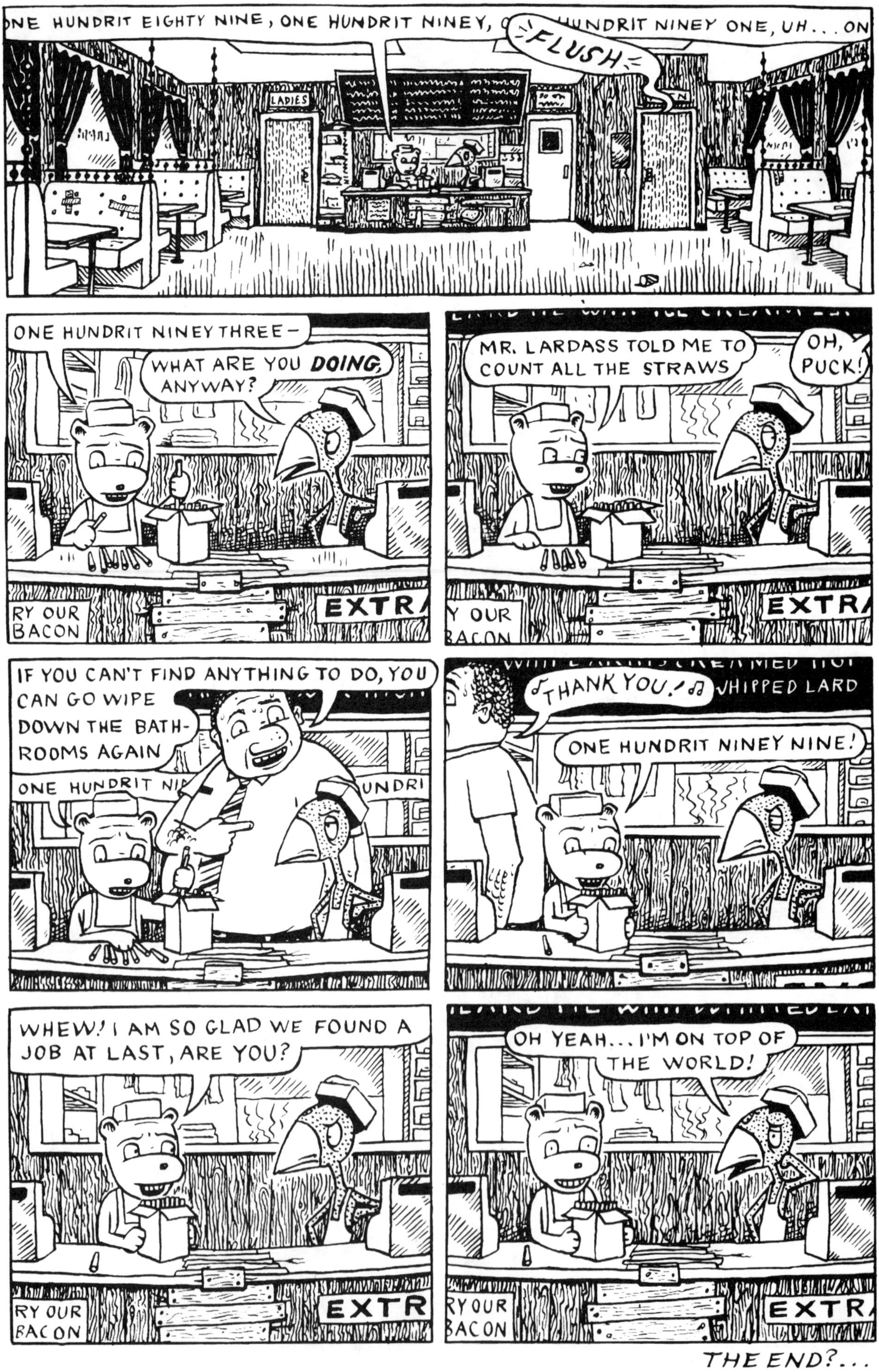
ONE HUNDRIT EIGHTY NINE, ONE HUNDRIT NINEY,
HUNDRIT NINEY ONE, UH... ON
FLUSH
LADIES
ONE HUNDRIT NINEY THREE—
WHAT ARE YOU DOING, ANYWAY?
MR. LARDASS TOLD ME TO COUNT ALL THE STRAWS
OH, PUCK!
IF YOU CAN'T FIND ANYTHING TO DO, YOU CAN GO WIPE DOWN THE BATHROOMS AGAIN
ONE HUNDRIT NI
UNDRI
THANK YOU!
ONE HUNDRIT NINEY NINE!
WHEW! I AM SO GLAD WE FOUND A JOB AT LAST, ARE YOU?
OH YEAH... I'M ON TOP OF THE WORLD!

THE END?...

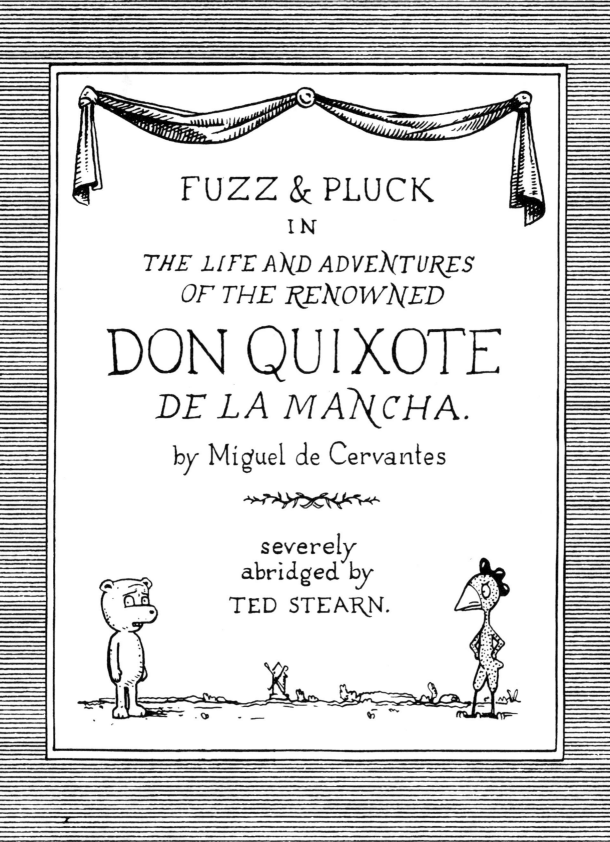

FUZZ & PLUCK
IN
THE LIFE AND ADVENTURES OF THE RENOWNED
DON QUIXOTE
DE LA MANCHA.

by Miguel de Cervantes

severely
abridged by
TED STEARN.

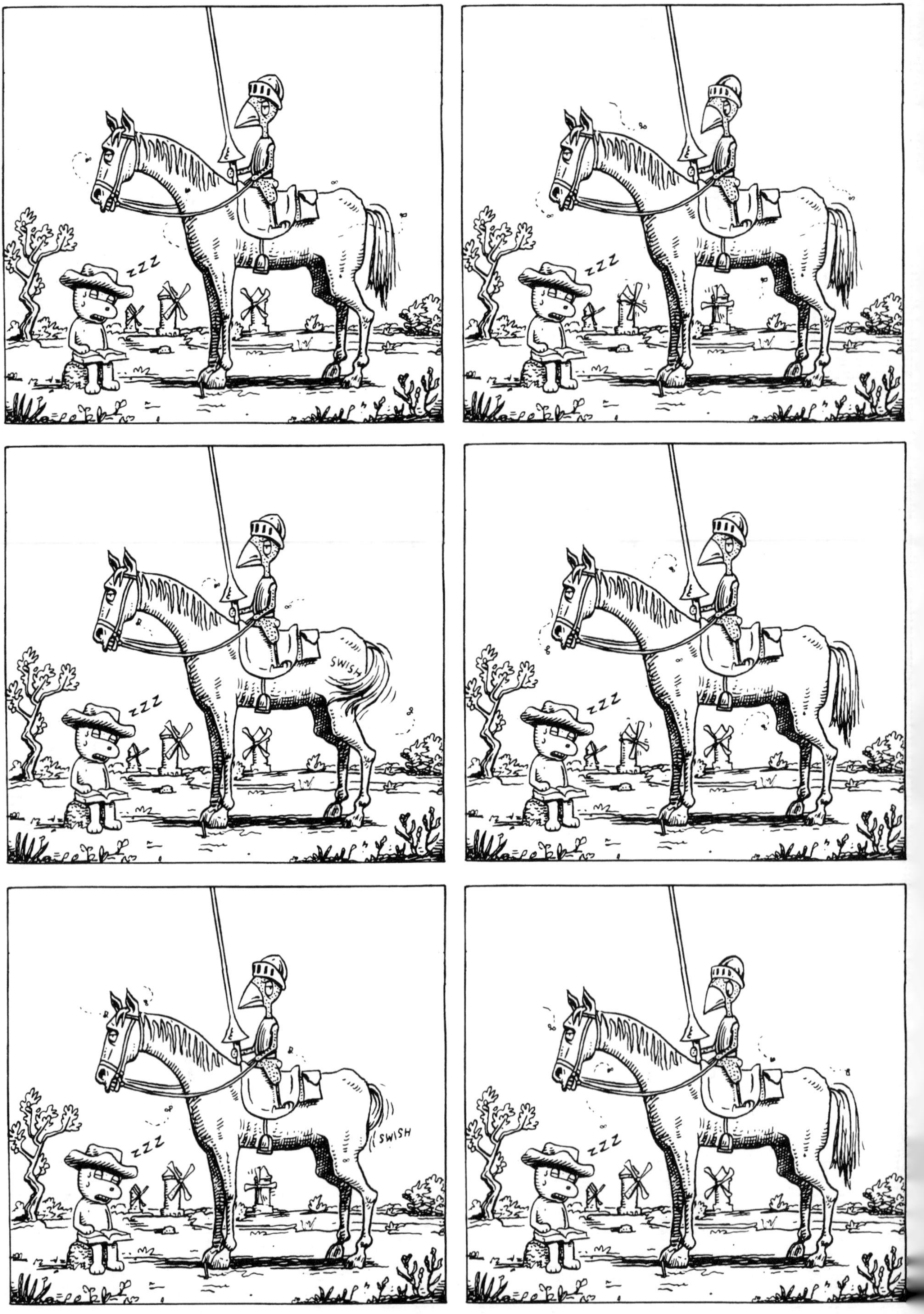

ZZZ
ZZZ
SWISH
ZZZ
ZZZ
ZZZ
SWISH
ZZZ

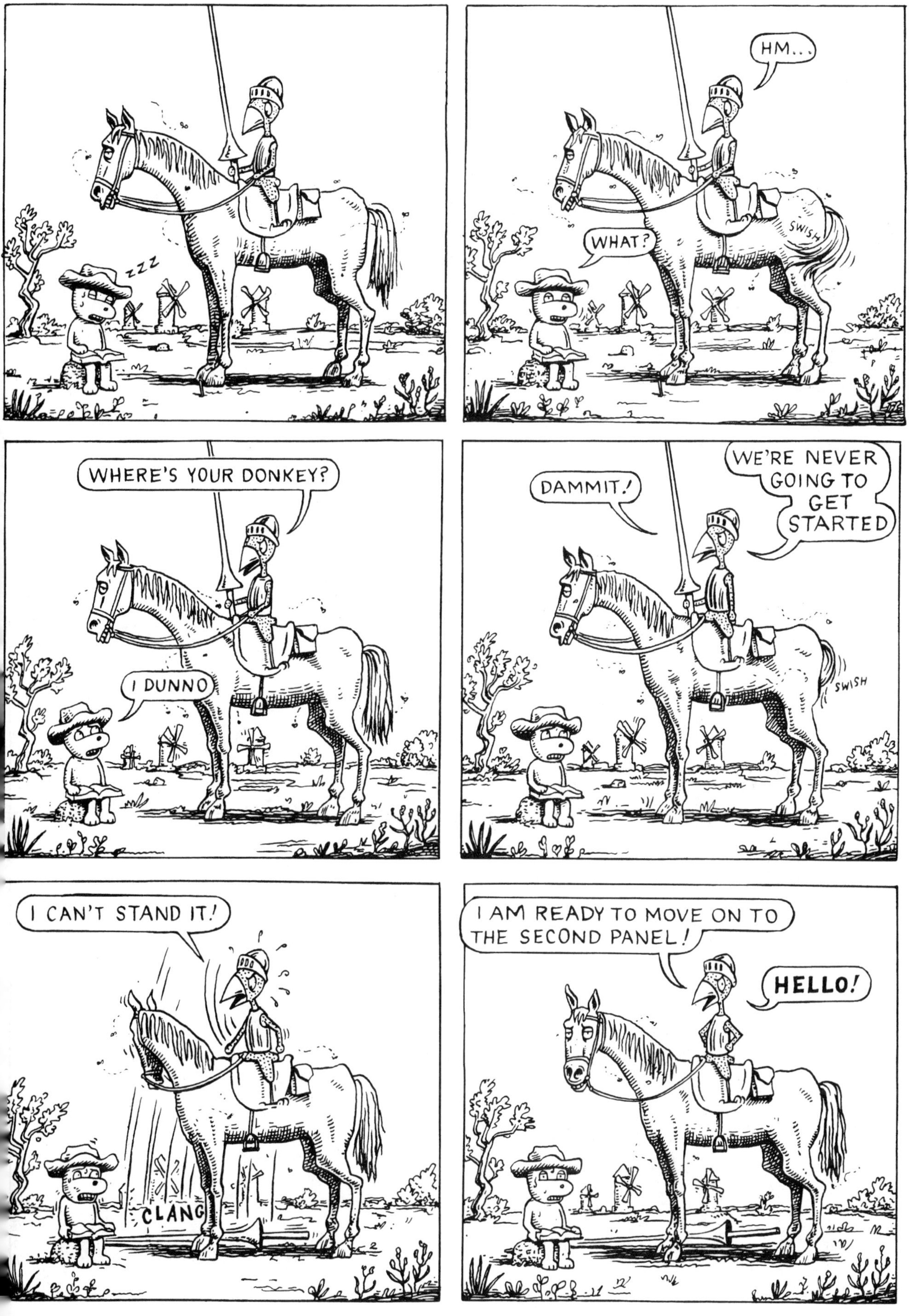
ZZZ
HM...
WHAT?
SWISH
WHERE'S YOUR DONKEY?
I DUNNO
DAMMIT!
WE'RE NEVER GOING TO GET STARTED
SWISH
I CAN'T STAND IT!
CLANG
I AM READY TO MOVE ON TO THE SECOND PANEL!
HELLO!

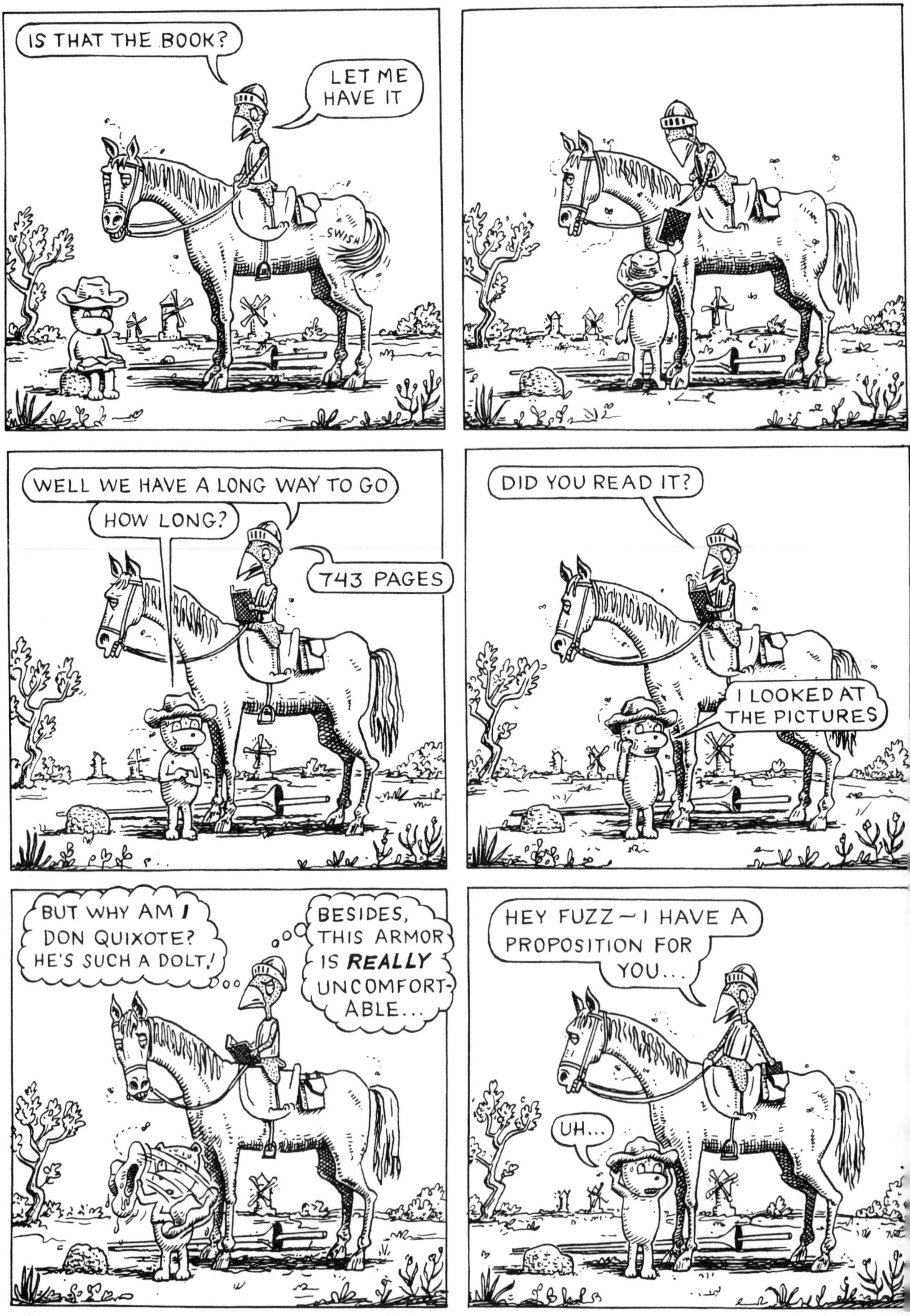
IS THAT THE BOOK?
LET ME HAVE IT
SWISH
WELL WE HAVE A LONG WAY TO GO
HOW LONG?
743 PAGES
DID YOU READ IT?
I LOOKED AT THE PICTURES
BUT WHY AM *I* DON QUIXOTE? HE'S SUCH A DOLT!
BESIDES, THIS ARMOR IS **REALLY** UNCOMFORT-ABLE...
HEY FUZZ — I HAVE A PROPOSITION FOR YOU...
UH...

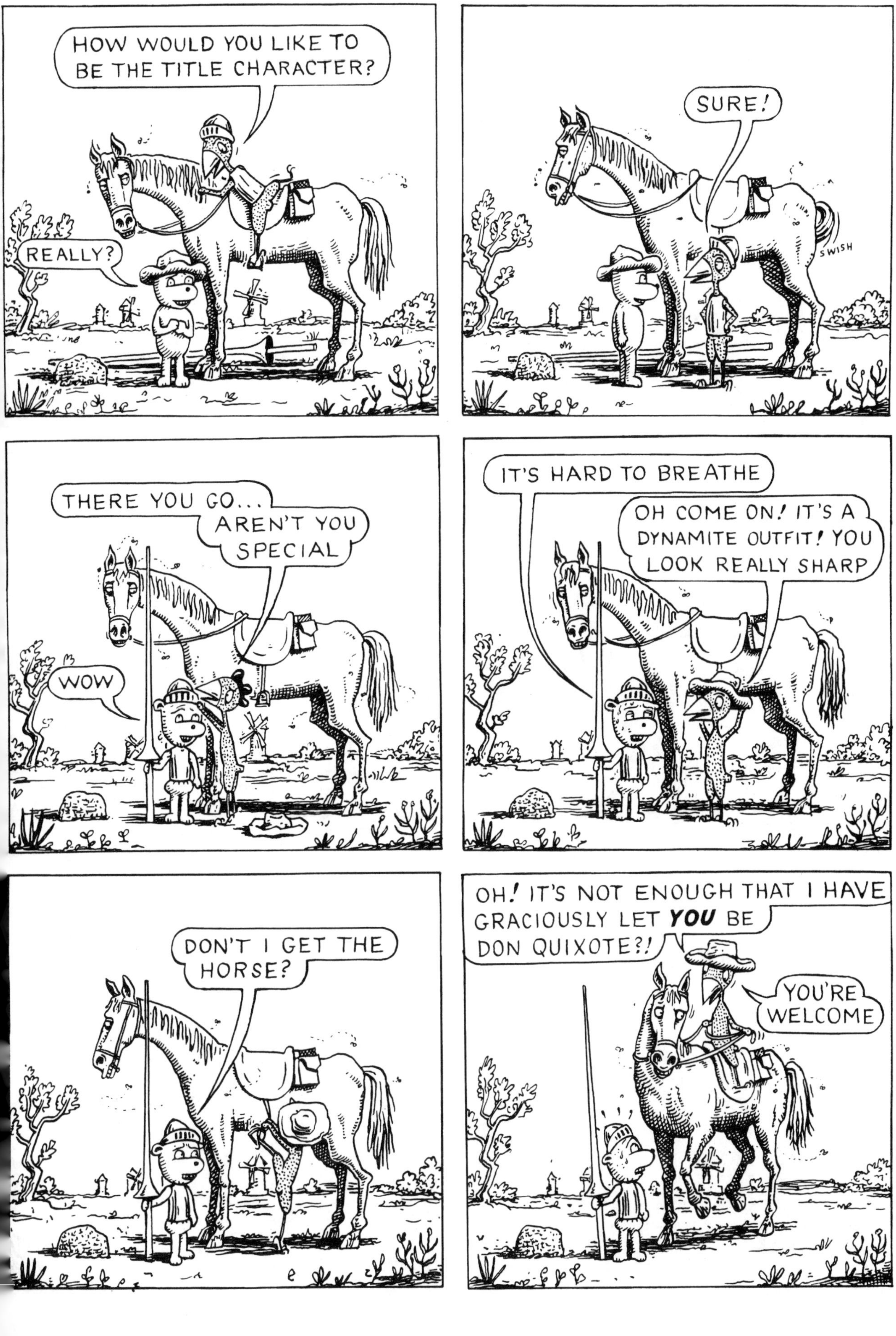
HOW WOULD YOU LIKE TO BE THE TITLE CHARACTER?
REALLY?
SURE!
SWISH
THERE YOU GO... AREN'T YOU SPECIAL
WOW
IT'S HARD TO BREATHE
OH COME ON! IT'S A DYNAMITE OUTFIT! YOU LOOK REALLY SHARP
DON'T I GET THE HORSE?
OH! IT'S NOT ENOUGH THAT I HAVE GRACIOUSLY LET **YOU** BE DON QUIXOTE?!
YOU'RE WELCOME

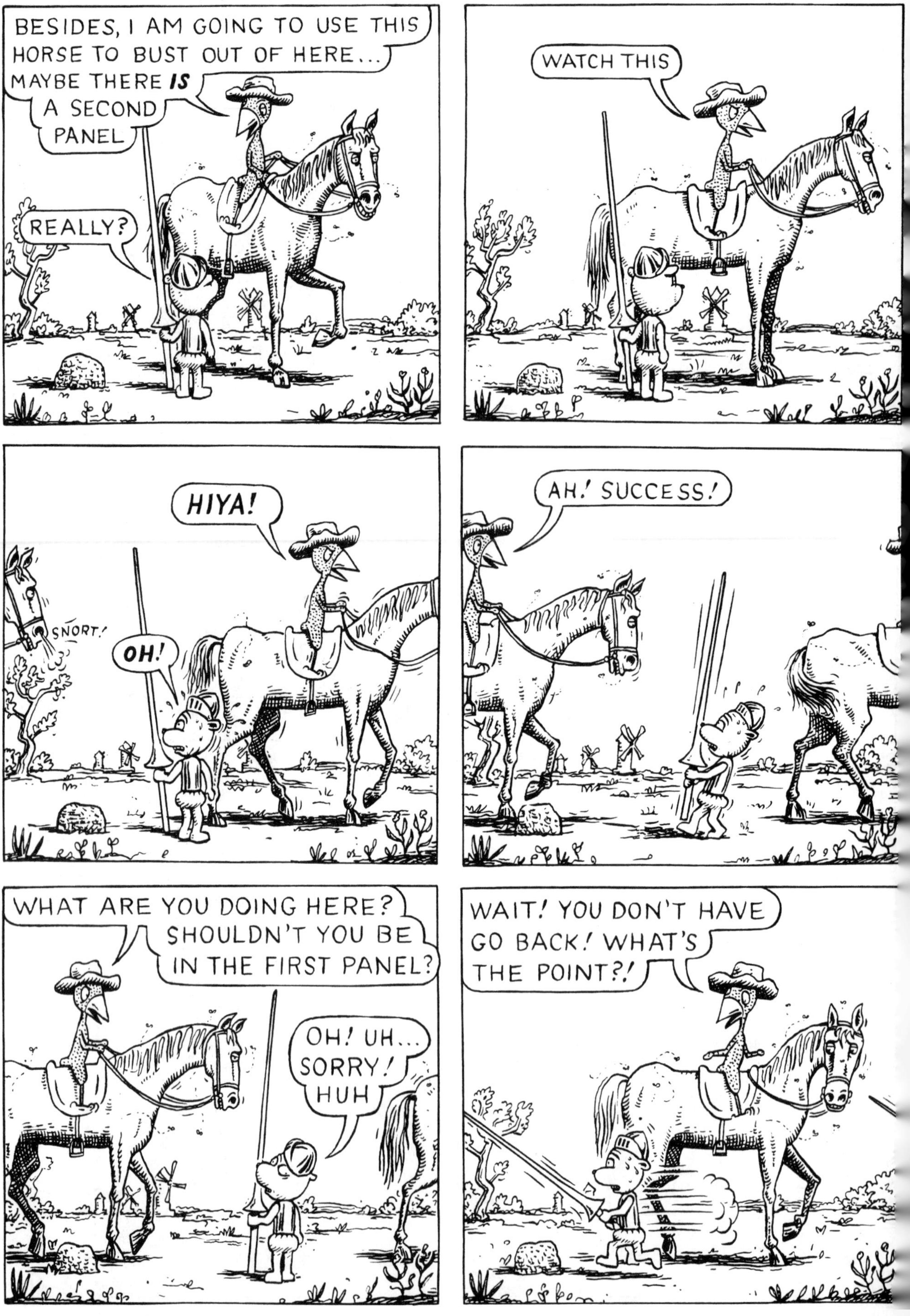

BESIDES, I AM GOING TO USE THIS HORSE TO BUST OUT OF HERE... MAYBE THERE **IS** A SECOND PANEL
REALLY?
WATCH THIS
HIYA!
SNORT!
OH!
AH! SUCCESS!
WHAT ARE YOU DOING HERE? SHOULDN'T YOU BE IN THE FIRST PANEL?
OH! UH... SORRY! HUH
WAIT! YOU DON'T HAVE GO BACK! WHAT'S THE POINT?!

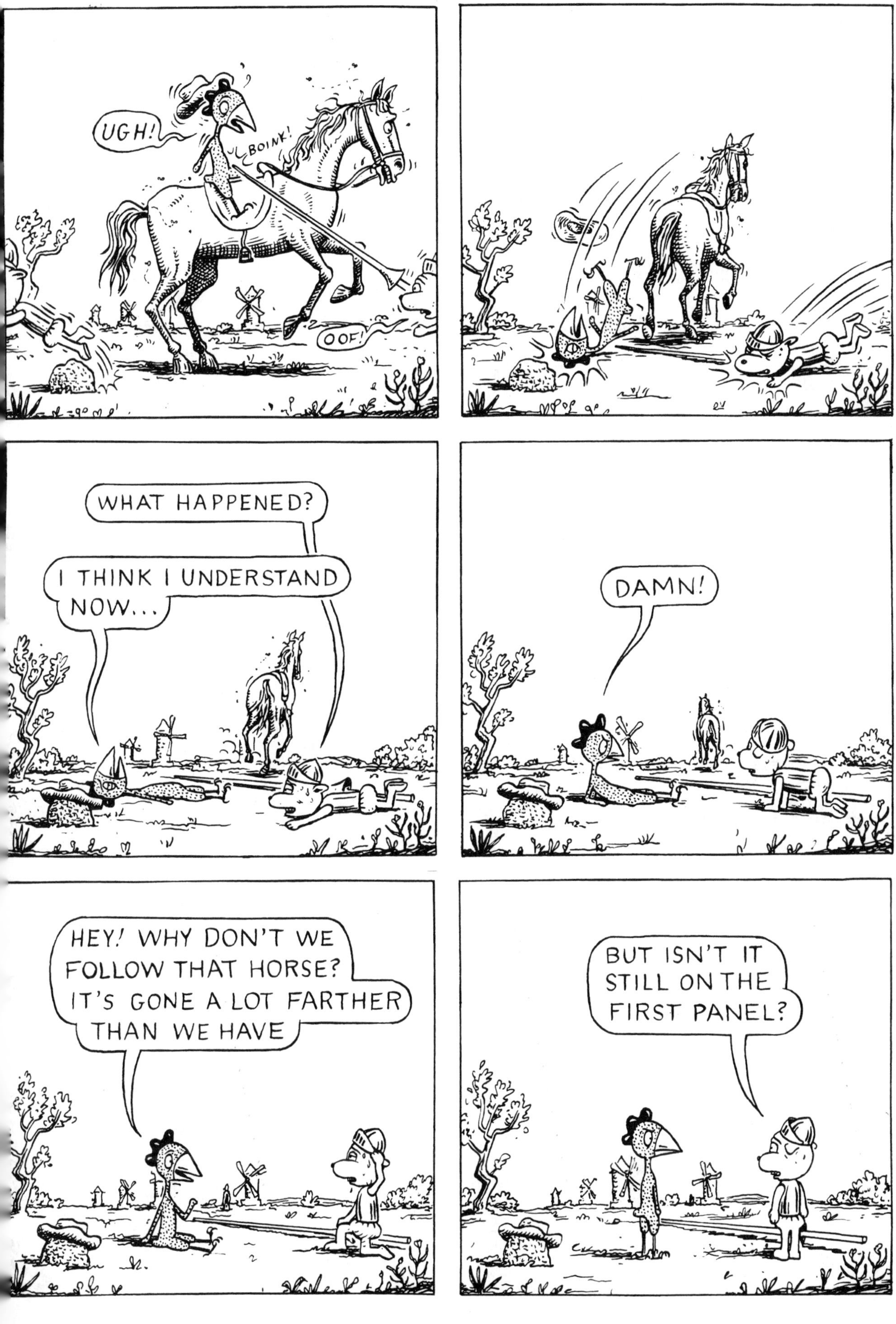
UGH!
BOINK!
OOF!
WHAT HAPPENED?
I THINK I UNDERSTAND NOW...
DAMN!
HEY! WHY DON'T WE FOLLOW THAT HORSE? IT'S GONE A LOT FARTHER THAN WE HAVE
BUT ISN'T IT STILL ON THE FIRST PANEL?

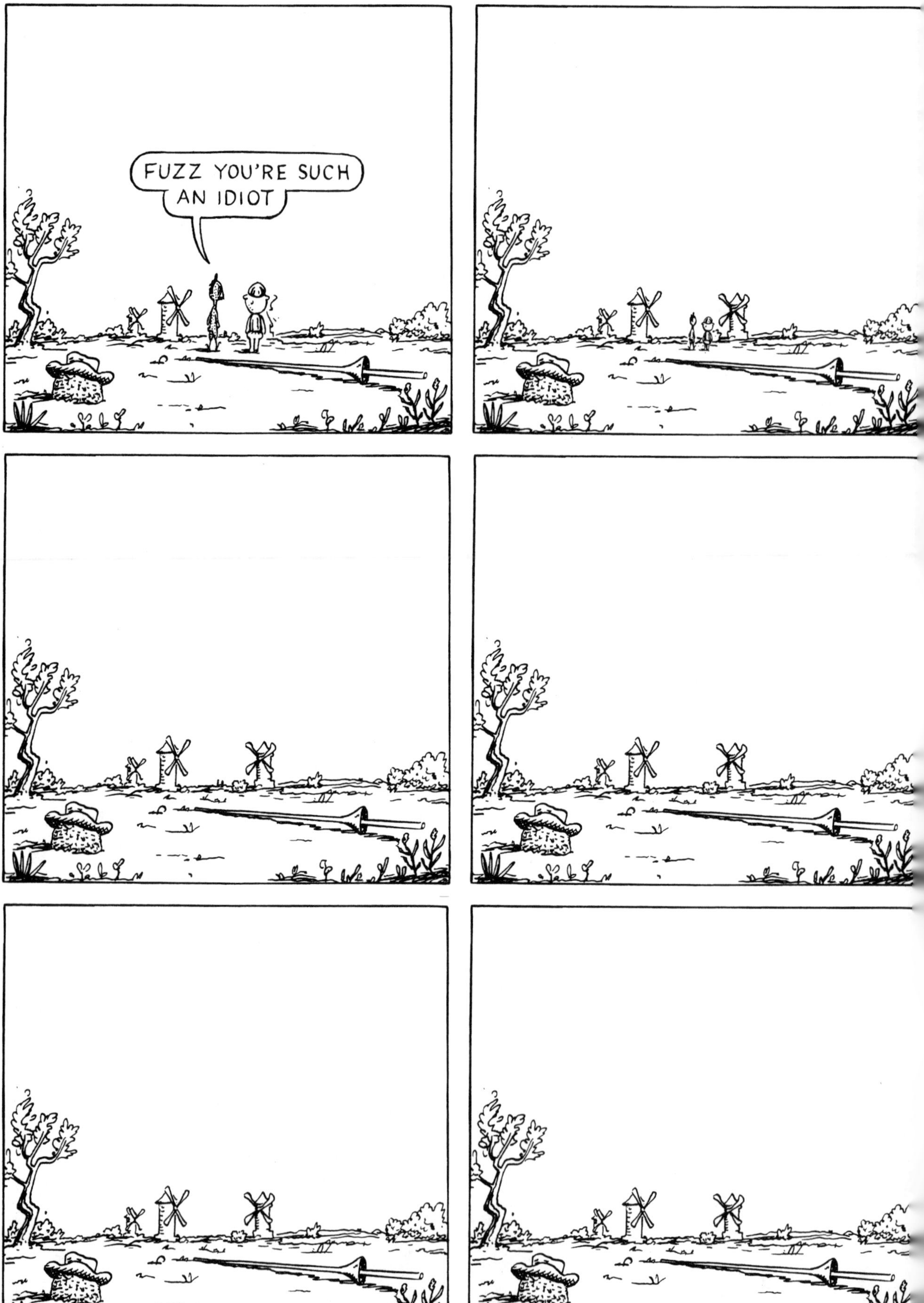
FUZZ YOU'RE SUCH AN IDIOT

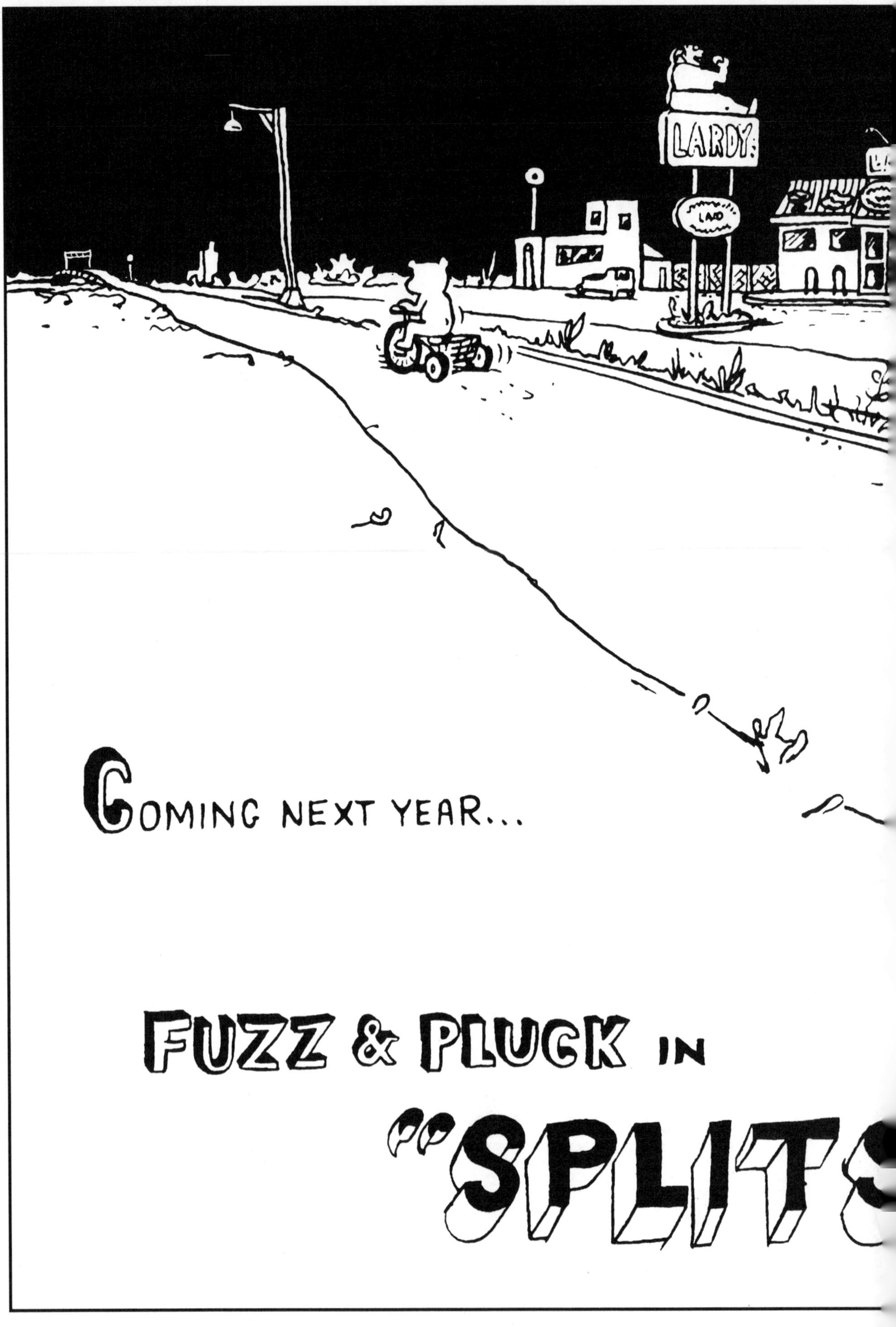
LARDY
COMING NEXT YEAR...
FUZZ & PLUCK IN
"SPLIT

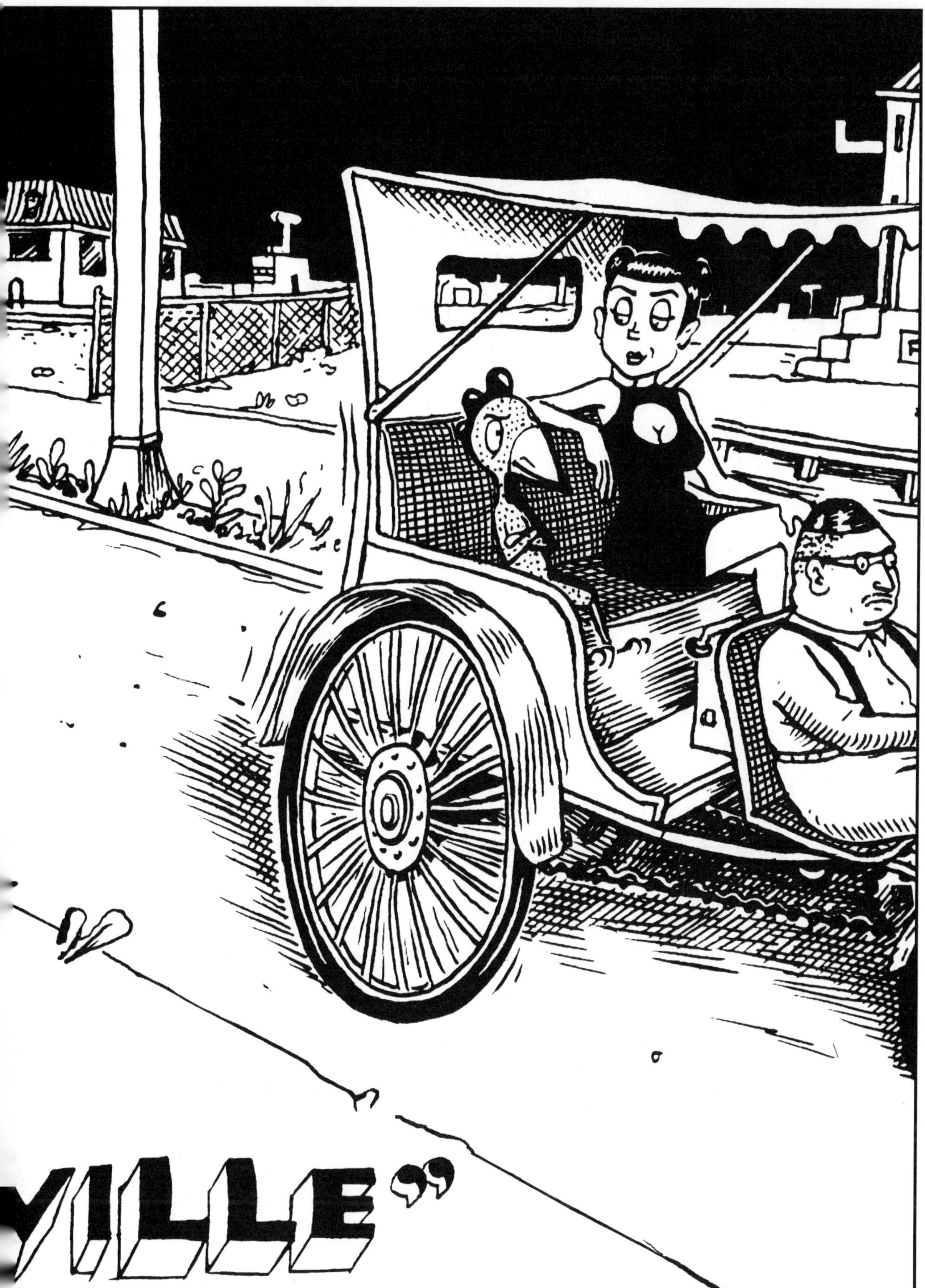
VILLE"